Great Thinkers in Economics Series

Series Editor: A.P. Thirlwall is Professor of Applied Economics, University of Kent, UK.

Great Thinkers in Economics is designed to illuminate the economics of some of the great historical and contemporary economists by exploring the interactions between their lives and work, and the events surrounding them. The books are brief and written in a style that makes them not only of interest to professional economists, but also intelligible for students of economics and the interested lay person.

Titles include:

Julio López G. and Michaël Assous
MICHAL KALECKI

Alessandro Roncaglia
PIERO SRAFFA

William J. Barber
GUNNAR MYRDAL

Paul Davidson
JOHN MAYNARD KEYNES

Peter D. Groenewegen
ALFRED MARSHALL

Michael Szenberg and Lall Ramrattan
FRANCO MODIGLIANI

Gavin Kennedy
ADAM SMITH

John E. King
NICHOLAS KALDOR

Gordon Fletcher
DENNIS ROBERTSON

Geoffrey Harcourt and Prue Kerr
JOAN ROBINSON

Forthcoming titles in the series include:

Esben Sloth Anderson
JOSEPH A. SCHUMPETER

Michael A. Lebowitz
KARL MARX

Gerhard Michael Ambrosi
ARTHUR C. PIGOU

J.R. Stanfield
JOHN KENNETH GALBRAITH

Warren Young and Esteban Perez
ROY HARROD

Roger Middleton
ROBERT SOLOW

Paul Mosley and Barbara Ingham
SIR ARTHUR LEWIS

Robert Dimand
JAMES TOBIN

Great Thinkers in Economics
Series Standing Order ISBN 978–14039–8555–2 (Hardback)
978–14039–8556–9 (Paperback)
(outside North America only)

You can receive future titles in this series as they are published by placing a standing order. Please contact your bookseller or, in case of difficulty, write to us at the address below with your name and address, the title of the series and the ISBN quoted above.

Customer Services Department, Macmillan Distribution Ltd, Houndmills, Basingstoke, Hampshire RG21 6XS, England.

Michal Kalecki

Julio López G.

and

Michaël Assous

palgrave
macmillan

First published 2010 by
PALGRAVE MACMILLAN

Palgrave Macmillan in the UK is an imprint of Macmillan Publishers Limited, registered in England, company number 785998, of Houndmills, Basingstoke, Hampshire RG21 6XS.

Palgrave Macmillan in the US is a division of St Martin's Press LLC, 175 Fifth Avenue, New York, NY 10010.

Palgrave Macmillan is the global academic imprint of the above companies and has companies and representatives throughout the world.

Palgrave® and Macmillan® are registered trademarks in the United States, the United Kingdom, Europe and other countries.

ISBN: 978–1–403–99937–5 hardback

This book is printed on paper suitable for recycling and made from fully managed and sustained forest sources. Logging, pulping and manufacturing processes are expected to conform to the environmental regulations of the country of origin.

A catalogue record for this book is available from the British Library.

A catalog record for this book is available from the Library of Congress.

10 9 8 7 6 5 4 3 2 1
19 18 17 16 15 14 13 12 11 10

Printed and bound in Great Britain by
CPI Antony Rowe, Chippenham and Eastbourne

Contents

Preface

This is a book about Michal Kalecki's economic theory of the capitalist economy. It purports to be a thorough guided tour through Kalecki's published works.[1]

Kalecki is a very important, and also a very peculiar, figure among twentieth-century economists. His ideas had their moment of glory and wide international recognition during the period when Keynesianism pre-dominated in the economics landscape. The coincidence is unsurprising: Joan Robinson and Austin Robinson, two of Keynes's closest collaborators, had recognized the priority of Kalecki in having put forward many of the basic concepts contained in the principle of effective demand. Later on, Kalecki's economics went out of fashion, simultaneously with, but at a faster rate than, Keynesianism loosing its central place in economic thinking and policymaking. Today, when the world economic crisis forces authorities and pundits to acknowledge the importance of Keynes's legacy, very few call for a reassessment of Kalecki's economics. The main objective of this book is to contribute to such a reassessment, and in this context to arouse the interest of readers in knowing more about, and hopefully reading directly from, this extraordinary Polish and socialist economist. In this Preface, we intend to give a glimpse of what they can find in this book.

When Kalecki arrived to England in 1936, a few months after the publication of Keynes's masterwork, *The General Theory of Employment, Interest and Money,* he was a complete unknown to British economists. However, without any university degree, and having spent less than five years, working as an academic economist, he had developed a brilliant career in his native Poland, both in theoretical and in applied economics. Among other things, he had produced the first national accounts estimates for his country. Besides, and this is what has given him most of his reputation in economics, in different pieces written in the first half of the 1930s, he had anticipated many aspects of the principle of effective demand, which Keynes was to put forward some years later.

Kalecki however gave to this principle a distinctive flavour, much closer to the Marxian than to the Marshallian tradition. Embedding it in the framework of business-cycle analysis, he had produced the first mathematical model of the cycle within this framework; a model which at the time gave him credit among such renowned mathematical economists as Ragnar Frisch and Jan Tinbergen. Also, he had linked the principle of effective demand with a theory of how profits come into being, giving birth to the sentence encapsulating his theory, "when workers spend what they earn capitalists earn what they spend". He had also shown that profits, and with them demand, can be augmented when a country is able to gain a trade surplus, and when the government engages in deficit spending. He applied this latter idea to a study of Germany in the early 1930s, in a short and brilliant article which was surely the first one where the Nazi economy was analysed using the principle of effective demand.

Finally, in a comprehensive and rigorous article, he had shown how the real and the monetary sectors interact in an economy where the classical assumptions rule. This piece came almost as an aside to his main subject of interest, and Kalecki never referred to it and never republished it during his lifetime. But here Kalecki put forward, for the first time, what later came to be known as the "Keynes effect", and this is probably the first publication where a complete and precise exposition of the working and the logic of Say's Law was made. Had Keynes read Kalecki's paper, he probably would not have written "Prof. Pigou's theory of unemployment ... is the only attempt with which I am acquainted to write down the classical theory of unemployment precisely" (Keynes 1964: 279). But then, Keynes did not read Polish!

This was Kalecki's background when he came to England. At the time, the "Keynesian revolution" was raging, and in such an intellectually fertile milieu Kalecki was able to proceed with his academic career, first at Cambridge University and later at the Institute of Statistics at Oxford University.

In this stage of his professional life, Kalecki completed his theory of the capitalist economy with a theory of price formation and of income distribution. He combined the latter with his theory of profits, arriving at a formulation of the principle of effective demand where the latter has, to use the modern parlance, rigorous microeconomic foundations. However, these foundations were radically different from the conventional ones, because Kalecki recognized that firms have to make their living and to take decisions in an environment where uncertainty is pervasive, and thus agents cannot optimize a known function under definite restrictions. And Kalecki also showed that, in taking their pricing decisions and in setting what he called their "degree of monopoly", firms also determine income distribution; and thus they also affect the macroeconomy.

World War II soon came to occupy a large part of Kalecki's scholarly efforts, and he wrote on several aspects of war finance, having as his main concern how to guarantee that the burden of the war effort be borne equitably, ensuring an egalitarian distribution of the available consumer goods. But he also found time to further develop his theory of the capitalist economy, and he was able to give a more complete and realistic foundation to his theory of the determinants of investment decisions, crucial for his theory of the business cycle. In this context, he brought into being his "principle of increasing risk", where he emphasized the dual role of profits in the determination of investment, both as a source of finance and as an indicator of profitability. Apart from that, he participated in one of the most original and insightful reflections on economic policies to overcome massive unemployment in a developed capitalist economy. The book issued on the subject, *The Economics of Full Employment*, included as its central piece "Three Ways to Full Employment", which was to become one of Kalecki's most renowned papers. In this paper Kalecki showed that if the government had the will, it could with appropriate policies bring about full employment, relying mostly on public expenditure and income redistribution in favour of the poor. At about the same time, however, Kalecki warned that important political changes would occur under full employment, and that these changes, or the fear they arouse among the dominant classes, would give birth to obstacles which would prevent the government from carrying out its full employment measures in full strength. These were the *Political Aspects of Full Employment*, the title he gave to one of his best-known and most-quoted papers, where he put forward his theory of the political business cycle; another one of his pioneering ideas.

Kalecki spent the next stage of his professional life, between 1947 and 1954, working at the United Nations in New York; and most of what he wrote during this period is hidden in various collective documents of that organization. McCarthyism was in full rage during his stay in the US, which limited his professional contacts, as well as his influence, on economic thinking in that country. Anyway, while there, Kalecki could complete his *Theory of Economic Dynamics*, his *magnum opus* summarizing his overall theory of the capitalist economy. Also, he could find time to reflect on the economics of underdeveloped nations. Though he wrote only a few papers on the subject, his approach and ideas showed a profound perception of the domestic institutional and structural obstacles facing economic growth in this type of country; a perception which was surely aided by his Polish origin and experience. His work at the United Nations brought with it invitations to visit as consultant Latin America and India; and these visits left a lasting imprint in those parts of the world. This is why Indian and Latin American Structuralist economic thinking had, and still have, a very distinctive Kaleckian flavour.

Kalecki returned to Poland in 1955, remaining there until his untimely death in 1970. Poland was a relatively liberal communist country in the mid-1950s, and at the moment of his arrival Kalecki was given a position of certain responsibility in economic planning. But the political situation deteriorated, and soon he lost his capacity to have any influence on the economic strategy and economic policy decisions. He therefore dedicated himself entirely to the academic interests, and devoted most of his effort to reflect on the economic growth of the socialist economy. His reflections resulted in another one of his masterful works, *Introduction to the Theory of Growth of the Socialist Economy.* Moreover, his enormous intellectual appeal brought him close to an important number of Polish economists, and that gathering soon gave life to a very lively and idiosyncratic Polish School of economics. As any attendant to the seminars that Kalecki conducted at that time at the Central School of Planning and Statistics will surely recollect – and one of the present authors (JL) attended those seminars – the liveliness of the discussions there had nothing to do with the dullness of economic debate in most of the other communist countries. Sadly, that School of thought was attacked and dismantled by the authorities during the political repression Poland suffered in 1968; and two years later, on April 17, 1970, Kalecki died.

The above is a brief summary of the life and work of the man about whose economic ideas we are writing this book. We do not make apologies about our prejudices and sympathy. We are not writing a book about a person chosen at random, but about the ideas of the economist from whom we have learned most of our economics, and who has had the greatest influence in our professional lifes. And one of us – JL – actually had the enormous fortune to study with him in the late 1960s. Our enthusiasm for Kalecki's economics is the most important message we want to convey to our readers.

There are several books on Kalecki's economics which we have consulted extensively in the process of writing this book. Without being exhaustive, we want to mention Bhaduri (1986), Feiwell (1975), Kriesler (1987) and Sawyer (1985). Of course, we would not have been able to write this book without the masterful edition of the *Collected Works of Michal Kalecki*, edited by Jerzy Osiatinsky. We are also thankful to Tony

Thilrwall, the editor of this series, who read the entire manuscript and made important observations, which we have tried to incorporate in this final version.

Julio López would also like to express his gratitude to colleagues and friends with whom he has been discussing Kalecki's economics for a long time, especially Martín Puchet, Tracy Mott, Emilio Caballero, Jorge Ibarra, Amit Bhaduri, Malcolm Sawyer, Philip Arestis, Marc Lavoie, Alberto Moritz Cruz, Armando Sanchez, Arturo Huerta, Juan Carlos Moreno-Brid, Jerry Courvisanos, Rune Skarstein, Gerardo Fujii, Guadalupe Mántey, Fernando Cardim de Carvalho, Jan Toporowski, Jan Kregel, Ignacio Perrotini, Rogelio Huerta, Eloisa Andjel and Robert Blecker. But most of all, he would like to thank his teachers and friends Ignacy Sachs, Kazimierz Laski and Adam Szeworski, close collaborators of Kalecki in Poland in the 1950s and 1960s, who taught him most of his Kaleckian economics while I studied in Poland in the late 1960s.

I am indebted to Professor Alain Béraud for supervising the dissertation from which this book is partially derived. Professor Rodolphe Dos Santos Ferreira – who served as an examiner and as a second adviser provided crucial suggestions as the dissertation neared completion. Several scholars – Richard Arena, Carlo Benetti , Jérôme de Boyer des Roches, Gilbert Faccarello, Heinz Kurz, Catherine Martin and Antoine Rebeyrol have distinguished themselves as friends and colleagues over the entire course of the project. Finally, I wish to thank my companion, Marjolaine Saraf, who showed unusual understanding and patience as I "disappeared" for many evenings.

1
Michal Kalecki's Life and Work

Initial steps

In 1933 Michael Kalecki, a young self-taught economist, published in Poland a small book: *An Essay on the Theory of the Business Cycle*. In this book he proposed his version of the theory of effective demand; a theory which was to initiate, albeit in John Maynard Keynes's version, a new phase in the history of economic ideas and policymaking.

When he published his book Kalecki was in his early thirties (he was born in June 1899). He came from an assimilated Polish–Jewish family,[1] who probably had been relatively well-off. However, his father had lost the small cotton-mill he owned and had to accept a job as a bookkeeper in his brother's company. Kalecki had first begun mathematical studies at the Warsaw University, and then started a university degree in engineering at the Gdansk University Engineering College. However, he discontinued studies shortly before graduation because of the difficult economic conditions of his family.

Kalecki had had no formal economic studies, and in his youth he had been rather attracted by engineering and mathematics. But his socialist political inclination had led him to study Marx's *Capital*, as well as the Marxian economic literature, which was rich and lively in those days preceding the advent of Stalinism.[2] Poland was at the time a backward agricultural country on the periphery of Europe and of capitalism; whose per capita income may have been about one-third of the average for industrial Europe. However, we must not forget that, as most countries in a similar situation it had a sophisticated *intelligentsia* which excelled in many areas.

In any case, Kalecki further developed his practical knowledge of economics working for a credit rating agency, and this probably led him to begin more systematic studies of economics. In the late 1920s, he entered into regular relationship with two Polish economic journals; writing many reports on important concerns, on economic conditions in particular markets, and on international economic relations. At the end of 1929, he got a job at the Institute for the Study of Business Cycles and Prices,[3] and he could thereafter devote himself entirely to work as an economist. It was at the Institute for the Study of Business Cycles and Prices where he published his *Essay* booklet.

However, Kalecki never completely discarded his interest for engineering, and in the early 1930s he published papers on the subject (reproduced in Kalecki 1997, part 4). Also, he would never abandon his attraction for mathematics, and would later publish papers on probability theory and on pure mathematics.[4] Anyway, in spite of his attraction to, and his good training in, mathematics, he was very careful as to the use of mathematics in economics. Here are two anecdotes told by two close collaborators of Kalecki:

> At a certain period I…had great optimism with regards to the possibilities of mathematics. Kalecki warned me of that, and he also warned me of the computer: he suggested that both were ideally suited as a scientific cloak to cover the lack of economic substance. (Steindl 1990b: 246)

And:

> Having written a rather formalized paper for **Ekonomista**, the main Polish journal of economics…I asked the Editor to submit the paper to Kalecki…One day I had a phone call…from Kalecki…who told me 'you should know that you must never use mathematics when you can say the same thing in a simpler way, in common language'. (Sachs 2007: 184)

During his period at the Institute Kalecki also entered into collaboration with, and contributed several papers to, the Socialist Review (*Przeglad Socjalistyczny*), under the pseudonym of Henryk Braun. In this Review, Kalecki published some papers where he took usually as a point of departure the peculiarities and impact of the world economic crisis and, interestingly, already in that period his short-run analysis was embedded within the framework of the course of business cycle. Besides putting forward his basic ideas regarding the cycle, he discussed above all the following issues. First, whether falling wages caused by the slump could contribute to an economic revival. Second, what would be the consequences on the world crisis of monetary and fiscal policy. Finally, whether a concerted expansionary policy carried out by the main developed countries, which he called the "'capitalist' overcoming of the crisis", could be implemented and thus would put a halt to the world crisis. Below are relevant quotes showing his opinions in the very early 1930s on each one of these issues.

On the impact of falling wages Kalecki said,

> during a crisis – such as we are now experiencing – reduction of wages causes a reduction of price, but the interval between these events does not permit workers to benefit immediately, while further reductions of wages eliminate altogether the possibility of their being able to do so. As a result, the standard of living of the working class and its share in the social income fall, but at the same time the increased share of the capitalists in the social income flows more into unsold stocks. This in turn further shrinks output and intensifies the crisis. (Kalecki 1932a [1990]: 43–44)

On monetary policy:

> Inflation[5] is the single "surgery-type" means of mitigating the crisis system, however, this instrument is of a merely theoretical significance now, since its use the concrete conditions of contemporary capitalism encounter insurmountable difficulties. For ... credit inflation, i.e. a more liberal supply of credit by the central bank, may be of minor significance only when the business crisis is deep as at present. Entrepreneurs will not, as a rule invest the newly received credits because easier terms of the credit will not induce any investor to build a factory that will have no chance of finding a market for its products. New credits will be used rather to pay back the old ones and the surprised creditors will bring their repaid credits back to banks thus happily closing the circle.
>
> What indeed could change the situation is fiscal inflation on a large scale. (Kalecki 1932c [1996]: 175)

On the impact of increased government expenditure:

> What processes take place with the financing of the public works through monetary inflation? Let us assume that the government is constructing public works, financing them by raising loans from

> the bank of issue. Prices, output, and hence profits increase with the overall growth in demand. The increase in profits will be equivalent to the accumulation of capital tied up in the completed public works. In what form do the profits reach the hands of the industrialists? They will reach them either in the form of an increased number of banknotes in their possession or in the form of repayments of their obligations to the bank of issue. This process is reflected in the latter's balance sheet in an increase in the portfolio of treasury bills, an increase of money in circulation, and a decrease in the portfolio of private bills. Yet another shift in the balance sheet takes place. Since the increase in output is accompanied by increased imports of foreign raw materials and semifinished products, part of the money put into circulation will be exchanged for gold or foreign currency to pay for this increase.
>
> In turn, the increased profits of industrialists will encourage the latter to undertake investments; private investments will begin to grow around public investments and the business upswing will be stimulated. (Kalecki 1932b [1990]: 61–62)

On the capitalist overcoming of the crisis:

> we should mention [the] ... possibility [of] ... a certain form of inflation consisting of individual states, or groups of states, starting up major public-investment schemes, such as construction of canals or roads, and financing them with government loans floated on the financial market, or with special government credits drawn on their banks of issue. This kind of operation could temporarily increase employment, ... [but] ... if it were to be carried out on a large scale, it would have to be co-ordinated by an international agreement of the individual capitalist governments, which, given today's quarrelling imperialisms is almost out of the question. (Kalecki 1932d [1990]: 53)

All in all, on reading Kalecki's early papers, one (or at least the present authors) cannot but conclude that early in the development of his thought, he had achieved an overall vision on the functioning and the dynamics of the capitalist economy he would preserve until his mature age. Of course, in each and every theoretical issue he would refine and make more precise his viewpoint. But his global outlook would only change marginally.

Let us now resume our narrative of Kalecki's career. At the Institute, Kalecki showed the impressive intellectual productivity that characterized his professional life. We already mentioned his booklet on the business cycle and quoted some of his short papers. Besides that, he produced (together with Ludwik Landau) the first estimates of investment, consumption and social income in Poland; and a study on the fluctuation of prices, costs and industrial production in Poland. To this we should add many additional articles, as well as academic and more popular papers, where he further discussed his theory of the business cycle and his general economic ideas. In this context, there are two academic papers which, in our opinion, are of particular importance. One is a theoretical paper, "Three Systems", (1934a [1990]) where Kalecki contrasted his own view with those of the ruling economic mainstream, showing an in-depth knowledge of the latter.[6] The other one is an applied paper: "Stimulating the Business Upswing in Nazi Germany" ((1935a) [1996]), which is probably the first study where the Nazi experiment was analysed using the principle of effective demand. We will discuss these two papers later on in this book.

In 1933, shortly after the publication of his *Essay*, Kalecki attended the meeting of the Econometric Society in Leyden, where he presented a paper exposing the main ideas from his *Essay* (Kalecki 1935b [1990]). The paper dealt not only with the theory of the cycle, but also with the theory of profits and (though not fully elaborated at that time) the theory of effective demand and output. Interestingly, the parts pertaining to the theory of profits and of effective demand and output, where he anticipated (in our view) important results which Keynes would reach later in the *General Theory*, were completely neglected by attendants to the conference. In contrast, the business-cycle model attracted favourable comments from Ragnar Frisch and Jan Tinbergen, who were at that time leading figures in the field of economics.[7]

Surely thanks to his participation in the Leyden conference, in 1935 Kalecki received a Rockefeller scholarship to study abroad, and in January of 1936 he left for Sweden. We do not know for sure why he chose Sweden, but we conjecture that it was because of his interest in Swedish economic thinking, and probably also due to his poor command of English (although he mastered German). However, he stayed in Sweden only a couple of months, and apparently did not make many professional contacts.[8] Here he read the *General Theory*, which had been published a couple of months earlier. Joan Robinson recollects the following story told to her by Kalecki: "In Stockholm someone gave him Keynes' book. He began to read it – it was the book that he intended to write. He thought that perhaps further on there would be something different. No, all the way it was his book. He said: 'I confess, I was ill.

Three days I lay in bed. Then I thought – Keynes is more known than I am. These ideas will get across much quicker with him and then we can get on to the interesting question, which is their application. Then I got up'" (Robinson 1977: 8–9). Anyway, Kalecki immediately published (in the Polish leading economic journal *Ekonomista*) an incisive review of that book, contrasting Keynes's with his own views. He also decided to go to England.

Cambridge and Oxford

In March 1936, Kalecki arrived in England. Here, he made efforts to contact Keynes's closes collaborators and was able to meet Joan Robinson. Let us hear the story from Robinson herself: "I received a letter, evidently from a foreigner visiting England, who said that he was interested in my article as it was close to some work of his own. I thought this very strange. Who could claim to be doing work that was close to this – the first fruits of the Keynesian revolution? When Michal Kalecki turned up, I was still more astonished. He cared little for party manners or small talk and plunged directly into the subject. He was perfectly familiar with our brand new ideas and he had invented for himself some of Keynes' fanciful concepts, such as the device of burying bank notes in bottles and setting off a boom in mining them. As we talked, I felt like a character in a Pirandello play, I could not tell whether it was I who was speaking or he. But he could challenge a weak point in Keynes' formulation and quickly subdued my feeble attempt to defend it. He told me that he had taken a year's leave from the institute where he was working in Warsaw to write the *General Theory*" (Robinson 1977: 8).

Kalecki's name and ideas were not unknown only to Robinson. In fact, though he had published sections of his *Essay* in English and in French, he was a complete newcomer in British academic circles. He remained in England thanks to an extension of his Rockefeller scholarship,[9] and published new papers in British economic journals. He also travelled to Norway (where he renewed contact with Ragnar Frisch); and to France, where he studied the economic policy of Leon Blum's government. In 1938 he received a scholarship from the University of Cambridge[10] and attended Pero Sraffa's seminar held at Cambridge. In autumn, in the same year, he embarked on the supervision, with Austin Robinson, Richard Kahn, Piero Sraffa and Keynes as chairman of the Cambridge Research Scheme of the National Institute of Economic and Social Research into Prime Costs, Proceeds and Output. We may conjecture that Kalecki's objectives were twofold: First, to collect and analyse evidence relevant to his income distribution theory purporting to explain the stability of the share of wages in national income, and second, to devise a new price theory taking into account both monopolistic and oligopolistic factors.

Kalecki was surely aware that several recently published works, including Colin Clark's (1937) *National Income and Outlay* and Simon Kuznets's (1937) *National Income and Capital Formation 1919–1935*, showed stability of the wage share in the long run. This result puzzled him, because an implication of his initial work was that the wage share should vary counter-cyclically. This would occur due to his assumption of "free" competition: each firm faced with a perfectly elastic demand curve, sets its output at that level where its marginal prime cost equals its selling price. Equilibrium of the firm would be possible only if the firm had a rising marginal cost curve. Kalecki believed this to be the case because there would be diminishing returns when additional labour was used with the given capital equipment. If the marginal prime cost was rising with output (at any rate, if it was rising with a constant or increasing slope, which was taken for granted) the ratio of the wage-bill to sales proceeds would fall (and the ratio of profits to proceeds would rise) with every increase in output.

We will have time later in this book to discuss in detail Kalecki's theory of prices and distribution; but here some brief comments may be useful. To explain the stability of the share of wages in national income, Kalecki made three assumptions: i) The short-period marginal cost curve does not differ considerably in the majority of firms from the average cost curve of manual labour and raw materials up to a certain point corresponding to "practical capacity"; ii) the output of the firms is usually below this point when firms act in a context of imperfect competition; iii) firms set a mark-up on their marginal cost.

Kalecki's assumption i) meant a radical departure from the extant cost and price theory. But Kalecki thought that it was much closer to the actual situation than the assumption whereby unit prime costs rise when output expands.[11] He rationalized it with the argument that increases in output are typically achieved not by increasing workers per machine or bringing inferior machines into use, but by increasing working hours per week.[12] Assumption ii) needed little defending in the depression of the 1930s. To give reason for the point, Kalecki (1939a [1990]: 28n) drew on the arguments of Harrod (1934) and Kaldor (1934) that surplus capacity is a normal consequence of imperfect competition. To substantiate assumption iii), Kalecki turned also to the doctrine of imperfect competition. Referring to Lerner (1934), he explained that the mark-up is determined by the "degree of monopoly", itself equal to the inverse of the elasticity of demand. If a firm's demand curve is determinate and known, the firm will set its output to equate marginal revenue with marginal cost, and at this level of output its selling price will exceed its marginal prime cost.

If marginal prime cost curves are horizontal (assumption i) up to the point of practical capacity (assumption ii), the degree of monopoly (assumption iii), by determining the ratio of price to marginal prime cost, determines the ratio of profits to sales proceeds, and likewise the relative shares of total sales proceeds going to profits and wages.

This was at the time the basis of Kalecki's theory of the distribution of the national income, enabling him to argue that the observed constant labour share in national income is attributable to the approximate stability of the degree of monopoly. And in so far as the degree of monopoly changes at all, it tends to be higher during slumps, while its effect on selling prices would be offset by a cyclical fall in the prices of "basic raw materials" (Kalecki 1939a [1990]: 31).

Kalecki's study for the Cambridge Research Scheme was very important for the completion of his principle of effective demand. Indeed, thanks to his study he came to the notions of "mark-up pricing" and "degree of monopoly", and he was also able to integrate in a more precise manner his theory of prices and distribution with his theory of effective demand. He presented his results on price formation and mark-up pricing in the form of individual reports on the single industries, which attracted a lot of discussion. For example, Richard Stone and Richard Kahn objected to the statistical methodology employed while Joan Robinson and Keynes criticized the "degree of monopoly" concept.[13] Soon afterwards, Kalecki resigned from the Cambridge post and moved to Oxford, where he had obtained a post as a research fellow at the Oxford University Institute of Statistics, and set himself to "writing" a theoretical interpretation of his results (letter from Kalecki to Kahn, 9 June 1939, in RFK 5/1/147 quoted by Marcuzzo, 2008).

Kalecki would remain in England until March 1945. There, his most important professional contact, and friendship, was with Joan Robinson. Mrs. Robinson was the first of the members of Keynes's closest circle to recognize Kalecki's anticipation of the main ideas of Keynes's *General Theory*, and during all her life she would call attention to the importance and pioneer nature of Kalecki's economic theories. Also, Richard Kahn, Maurice Dobb and Piero Sraffa, would become close friends of Kalecki.[14] Apart from them, he worked directly with other members of the Institute of Statistics, such as Thomas Balogh, Ernst Friederich Schumacher, David Worswick, Kurt Mandelbaum (Kurt Martin since

1947), F.A. Burchardt and Josef Steindl. He also had contact with Roy Harrod and Nicholas Kaldor.

Naturally, Kalecki also had professional contact with Keynes. Joan Robinson tells us: "When Kalecki came to Cambridge in 1936, we told Keynes about him, but he was not much impressed...He picked on a phrase in [Kalecki's] *Econometrica*[15] paper that seemed to him too 'monetarist', though in fact it contained a point of view which he later came to himself... Keynes did not sympathize with Kalecki's political presupposition and by background and temperament they could not have been further apart...However, Keynes took the trouble to get a research project set up to provide Kalecki with a job" (Robinson 1977: 9).

Keynes had mixed feelings about Kalecki. He published several of his papers in the *Economic Journal*, of which he was the editor, and he appreciated some of his papers.[16] But sometimes he was very critical and even scathing towards him. Here are some of the comments Keynes wrote to Joan Robinson on a paper Kalecki sent to the *Economic Journal* and which Keynes rejected for publication[17]:

> Kalecki's article,...after a highly rational introduction...my first impression is that it becomes high, almost delirious nonsense. I am ready to believe that there are some assumptions in relation to which his conclusions are correct. But so many are latent and tacit that no-one could say...whether he has proved his proposition. Indeed I do not feel perfectly sure whether the hypothesis may not be self-contradictory. Is it not rather odd when dealing with "long-run problems" to start with the assumptions that all firms are always working below capacity? (Kalecki 1991: 530)

And further

> You tell me that it is a kind of sinful pride which makes Kalecki write like this. I think it is a form of profound stupidity, though physical and aesthetic, perhaps, rather than intellectual...I do not doubt that he is saying something. But I suspect him of being at one of his old tricks in an extreme form, namely, of taking artificial assumptions which have no possible relation to reality or any other merit except that they happen to lead up to a needed result. (Ibid: 531)

Nevertheless, Kalecki soon became a prominent member of the "Keynesian" group,[18] and his research at the Institute of Statistics amplified his reputation, especially in England.

At the Institute, Kalecki further developed his theoretical study of the functioning and dynamics of the capitalist economy, publishing his celebrated *Essays in the Theory of Economic Fluctuations* (Kalecki 1939a [1990]) and a series of papers on the subject; but he also did research on the most pressing problem of the time, namely war economics. The Institute assigned him to work on War Finance; and he produced many papers on this issue, and particularly on rationing. He strongly supported rationing to face the scarcity caused by the war effort, and thus took the contrary stance to Keynes, who instead advocated compulsory savings through taxes in his famous pamphlet "How to Pay for the War?". Here is an informed opinion of someone who worked with Kalecki at the Institute: "I thought at the time, and I still think, that the paper on General Rationing was the most important single thing which Kalecki did in war economics. It is natural to ask what influence it had on actual policy. Of direct influence there is little, if any, evidence... Nevertheless I think that Kalecki's exposition may have helped along the cause of rationing in general" (Worswick 1977: 23).[19]

Kalecki was very skeptical as to the possibility of a crucial reform of capitalism which would make it deliver full employment. His skepticism was based on political considerations, and his view is clearly stated in one of his most famous articles, also written during his stay at the Institute, "Political aspects of full employment" (Kalecki 1943a [1990]; see further Chapter 9). Nevertheless, he also devoted attention to this issue: how to achieve full employment and how to maintain it in a reformed capitalist economy. Thus, together with other members of the Institute, he published "The Economics of Full Employment". This is an outstanding set of papers – one of the best collections of propositions ever published by academic economists – where the issue is tackled from different angles; and Kalecki's paper "Three ways to full employment" (1944a [1990]) would gain a lot of attention. A year earlier he had published, together with Schumacher, "International clearing and long-term lending" (Kalecki 1943b [1997]), which is on a related subject, but this time dealing with the international dimension of the problem; where the authors went beyond Keynes's proposal for reform of the world international monetary and financial arrangements.

We will discuss in detail Kalecki's most important papers from this period in other chapters of this book. Let us now hear opinions regarding his influence from two of his collaborators at the Institute:

> In those days, for me, he was the best economist in the world: there was no doubt about it.... A few years ago at the British Association

> I sounded off about the state of economics and I contrasted some of the activities which go on under the umbrella of economics with "serious economic science". I did not offer a definition of that term. When I think about it now, I realize I must have had at the back of my mind a model of a "serious economist" – Michal Kalecki. I thought him the best when I knew him in the war, and I still think so. (Worswick 1977: 29)

And let us hear one who was perhaps Kalecki's most inspired and original follower, Josef Steindl:

> My years at Oxford were mainly spent at the Oxford Institute of Statistics...The inspiration of the Institute and my guru was Kalecki. Kalecki had a penetrating mind and a passionate interest in what was going on in the world. He continuously absorbed, analysed and discussed the daily flow of events in the economic and political sphere and his judgement almost always proved right. It was due to the availability of Kaleckian solutions that we of the Oxford Institute felt very confident...He remains my inspiration and my reference system till today. (Steindl 1990b: 245–246)

The immediate post-war period

Kalecki remained at the Institute until March 1945, when he left England, going to Montreal to take a post at the International Labour Office (ILO). He worked there mostly on problems of employment and economic reconstruction, but he did not stay long at the ILO. In December 1946, he left to take a position as Assistant Director of the Economic Stability and Development Division in the Department of Economic Affairs of the UN Secretariat, in New York. He would remain there until January 1955, and apparently he did not make many professional contacts with US economists. We know (personal communication to one of the present authors) that he met and frequently discussed with Paul Sweezy (who had already left his academic work to devote himself to his recently founded magazine *Monthly Review*); and we also know that he participated in a Symposium on Fiscal and Monetary Policy at the University of Chicago, together with Lloyd Mints, Alvin Hansen, Howard S. Ellis, and Abba Lerner. But we do not record any other activity at US universities, and we know that he did not have practically any influence on economic thinking in that country.[20]

Let us have the opinion of a collaborator of Kalecki, Sidney Dell, regarding his work at UN:

> It is hardly necessary to say that Kalecki's creativity and brilliance, and above all his deep understanding of the economic and social forces required for growth and development, had a profound influence on most of those with whom he came into contact, whether on the staff or in the councils of the UN. Yet international organizations, like national civil services, are not always able to accommodate men of Kalecki's individuality, notwithstanding certain celebrated exceptions. Moreover the intellectual climate of the early fifties was not conducive to dispassionate consideration of unorthodox ideas such as those espoused by Kalecki. Without going into the details of the matter, it must be noted that a situation was created in 1954 that led to Kalecki's resignation. Bitter as was the moment of his departure, he felt that it was a blessing in disguise to be relieved of the constraints on freedom of expression that any international civil servant must accept. And yet these constraints had been readily accepted by him. In fact, although he was a man of exceptional originality and independence of mind, Kalecki had an austere concept of the discipline to be observed by an international civil servant in the discharge of his duty. As he saw it, the Secretariat could be expected to command the confidence of governments only if it abstained from judgments on their politics and policies. At the same time, reticence on political and policy matters should, Kalecki believed, be accompanied by complete objectivity and fearlessness in discussing the facts and the relationship of those facts to internationally agreed goals. (Dell 1977: 31)

At the UN Kalecki was responsible for the analysis of the current domestic economic problems. These were surveyed in the *World Economic Report* series and a large part of the analysis concerned the problems of full employment and inflation in both developed and underdeveloped countries, including the socialist ones. Dell recalls:

> Kalecki's associates would readily agree that his was the guiding and controlling spirit not only as regards the theoretical framework of the work done but also in the practical analysis carried out. Unlike many theoretical economists of his generation, he was thoroughly familiar with the methods of statistics and econometrics, and he

> directed the analytical work on each and every country studied down to the last detail, and to an extent that was and is unusual for research directors. He also insisted on the greatest possible precision and conciseness of expression, and went over every single word of the text to that end. (1977: 32)

Kalecki also continued with his previous theoretical research, and it was while at the UN that he published, what was perhaps his greatest *opus*, namely his *Theory of Economic Dynamics*. He also gave advice in Israel as a UN official, and a lecture in Mexico; and thanks to this experience during which he produced two very important papers, dealing with the semi-industrialized economy and with the underdeveloped one. He finally resigned because of political considerations, and, in particular, US pressures were affecting his work at the UN. Here is a brief account of the situation:

> The last years of Kalecki's service with the United Nations coincided with the worst phase of the cold war which culminated in the political witch-hunts of Senators McCarren and McCarthy in the United States ... Anyone daring to criticize, or even failing to co-operate with, McCarthyism, left himself open to the serious accusation of being a communist or a fellow traveller. A number of Kalecki's colleagues were dismissed by the Secretary General (Trygve Lie) for undeniably political reasons. (Eshag 1977: 83)
>
> It was because of his uncompromising attitude, that eventually his superiors decided to push him out of the United Nations ... The opportunity for pushing Kalecki out of the United Nations finally came when a scheme for the reorganization of the Secretariat was introduced under which a number of senior Director posts were created. Because of his seniority and his exemplary services to the Secretariat, Kalecki would in the normal course of events, have been entitled to promotion to one of these senior posts from his rank of Assistant Director. But instead, under the reorganization plan Kalecki's post, which carried the responsibility of producing Part I of the World Economic Report, was eliminated and he was asked to perform the lower grade functions of a Chief of Section. It was said that the World Economic Reports were in the future to be written by outside experts and Kalecki and his staff were to have the simple duty of collecting and presenting the data to these experts. Kalecki was thus presented with the option of being humiliated into accepting a sinecure with

> a lower status or resigning. He decided to resign and to return to Poland. (Ibid: 84)

At the end of February 1955 he returned to Poland.

Back to Poland

Kalecki had already made a three-month visit to his home country in 1946. He had been invited by Michal Kaczorowski, then Minister of Reconstruction, and did some work on rationing and the price system, on monetary circulation, and produced a draft project on financial plans for 1946 and 1947. We do not know why he did not decide to settle then in Poland, but we may guess that this was because he was not very optimistic about the political future of his country. At the time the Polish Communist Party was consolidating its power with a blunt offensive against its rivals, and this affected not only those parties and persons who opposed its intention but also all voices different from the communist orthodoxy. After the death of Stalin in 1953, however, the situation had dramatically changed in the communist bloc, and especially so in Poland, where several circumstances left room for optimism. Thus, for example, the government officially recognized that the security apparatus had engaged in anti-democratic activities, and its former head had been dismissed. Journalists and writers gained more freedom of expression and in 1955 the democratization campaign became more visible in cultural reviews. In June 1956, an insurrection begun in Poznan ultimately led to an invitation to Gomułka to serve as First Secretary of the Party.[21] Once in power, he launched some reforms that made him initially very popular, apparently seeking a "Polish way to socialism". However from 1960 onwards the regime became increasingly harsher with dissident voices and communist orthodoxy regained the upper hand. Nevertheless, some degree of freedom of opinion still existed, and it was much larger in Poland than in the other countries of the communist camp.

Shortly after his arrival, in April 1955, Kalecki was appointed adviser to Hilary Minc, then deputy Prime Minister. All along the period going from that date until the beginning of 1960 he held different posts as advisor or consultant mostly on matters dealing with economic planning, and participated in a great number of committees. In fact, he played an important role during 1958 and 1959 in the elaboration of the Outline Perspective Plan for the years 1961–1975. But this Plan was subsequently severely criticized, above all because its targets were considered too modest; and most probably also because it reflected Kalecki's departures from the communist orthodoxy regarding the "laws of development" of the socialist economy (on which more later). Let us hear the story: "In Dec. 1959, Kalecki went for three months to India...During his absence, a conference was held at the Planning Commission...The meeting expressed sharp criticism of the perspective plan. It was denounced for projecting an inadequate rate of development, and in particular an insufficient growth of industrial production...Another pretext which apparently served for the rejection of this version of the plan was the desire (not substantiated by any reliable and consistent economic analysis) to catch up with and even overtake at least one advanced capitalist country in terms of national income...Shortly after this conference and his return from India, in May 1960, Kalecki was removed from his position of a member of the Planning Commission's Board and made 'scientific adviser' to his chairman. This limited his influence on the work of the Planning Commission in general, including its subsequent course of work on the perspective plan" (Osiatynski 1992: 400).

This episode marked the beginning of Kalecki's withdrawal from active participation in the definition of the economic strategy for his country. He would still be nominated for, and take part in, different commissions and committees, but from now onwards, and until his death, he would devote himself mostly to theoretical work and to teaching activities. His last important pronouncement regarding Poland's macroeconomic development and strategy came in his paper "Observations on the 1966–1970 economic plan" (Kalecki 1964 [1992]), which was very critical of the assumptions underlying that plan and on the targets proposed. According to Kalecki's editor:

> The only reply to Kalecki's "Observations" was [Wladyslaw] Gomulka's contemptuous dismissal..."Professors with titles, grown-up people, instead of conducting research, or helping, write nonsensical theses"...Kalecki often said later that it was this reaction of Gomulka that finally persuaded him to leave the Planning Commission. (Osiatynski 1992: 422)

Surely, misgivings towards Kalecki from the authorities were greatly motivated by the attraction he had on that relatively large non-orthodox and more open section of the Polish intelligentsia. Since his arrival, and probably thanks to the relatively open character of the communist rule in Poland at the time, Kalecki's unconventional and non-orthodox outlook provoked a great impact on economic thinking in his country. Let us hear an eyewitness account of this impact:

> My professional life consists of two distinct periods and the border line between them is linked with the definitive return of the Kaleckis to Poland in 1955. Before being confronted with his teaching I was a rather dogmatic Marxist, much more a priest of the "new religion" than a scientist... In November 1955 [Kalecki gave] two lectures on "The impact of militarisation on the business cycle after the Second World War". I knew his name from reading, but since in the Manichaean world of finely drawn divisions between Marxian and bourgeois economics he was not considered a Marxist, I classified him accordingly and was rather sceptical towards the expected benefits of his lectures... It is difficult to describe the first impression Kalecki's lecture made upon me. I saw in front of me a man of a rather small stature, who spoke in a loud voice, but intellectually a kind of sorcerer who played with the familiar schemes of reproduction but used them for asking the most important and pertinent economic questions to arrive at conclusions that were completely opposed to the canons of the "Marxian faith". One of them was that inflation was bad, especially for workers, and a balanced budget was good. This was exemplified by his analysis of the effects of militarisation, which according to the ruling ideology at the time was the main determinant of the successful development of capitalist countries. Kalecki did not deny at all the expansive role of militarisation expenditures but showed that their consequences for the capitalist economy depended on the method of their financing... [He] slightly redefined the notion of two departments by assuming that they are vertically integrated, each of them producing only final goods, while in Marx's schemes of reproduction the first sector produces not only final goods but also intermediary goods for both sectors... The small change introduced by Kalecki clarified immensely the meaning of Marx's schemes of reproduction and put in the centre of analysis the relation between investment goods... and consumption goods... i.e. the relation which became the cornerstone of Kalecki's theory of effective demand in the early 1930s. (Laski, AEPE Newsletter, 36: 2–3)

At first, Kalecki had been reluctant to participate in the discussion concerning the construction of socialism in his country. However:

> The fast changing political circumstances in Poland, boosted ***inter alia*** by Krushchev's denunciation of Stalin at the XX Congress of

> the Soviet Communist Party, opened the way for Kalecki to drop his reservations about the inadvisability of engaging in theoretical discussion of socialist economics. The most significant manifestation of this new attitude came during the National Congress of Economists in June 1956 in the paper on "Investment and national income dynamics in socialist economy". The paper was directed against the so-called law of faster development of the producer goods sector ... as an allegedly absolute condition for sustained growth. By using a simple growth model ... Kalecki demonstrated how inadmissible the absolutist conclusions were. The strong impression Kalecki's paper made on me, as well as on the gathering as a whole, was not because he endorsed or refuted a specific development policy in absolute terms, but because he showed that conclusions have to be derived from assumptions and interrelations clearly defined and without the vagueness that provides the breeding ground for fetishist beliefs planted behind a smoke-screen of "holy Scriptures", in this case of wrongly interpreted Marxian theory. (Brus 1999: 258)

Anyway, apart from his engagement in practical economic matters, after his return to his home country, Kalecki's first-hand knowledge of the working of the socialist economy motivated him to elaborate his major work of this period, the *Introduction to the Theory of Growth in a Socialist Economy* (Kalecki 1963 [1993]), as well as many other more applied papers on the subject. It was around his new theory that he rallied around him a large group of Polish economists in a very lively seminar, creating in fact a whole school of thought on the subject. Let us hear again the opinion of a prominent participant of that school:

> Perhaps most inspiring in the Kaleckian way of practising economics was his constant awareness of the need to combine rationality with full appreciation of its socio-political implications. In no other field, probably, did this come out more clearly during his Polish years than in his work on the theory of growth under socialism and the related problems of long-term planning ... Each step in his analysis contained a careful scrutiny of the consequences of a particular growth policy for living standards. Even with an existing pool of unemployed labour warranting an acceleration of growth, the trade-off between the relative loss in consumption at early stages against later gains was meticulously examined ... I mention the growth theory as an example, but evidently it carried a wider message: all the beloved slogan-type objectives of socialist planners (such as raising productivity as much as possible or aiming at the highest possible levels of

> technology) should not be regarded as fetishes and must be subjected to rational examination in the light of existing circumstances and in relation to their social effects. (Brus 1999: 258–259)

Besides his work on the socialist economy, Kalecki further developed his analysis and his theory of the advanced capitalist economy. At the end of 1955 he had been given a post at the Institute of Economics of the Polish Academy of Sciences. There he set up a small group of young economists working on the economic situation of advanced capitalist countries, which produced a series of papers applying his theory.[22] In fact, it was in this period that he produced three of the papers he would include in his posthumous *Selected Essays on the Dynamics of the Capitalist Economy, 1933–1970*; as well as other equally important theoretical and applied papers.

A third important aspect of Kalecki's activity in those years was his work on the economic problems of the less developed economies. Here is a quotation of the experience of one of his closest collaborators in this area, which we reproduce in full in spite of its length:

> In Warsaw, together with Oscar Lange and Czeslaw Bobrowski, Kalecki started in 1958 an advanced seminar on underdeveloped economies and convened it with great regularity for almost 10 years. The seminar became a focal point for all researchers and practitioners dealing with the less developed economies. It was addressed by a large number of distinguished foreign speakers many of whom came from the Third World. It discussed many reports from the field, analysed actual plans and played with enthusiasm Kalecki's famous planning games. Thus a group produced a draft plan for "Cocolandia" building on the experience gained by Polish planners in Ghana. Another addressed itself to the strategies that could be initiated by an enlightened monarch in an oil-rich country. A third game was concerned with building the model of an economy based on extensive cattle breeding made possible by exceptional natural conditions; data from Mongolia were used, but discussions were also held on the historical experiences of Argentina and Australia.
>
> In 1961 a small Research Centre on underdeveloped economies was started under the joint sponsorship of the Central School of Planning and Statistics and Warsaw University. Kalecki became the Chairman of its Scientific Board and took a very active interest in the day to day affairs of the Centre…The standards imposed by Kalecki were stringent and his criticism was very sharp. But he was so generous with

> his time and so objective in his judgement that most of us considered his proverbially uncompromising attitude as a unique opportunity to learn from him. Some of Kalecki's own papers were prompted by the research projects carried out at the Centre….
>
> A third institution closely associated with the two mentioned above was the Higher Course in National Economic Planning for economists from less developed countries. About 25 students from Latin America, Africa and Asia would spend several months in Warsaw, attending lectures given in English, writing diploma papers and eventually staying for a couple of years to prepare a doctoral dissertation. Kalecki was the central figure in the teaching staff and supervised several doctorates. He had a major role in designing the curricula and saw to it that they gave an unbiased picture of the working of a socialist economy with its bright and dark sides. He would repeatedly warn the students against transposing Polish experiences to the institutionally different context of less developed economies. (Sachs 1977: 47–49)

On the other hand, Kalecki was very active in teaching; and he remained involved, practically until his death. In 1956 the Central Qualification Commission conferred on him his first academic title: Professor of Economics; and somewhat later in that year he was appointed Professor of Economics of the Polish Academy of Sciences. In 1960 he was appointed a member of the Committee of Economic Sciences of the Polish Academy of Sciences. In 1961 he began lecturing at the Central School of Planning and Statistics (SGPiS), and then resigned from his other posts and took a full-time job there.[23] In 1962 the Minister of Higher Education appointed him deputy chairman of the board of the newly founded Centre of Research on Underdeveloped Economies, also located at SGPiS; and in that same year he was appointed member of the research council of the Advanced Course in National Economic Planning for economists from less developed countries, closely linked with the Centre. At the beginning of that year he was also appointed full Professor in the Chair of Political Economy at the Foreign Trade Faculty of the SGPiS.

During this period Kalecki gave two regular courses at the SGPiS, based on this own theories, and conducted two seminars. The first one was based on his *Introduction to the Theory of Growth of the Socialist Economy*; and this was also the course he gave at the Advanced Course in National Economic Planning. The second one, on his theory of the functioning and dynamics of the capitalist economy, led in 1968 to a proposal to Penguin, the publishing company, following a request from them:

> I have been giving for a number of years a course on [the] economic dynamics of [the] capitalist system ... consisting of about ten lectures. It includes the problems of government intervention and ... my new ideas on investment decisions and trend. I may try to write it up which, however, will take some time because I lecture without notes.
>
> I have to say in advance that this would be less precise than my other writings, because the purpose of the course is to give to the students a general idea of the functioning of the **laissez faire** and the present capitalist system. It is therefore necessary to skip over some intricate points. (Osiatynski 1991: 605–606)[24]

In each one of his two courses, Kalecki presented exclusively his own theory, without much reference to other theories. The classes were attended not only by students, but also by teachers. In the first hour he would expose the relevant part, and he would then give attendants a fifteen-minute break, in order to reflect on the points presented and prepare their questions. During this break, he would slowly pace in the corridor, with his hands on his back, immersed in his thoughts. Then he would come back to the classroom and would write on the blackboard the main ideas presented in the first hour of the class. Attendants would then be invited to put forward their questions and comments; and of course, everybody would prepare very carefully their question, because this was like an exam for them. If there was not any question to one of the points on the blackboard, he would synthesize the argument previously developed and go on to the following point. He would answer with extreme politeness to all questions, and from his answers one always got the impression that he had already reflected carefully on any possible objection or counter argument to his theory to the last detail.

Kalecki had his office at SGPiS, and he would arrive to work very early in the morning, and would remain there all the time except for brief breaks to have a tea at the cafeteria or at lunchtime. His office, a rather large one, would be open to anyone wanting to consult him, and you would find him usually pacing slowly, thinking or reading. The books on his desk would most of the time not be of economics, and those of economics would not deal with theory, but rather with applied economics. If he was busy when one came to see him, he would give another appointment, in very precise terms. At the time of the meeting, he would listen carefully, and then would answer the questions or the points that have been raised in very neat terms, very politely and without trying to prove the other person utterly wrong; even when that's the case. If he was consulted by letter, his answers would come relatively quickly, and would have the same respectful tone. He carefully kept all the incoming and outgoing correspondence; even when his original letter had been handwritten.

Kalecki was conscious of his importance as an economist and of the relevance of his theory. In the Preface to a collection made of some of his early papers, *Studies in the Theory of Business Cycles. 1933–1939* he wrote: "As the reader will find, I had dealt in these essays with a number of basic issues which were in the centre of economic discussion during the subsequent twenty years". However, later in life he realized that economic thinking had been changing, and that a new fad had arrived which did not attach the necessary importance to what he saw as the crucial theoretical issues of capitalist economies. One of us (JL) recalls a conversation with Kalecki after he returned from a visit to Cambridge, where he had been invited for a term in the spring of 1969. He remarked that he was not given the intellectual positive reception he was expecting, and had the feeling that the new developments he had made to his theory were not sufficiently appreciated. He mentioned in particular that he had not received practically any academic feedback from his last version of his business-cycle theory (Kalecki 1968a [1991]).

Kalecki's last years of life were gloomy. He was in bad health, having had a heart attack in December 1965 which left a lasting imprint. Moreover, his health and his inner-self were also negatively affected by external factors, and particularly by the deteriorating political situation in his country. The Israeli Arab war of 1967, when all the communist camp had sided with the Arabs, and the liberalization attempts carried out in Czechoslovakia, led to a repressive move in Poland; which had also an anti-Semitic connotation.[25] The situation worsened after March 1968, due to the emergence of student unrest and street protests. In that same month a conference was organized at the SGPiS, in which Kalecki's theories were attacked as being non-Marxist and bourgeois (!). Universities were purged against anyone not aligned with orthodoxy, and almost all of Kalecki's closest collaborators were sacked. Thus, the very lively and original Kaleckian school of thought that had been created in that country was dismantled.

One of us (JL) can convey to the reader a brief final recollection. I visited him in his flat in June 1969, when he had already resigned his post at SGPiS. He was lying on his bed dressed, and he looked pale and tired, speaking in a low voice; something unusual in him. He was sad and pessimistic about Poland, and he called attention to me on how he had tried to help his home country and how badly it had treated him; he was not bitter, though. But he had not lost his interest on world events and on economics. Afterwards, I corresponded with him, and was thrilled when he responded positively to my invitation to write something on "economic dependency" for a Latin American journal. Alas, this was never completed. Michal Kalecki passed away on April 17, 1970.

2
Kalecki's Theory of Profits and Output

Kalecki formulated the principle of effective demand in the context of his theory of economic dynamics, dealing with the equilibrium of income occurring at a given point of the cycle. Thus, he put forward his short-term analysis in the framework of a dynamic process, whereby the economy is subject to a long-run trend and cycles. The short- and long-term aspects of his analysis were a part of his methodology; first, allowing centring on situations he labelled "quasi-equilibria" or "short-period equilibria" situations in which the stock of capital is assumed given, and second, explaining how, as soon as the capital stock is assumed to vary, the economy is likely to enter in a continual movement through a series of short-period equilibriums or quasi-equilibriums.

The aim of this chapter is to present Kalecki's final formulation of his theory of profits and income determination, centring first on the short-term analysis, and afterwards discussing briefly the long-period theory.[1] In the next chapter we describe the process whereby Kalecki reached his final formulation. We also emphasize that in a short-period, Kalecki carried out an in-depth discussion of the macroeconomic effects of changes in variables that explain the cycle, such as investment. He also considered changes in variables that are assumed to either remain constant or move slowly in the course of the cycle, such as capitalist consumption, wages or interest rate.

Moreover, we note that Kalecki acknowledges the importance of monetary phenomena in his theory. Consistently, in his writings, adjustments between profits and capitalist expenditure are always conceived in an economy where the monetary and real sector interact. However, to simplify, we will first abstract from the complications of the monetary sector, taking into account the interactions occurring between the real and monetary sectors only in a second stage.

The basic short-period model

We will consider a capitalist economy made up of large number of firms that produce a variety of goods, and where government and foreign trade are negligible. We will first look at how equilibrium of production is attained. Here, we define "equilibrium" in a rather narrow sense; that is, as a situation where the level of production equals sales, and there is no undesired variation in the stocks of unsold goods of firms.

Production may vary within limits, depending on the availability of the workforce and the degree of utilization of the available capacity (which we assume as given in the short run). If we suppose that there is an abundant reserve of labour force, then the upper limit of production will be determined by the productive capacity and, more specifically, by the maximum utilization of that capacity.

Final demand for goods and services consists of two parts. First is the capitalists' demand for consumer and investment goods. Second is the workers' demand for consumer goods (wage goods). Kalecki assumed most of the time that workers do not save, and we will keep this assumption unless we state otherwise. We may also suppose that in any given short period the demand of the capitalists is independent of the value of production; we discuss this assumption in detail later on. Workers' demand does however vary with production. Upon increased production, the hired workforce will grow and subsequently, the total payment of wages will grow as well. Since wage earners consume all their wages, the higher the wages, the higher workers' consumption.

Furthermore, let us assume, with Kalecki, that in the short run labour productivity is given and is constant (in other words, unlike in the neoclassical story, we do not assume decreasing marginal returns to labour). Then, if money wages per worker are given and constant, unit prime costs and the unit wage cost are also constant. Now, if the profit margin (which we define as $[p-u]/u$, where p is the unit price and u is the unit prime cost) and the real wage are also positive constants, workers' consumption will rise in proportion to output.

Our assumption may give rise to an interesting question – Having assumed prices exceed unit costs (the profit margin is positive), how then can we simultaneously assume, with Kalecki, that firms have idle production capacity? In fact, with optimizing behaviour of the firms, or even simple "rule-of-the-thumb" behaviour, we would expect that all firms produce up to a limit of the existing capacity. By keeping idle capacity their total profits appear to be lower than they could be otherwise. Kalecki's (1939c [1991]: 33) answer to this puzzle was: "[According to] the theory of imperfect competition...the entrepreneur considers in fact that the extension of 'his' market would require such a reduction in prices that this would not be offset by increased sales...The establishments are in general not fully utilized, since they maintain a monopolistic (cartel) or quasi-monopolistic (imperfect competition) position in the market". We will come back to this issue later on.

Let us now return to our previous discussion and assume that the value of production rises, in turn increasing the workers' consumption. However, *this increase will be lower than the increase in the value of production*, because the latter must include a potential profit. Please note, *up until now profits are purely potential*. Their materialization, or *realization*,[2] requires that the goods be sold.

The total expenditure, or total effective demand, thus depends positively on the value of production, since part of this expenditure is linked to the value of production. To better understand our definition of "equilibrium" and Kalecki's reasoning in this aspect, we will now examine a situation of disequilibrium.

We may suppose that on the basis of, for example, optimistic expectations related to higher value of sales, entrepreneurs have decided to expand production,[3] without raising investment or their consumption *in that same period*. What would happen in a situation like this? At the new level of production, the value of production will be higher than the value of sales. Indeed, sales would have increased to an amount equal to workers' consumption. But then workers' additional consumption will equal their extra wages, which are lower than the value of the extra production. Therefore, relatively low demand will result in part of the production being unsold and stocked in the firms.

Firms may respond and deal with these unwanted goods in two different ways. First, they could lower prices so as to expand sales. According to Kalecki, and also to most empirical research, this is not a very common behaviour, at least in the short term. It appears that prices, and the profit margin, are not cut when sales are lower than expected. In any case, we consider the repercussion of reducing prices later on, because we need to introduce factors not considered hitherto.[4] A second response could be to reduce production in the next period.

If entrepreneurs take the second decision, this will have more or less the following consequences. Firms that have excess of unsold goods will reduce production. The lowering of production will lead to a drop in the level of employment. The drop in employment will result in lower wages. Lower wages will lead to lower consumption, and to lower effective demand. The latter will, in turn, lead to unwanted stocks of unsold goods, and so on. This process of repeated reductions will continue to a point where the value of production equals the value of sales.

In this light, we will now emphasize some essential aspects of this analysis. First, we can see that the equilibrium between aggregate supply and aggregate demand can be established below full employment. Second, when capitalist expenditure is given, the change in output (and hence income) itself acts as an equilibrating force. That is, when the economy is in a state of excess aggregate supply described above, then the resulting decline in output, and hence income, will depress supply more than demand and thus eventually bring the economy to equilibrium. Kalecki's theory of effective demand is concerned not only with the mathematical solution of the equilibrium between aggregate supply and aggregate demand, but also with the demonstration of the stability of this equilibrium.

We can draw here some important "Kaleckian" conclusions.

a) First of all, we need to emphasize the determining force of effective demand on levels of economic activity (production and employment). In effect, it is clear that the capital installed and the available workforce set the upper limit of production (potential output). In practice, however, the real level of production is determined by the ability to sell goods and therefore, in turn, by the level of effective demand.

The reason why we assign the role of the independent variable to effective demand can also be argued from a different angle. Let us suppose that, for whatever reason, effective demand changes autonomously. Then production will tend to change in the same direction. Indeed, entrepreneurs are stimulated to respond to demand whenever this allows profits to rise, and total profits will always rise if the profit margin is positive. On the contrary, if we suppose, that, for whatever reason, entrepreneurs decide to increase production without altering their expenses, it would create a situation of disequilibrium in which production would exceed demand.

In effect, when production changes autonomously, demand will follow suit, since the payroll and workers's consumption will change. But if capitalist demand for consumption and investment goods is fixed, absolute (and autonomous) changes in the value of production will always be higher than the absolute changes in the value of demand, since the latter only varies in relation to wages, which are inferior to the value of the goods. This leads to an undesired variation in stocks, which indicates a situation of disequilibrium, which tends to correct itself later.

This analysis proves how production adjusts to demand, and not the other way around.

b) Second, we need to clarify the casual, or derived, character of the equilibrium between production and sales. In effect, in a capitalist economy the forces underlying decisions of production and those underlying the market for that production do not coincide, and do not even respond to the same logic.

The first – within the boundaries of productive capacity – is determined by the short-term expectations of capitalists and stands in relation to its possibilities of sales and profits. The second, however, is determined by a group of factors, which determine capitalist expenditure; and where demand for investment goods plays a central role.

The normal pattern is, therefore, not so much a situation of equilibrium but of discrepancy between production and expenses. In Kalecki's framework, the (usual) short-run correction mechanism is the variation in stocks; not change in prices and in the profit margin.

Kalecki insisted that in a capitalist economy, existence of idle capacity and unemployed workers would be a normal situation . Even more so, he also showed that capitalism does not contain forces that spontaneously lead to the maximum use of the means of production, or a complete utilization of the workforce.

Kalecki's theory of gross profits and output

To summarize the conditions of the generation and utilization of output, it will now be useful to present the way in which the different parts composing the global output created during this period, are sold at the end of this period. In this context, we will be able to present Kalecki's theory of profits, one of his most original contributions.

Let us assume that all industries are vertically integrated, in the sense that they do not buy (or sell) raw materials or productive inputs. Accordingly, for any industry, and for the whole economy, the value of production is equal to the gross value added (inclusive of depreciation). To simplify the reasoning, we assume that only capitalists and productive workers exist. Then the total value of production can be decomposed into total wages plus (gross) profits. Also, from the point of view of sales, production can be decomposed into production of investment goods, production of consumption goods for capitalists, and production of consumption goods for workers (wage goods). But then, if workers do not save, profits will be necessarily equal to capitalist consumption plus (private) investment. Namely,

$$P = I + C_k \tag{2.1}$$

where P is gross profits, I is (private) investment, and C_k is capitalist consumption.

In accordance with what we have argued, while workers spend what they earn, capitalists earn what they spend: the amount of their expenditure determines the amount of profits they can make.

Kalecki explains in this context the sense of causality between profits and capitalist expenditure. He asks, "What is the significance of this equation [$P = I + C_k$]? Does it mean that profits in a given period determine capitalist consumption and investment, or the reverse of this? The answer to this question depends on which of these items is directly subject to the decision of capitalists. Now, it is clear that capitalists may decide to consume and to invest more in a given period than in the preceding one, but they cannot decide to earn more. It is, therefore, their investment and consumption decisions which determine profits, and not vice versa." (Kalecki 1954a [1991]: 239–240)". In other words, capitalist demand (for investment goods and consumption) determines the level of sales and production, and – given unitary costs – establishes a level of costs such that the difference between sales and costs – the amount of gross profits obtained from them – exactly equals capitalist expenditure.

We will now elaborate on this point. If total capitalists expenditure were the same in every period, then profits would be constant. However, in a capitalist regime the common rule is that the capitalists' consumption and investment fluctuate constantly over time. It is, therefore, necessary to identify the independent variables or data in the (implicit) model. In any given period, the level of expenditure is the result of decisions taken in the past, in previous periods. That is to say, in any given period, capitalists decide on their expenditure, but not on their profits. In fact, profits need not only be produced, but they also need to be realized. As we already said, until they are realized, that is, until the commodities are sold at their production prices, profits are purely potential.[5]

Two elements influence the delay in investment. First, the risk involved in any investment, which forces capitalists to carefully ponder and consider many elements before deciding whether or not, and how much, they will invest. The second element that influences the delay in investment is the period needed for the construction of the equipment that materially constitutes the investment.

The delay in consumption is explained by the fact that capitalist consumption is decided *before* profits come into existence. As we mentioned, profits are purely virtual before the goods are sold; unless capitalists consume and invest, they will make no profits at all. Furthermore, we may assume that capitalist consumption only slowly adjusts to changes in profits.

The point we previously discussed concerning the *predetermined nature of capitalist expenditure* is a very essential one in Kalecki's theory. The author did not give a detail explanation of this point, probably because he considered it obvious. But it appears that it is anything but self-evident; in fact, economic analysis has seldom given much thought to this issue.[6] It may be important, therefore, we say a few words about it; even at the cost of making a small detour in our exposition.

Early in the elaboration of his theory, Kalecki assumed the existence of a "decision period" of a certain length, and he distinguished between investment orders, investment outlays and delivery of capital goods. The process that he envisioned takes into account the existence of several short periods and can be described as follows. At the end of (say) period 0 all pending investment decisions have been carried out. During period 1 new profits are realized, which generate a certain rate of profits; new savings accrue to firms; and the whole economic environment evolves in a certain way that influences new investment decisions. New investment orders arise at the end of period 1. During period 2, production of capital goods takes place, which, together with capitalist consumption, determines profits and aggregate demand in period 2.

The process previously described implies that in Kalecki's model the investment process is time-dependent in a very precise sense. In any given short period, investment is *predetermined*. Moreover, it is unlikely to fall or rise based on the current situation; unless the latter abruptly and dramatically changes, due to, for example, "crises of confidence".[7] Here, we should consider that capital goods are not bought in a shop, but they are ordered from capital good producers, with very precise specifications. The latter incur costs when they carry out the fabrication of the goods ordered. Accordingly, they normally ask for monetary advances, and formal – that is, legal – commitments from the entrepreneurs who deliver the order. Therefore, Kalecki concluded that investment decisions once made are very difficult to cancel because then they prove very costly to both capital goods producers and the entrepreneurs who placed the orders.[8] Kalecki also supposes, which seems realistic, that the decisions of the capitalists on investment and consumption have been taken in *real terms*, so that when, for example, prices increase (or fall) in the time span between the moment in which these decisions were taken and the moment in which they materialize, *real* expenditure will not change (though *monetary* expenditure will be affected).

We come back now to the core of our exposition. We will show now that when we take income distribution as given, capitalist expenditure determines, together with the amount of profits, the total national income.

The argument is straightforward. In fact, in the case of a private and closed economy, the capitalist expenditure on income and consumption determines the amount of profits realized. Moreover, production of investment and consumer goods for capitalists implies a certain amount of employment; and gives rise to wages, which determine workers' consumption. Now, given the income distribution between profits and wages, the total of paid wages and the total consumption of the wage earners can be established. The latter appears, therefore, as an induced element entirely determined by capitalist expenditure and income distribution.

This means that there is a functional relationship between income, the expenditure of the capitalists and income distribution. Given the levels of (gross) investment and capitalist consumption, the amount of domestic income that can be created depends on income distribution. The higher the share of wages in domestic income, the higher the total of wages paid. Thus, the consumption of wage earners and total effective demand will be higher.[9] We specify this as follows:

$$Y = \frac{P}{e} \tag{2.2}$$

where Y is demand (and output), P is total gross profits, and e is the relative share of profits in value added.

Now, given that the level of output will be higher when the share of wages in income is higher, we can conclude that the degree of utilization of the existing productive capacity will also be higher. Given that employment directly depends on the levels of production and demand, we can affirm that when capitalist expenditure is given, the higher the share of wages in domestic income, the higher the levels of employment. In other words, both the levels of employment and the degree in which the installed capacity is utilized are closely linked to the existing income distribution in the economy.

The short-run dynamics

We will now examine how changes in effective demand create changes in the levels of economic activity. Our interest is an economy which is subject to changes. However, the changes we examine here is related to the short run; that is to say, a period in which we assume that productive capacity does not change.

We have said that, depending on the amount of idle productive capacity, upon an increase in effective demand, an increase in capitalist expenditure will, directly and indirectly, stimulate the level of economic activity. If thus, for example, a higher level of investment takes place, this will lead to an increase in the amount of wages paid, higher production of wage goods, and so on. Now, increased capitalist expenditure allows for an increase in profits and this can stimulate, with a certain delay, a new rise in investment and capitalist consumption. By considering in detail what happens when investment increases, we will study how higher profits influence capitalist consumption – that is, the dictum sometimes attributed to Kalecki: "when workers spend what they earn capitalists earn what they spend".

Changes in output and employment occur in response to changes in effective demand, which – in a private and closed economy – consists of the demand of the capitalists and the workers. We previously showed that, when income distribution is a constant and no saving out of wages takes place, workers' demand is not autonomous but induced. We will first examine the effects derived from a change in capitalist expenditure, our central autonomous variable.

We take as a point of departure an increase in capitalist expenditure, for example in investment, which is explained by, let us say, an important technical innovation that stimulates new investments because entrepreneurs expect a higher income-yield capacity from the new productive equipment. Accordingly, profits rise. Since the level of capitalist consumption depends to a certain degree upon the level of profits, it can be expected that an increase in profits would, at some point, lead to an increase in their consumption. However, let us assume, to simplify, that the time lapse we consider is short enough that higher profits (derived from higher investment) do not affect capitalist consumption.

If some capitalists decide to invest more (while maintaining their consumption at the same level) they will increase their demand for investment goods. Their increased purchase of these goods will imply an increase in the demand for those industries that produce capital goods, which leads to an expansion of production and employment (and, therefore, higher profits) in the sector producing these goods. The higher level of employment in this sector brings about a higher demand for wage-goods and this leads to higher production and employment in the group of industries that produce wage-goods. This higher level of production and employment, obviously, also increases profits in this sector. Thus, profits and wages increase in the entire economy. That is to say – assuming that income distribution does not change – higher investment creates an expansive process; that is, there will appear a "multiplier" of the original investment.

Now, income must increase at a level that equals the increase in wages and profits. Moreover, this increase should be such that the profits it creates equal the increase in investment.

There is one crucial point underlying the previous reasoning: the degree of utilization of the productive capacity. Supply will only expand if the industries concerned have a certain margin of idle capacity. This is a realistic assumption in developed countries; but is not necessarily the case in underdeveloped economies.[10] On the other hand, it is evident that in order to have the new investment provoke an increase in employment, new workers are needed. This comes from the reserve of the unemployed.

When we consider the increase in capitalist expenditure, it's vital to study another aspect – investment. We will discuss this theme in detail at a later stage. Spending on additional means of production increases productive capacities in the long run, but in the short run it only acts as effective demand. This occurs because the rapid increase in production and profits *presupposes the previous existence of idle productive capacity*. So, we ask, does investment not create productive capacity also? Yes, but it is only being made concrete in the time span that stretches from one period to another, or in other words, there is a gestation period for investment during which the installed capacity is not yet being increased.

The previous analysis, and in particular the one related to the increase in capitalist expenditure, presents us a question we need to answer. We need to explain where the money comes from that pays for the increase in expenditure. We must note at the outset that this is a different question from the one referring to the relationship between savings and investment. More concretely, we are not asking here, where does the saving which funds the increase in investment come from? The latter is an issue we will deal with afterwards.

Now, if we assumed that capitalists spend the same amount time after time, this question would be irrelevant. But we know that capitalist expenditure varies. Since previous profits are the main source to finance capitalist expenditure, it is unclear at first sight how capitalists can initiate a cycle of increased expenditure, which would imply higher profits that do not yet exist.

A first alternative is that they can spend more by taking money from their accumulated hoardings. In this way, the given capitalist expenditure increases with a certain factor, which creates a higher expenditure that allows for an increase in total profits, in an amount that equals the new expenditure. But let us assume that profits grow on a permanent basis. This implies that expenditure will also grow permanently, and that, therefore, the growing increase of expenditure will finally drain the accumulated hoardings. Expenditure cannot then grow more along this basis. What is the alternative left?

From a macroeconomic perspective, we have therefore to assume that capitalists need to have recourse to credit. The outcome of our analysis is then that capitalists will need to go into debt if they want to spend on a growing basis. In a simplified manner this process can be visualized as follows. We assume that capitalists decide to increase investment and that in order to finance this investment they turn to bank credit. When asking for and paying for the investment goods demanded, the capitalists of the sector producing these goods will receive the money and will return it as deposits to the banks.

As a consequence the question "what is the origin of the money that the capitalists use to finance increased expenditure?" can be answered by the assumption of bank credit elasticity, which allows the capitalists to get into debt.

At this stage, we should mention that Kalecki had quite a sophisticated view, although apparently neglected, of how money and the real economy interact.[11] Already in his first theoretical papers he clearly established that a stable flow of spending would tend to recreate the previous volume of bank deposits and hence also the lending capacity of banks (what Keynes would call "the revolving fund"). He also noted that availability of extra liquidity was required for private spending, and more so, for investment spending to grow. He also emphasized the strategic role of banks – commercial as well as the central bank – in providing the extra finance, and in avoiding drastic rises in the interest rate that might abort a business upswing.

Broadly speaking, in Kalecki's overall vision, money is an endogenous consequence of demand for finance. Supply of finance tends to accommodate for the demand of it, *but only if and when the banking system responds to that demand.* Finally, the price of finance (the rate of interest) can vary depending on the interplay between the central bank's monetary policy, the behaviour of commercial banks, and the level of output.

However, the question as to the origin of the additional savings, which are the counterpart of the additional investment, can also be answered here. Before the additional investment is being carried out, the *actual* additional savings do not yet exist, only the *potential* additional savings exist. These are embodied in the idle capacity that will be used when output increases thanks to the injection of additional demand. More concretely, the additional investment increases profits, which give rise to the additional savings. Over any short period, investment creates savings, and not the other way around.

Appendix 2.1

This Appendix, as well as the Appendices to the remaining chapters of this book, is largely based on the notes taken by one of the present author (JL) of M. Kalecki's lectures at the Central School of Planning and Statistics, Warsaw, during the academic year 1967–1968.

We will illustrate the reasoning of the first part of the text with the aid of Figure A2.1. The demand of the capitalists, symbolized by G_k, is independent of the value of production. Workers' consumption as symbolized by C_w, does however vary with production, and it appears as the straight line C_w in Figure A2.1. This straight line has a positive angle, which is, however, less than 1. The angle is positive because an increase in production leads to an increase in demand, since employment and salaried consumption C_w will be higher. The slope's value of less than one (the slope is below 45°) is explained because wages absorb only a percentage (less than 100%) of the value of production.

The total expenditure, or total effective demand, thus depends positively on the value of production since part of this expenditure is linked to the value of production. This is symbolized in the figure by the straight line $G = G_k + C_w$. It can been seen that production in equilibrium Y_e is achieved when the straight line OA crosses the straight line G_kG_k by a value of demand that equals G_e.

To fix ideas, let us consider a situation of disequilibrium, in which entrepreneurs have decided to expand production up until a certain value Y_a (in which $Y_a > Y_e$). At this level of production (and employment), demand equals the distance Y_aC. The value of production will, then, be

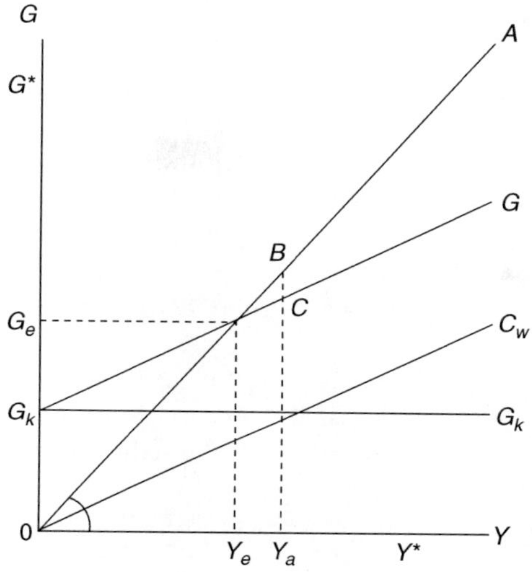

Figure A2.1

higher, and the excess of production over sales will equal the distance Y_aB. If the slope of the straight C_w is constant, production will then fall to the point $Y_e = G_e$ of graph I.[12]

In other words, the intersection of the aggregate-demand curve with the 45° line determines equilibrium real output on the left of that level of production Y^* entailing full employment of the labour force and of the capital.

Figure A2.1. above, shows a situation of equilibrium. However, this has to be understood as a simply fortuitous, and therefore highly unlikely, result of the qualitative equivalence between the decisions made in relation to production and those made in relation to expenses, or as a "terminal situation" in which initial disequilibrium has already been corrected.

We now put forward the following question: How is each part of the gross value of production realized? To simplify, let us assume that all sectors are vertically integrated.

a) The demand for an amount that equals the value of total wages, as contained in the product (W) comes from workers' consumption (C_w).
b) The demand for an amount that equals the value of the wear and tear of the means of production, plus a part of the profits, which

is contained in the value of production, comes from capitalists' expenditure in order to replace the means of production worn out during the production period, and to expand their means of production. This is gross investment (I).

c) The demand for amount that equals another part of the gross profits, contained in the output is sold by means of the consumption of the capitalist class (C_k).
d) Thus the consumption of the capitalists and their gross investment equal gross profits (before deduction of depreciation).

The results of the previous analysis can be also formalized as follows. The first two equations to follow relate income to, on the one hand, effective demand and on the other, to the incomes of the two main classes. The third equation links the net capitalist profits to capitalist expenditure. The fourth refers to gross profits. We assume a private and closed economy.

$$Y = I + C_k + C_w \tag{A2.1}$$

Y is income (gross of depreciation), I is gross investment (gross of depreciation), C_k is capitalist consumption, and C_w consumption out of wages.

On the other hand, given that income (gross) is distributed between capitalists and the wage earners, we have:

$$Y = P + W \tag{A2.2}$$

and therefore

$$P + W = I + C_k + C_w \tag{A2.3}$$

where Y stands for gross income (GDP), I stands for gross private investment (replacement investment plus net investment), C_k stands for the consumption of the capitalists and C_w for the consumption of the wage earners, P stands for gross profits (which includes the value of the depreciation of capital equipment and which equals net profits plus depreciation), and W for the total of paid wages. If we suppose that the workers do not save nor get into debt, we get:

$$P = I + C_k \tag{A2.4}$$

or

$$P = G_k \tag{A2.4}$$

where G_k stands for capitalist expenditure.

We can easily see that workers' savings would imply lower profits, and that their dissaving (e.g., because of debts) would mean higher profits.

$$P = G_k - S_w \qquad \text{(A2.5)}$$

In Kalecki's theory, in any given period, G_k is given, and the level of P is the dependent variable. Thus G_k determines P and never the other way around. Furthermore, capitalist expenditure determines, together with the amount of profits, the total national income. The argument is as follows. P is the level of gross profits. Y is the level of income and e stands for the relative share of profits in domestic income.[13] Then,

$$Y = \frac{P}{e} \qquad \text{(A2.6)}$$

Furthermore, we can assume that in a short period capitalist consumption can be broken up into two parts; a part that is fixed in the short run, and another part that is variable, since it depends on profits. We can specify this as follows:

$$C_k = A + \lambda P_{t-n}$$

where *A* represents the constant part of capitalist consumption, and λ is a parameter higher than zero but lower than one. "λP" is thus the variable component of capitalist consumption, that is to say, that part which adjusts according to the change in the level of profits. Subscript "*t–n*" simply states that this dependence is not immediate, but there is a certain time delay between the period in which the profits change and the one in which consumption finally changes. In order to simplify, we will suppose for the moment that this delay is infinitely small (or, that "*n*" is close to zero), so that we can write

$$C_k = A + \lambda P \qquad \text{(A2.7)}$$

Considering this new relationship and remembering that $P = I + C_k$, making the necessary changes gives us

$$P = I + A + \lambda P$$

which allows us to express P as

$$P = \frac{I + A}{1 - \lambda} \qquad \text{(A2.8)}$$

Thus, total profits of a certain period are linear function of investment and the stable part of capitalist consumption.

We can thus establish the following:

$$Y = \frac{I + A}{e(1 - \lambda)} \qquad \text{(A2.9)}$$

It follows that demand and output are inversely (positively) related to the share of profits (wages) in value added. They are, however, positively related to the capitalists' propensity to consume λ.

We will now return to the role of investment. From our previous equations we can also deduce that, for example, when technological innovations stimulate new investment, this would lead to an increase in profits. This level of increased profits can be calculated by means of the following equation:

$$\Delta P = \frac{\Delta I}{1 - \lambda}$$

and an increase in total income, also of a certain amount that is easy to establish

$$\Delta Y = \frac{\Delta I}{e(1 - \lambda)}$$

We can see that to the degree in which λ is greater than zero and less than one, the increase in profits will exceed the increase in investment. This can be explained by the fact that under these conditions the increase in profits triggers effects in capitalist consumption. Moreover, if we suppose that the distribution coefficient e is constant and less than one, we can demonstrate that the increase in income will be higher than the increase in profits. This occurs because part of the higher income consists of increased real wages. Thus higher production and employment create an increase in the demand of wage-goods. Therefore (if there is idle capacity in the sector producing wage goods) total real wages will increase. Thus,

$$\Delta Y = \Delta P + \Delta W$$

This shows that total income changes with such a factor that the amount of profits obtained from the change in income, equals the new amount of investment plus capitalist consumption.

We will now examine Kalecki's formulation of the principle of effective demand in detail. We will specify the intersectorial relations that exist in a modern economy and examine the problem related to the way in which the productive capacity is utilized and the employment level is determined. We will initially work with an economic model based on schemes of reproduction, or departments (Kalecki 1968b [1991]), which starts with the premises – the product generated equals the product realized, that is to say, we suppose that there is no undesired accumulation of unsold goods. The goods produced over a certain period will be sold at the end of this period. The wage earners consume all their income and do not save. The economy is closed and private.

We consider that the economy is divided into three sectors or departments, which are completely and vertically integrated. As mentioned, that is to say that each of them produces the total of its inputs. Sector I produces goods that cannot be used for consumption (the means of production that comprise gross investment), sector II produces consumer goods for capitalists, and sector III produces consumer goods for wage earners; that is, wage-goods.

In these conditions the gross global product of this economy can be established as shown in Kalecki's three department scheme in Table A2.1.

Table A2.1

Sector	**I**	**II**	**III**	**Total**
Gross profits	P_1	P_2	P_3	P
Wages	W_1	W_2	W_3	W
Gross value added	I	C_k	C_w	Y

Pi represent gross profits (gross of depreciation) for each sector (i = 1, 2, 3).

Wi, are the total of wages paid in each sector.

P and *W* are the global profits and wages.

Y represents the entire economy's domestic gross income. The gross value added is composed in the following manner: I = the product of sector I, C_k the product of sector II, and C_w the product of sector III.

To summarize: $Y = P + W = I + C_k + C_w$ = domestic gross income

We will begin our analysis considering only sector III. Part of the gross value added by this sector equals (both materially and in value) W_3 and is directly paid to the workers of this sector. Another part of the product remains and needs to be sold completely. These goods, by nature, need to be sold to the rest of the workers, that is to say, those of sectors I and II. Then the profits of the capitalists of sector III ($=P_3$) consist of the consumer goods that remain in their possession once the respective wages are spent. They fetch these profits by means of the sale of these goods to the wage earners of sector I and II who, following our assumption, do not save. Thus we have:

$$P_3 = W_1 + W_2 \quad \text{(A2.10)}$$

From this last equation we get (adding $P_1 + P_2$ on both sides)

$$P_1 + P_2 + P_3 = (P_1 + W_1) + (P_2 + W_2)$$

The total of profits = Gross investment + capitalist consumption.

We will now explicitly introduce the parameters defining income distribution of each of these sectors. These are:

a) Sector I: $w_1 = W_1/I$
b) Sector II: $w_2 = W_2/C_k$
c) Sector III: $w_3 = W_3/C_w$

The coefficients w_1, w_2, w_3 must be interpreted as the share of wages in the total income of the firms of each sector.

We had $P_3 = C_w - W3$. We will now introduce the known coefficients of income distribution. That gives us $W3 = C_w \bullet w_3$

and

$$P_3 = (1 - w_3)\, C_w \quad \text{(A2.11)}$$

Given that we know that P_3 equals $(W_1 + W_2)$ we can express workers' consumption as follows:

$$(1 - w_3)\, C_w = W_1 + W_2 = w_1 I + w_2 C_k$$

from which it follows:

$$C_w = \frac{w_1 I + w_2 C_k}{(1 - w_3)} \quad \text{(A2.12)}$$

Equation (A2.12) allows us to confirm that, with capitalist expenditure $(I + C_k)$ given, the consumption of wage earners will be higher in as much the participation of wages in the aggregate value is higher.

We have expressed total income as:

$$Y = I + C_k + C_w$$

We then have:

$$Y = I + C_k + \frac{w_1 I + w_2 C_k}{1 - w_3} \quad \text{(A2.13)}$$

We notice that when income distribution is constant, changes in capitalist expenditure are always linked to changes in the degree in which the installed capacity and employment are utilized. More precisely, when there is an increase in capitalist expenditure, the productive capacities and work force are more fully utilized. By the same token, when capitalist expenditure decreases, the level of exploitation of productive capacities and work force decreases.

The analysis of the growth and fall of capitalist expenditure can be graphically visualized as follows:

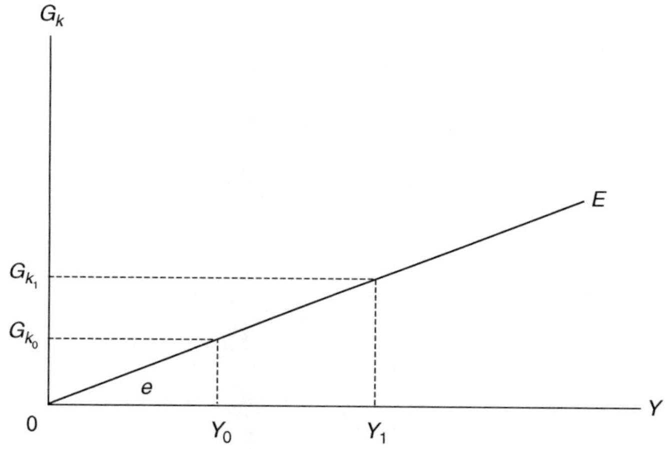

Figure A2.2

On the ordinate axis we see capitalist expenditure G_k, which, as can be seen, equals profits *P*. On the abscissa axis we see income (*Y*). The straight line, which starts from the origin relates profits to income. This line has a slope e ($e = P/Y$). Its angle is less than 1 ($e < 1$), given that profits are always lower than income. In any given period, expenditure G_k determines profits *P* and allows for, – given the ratio of profits in income, *e* – the creation of income *Y*. Another level of expenditure G_k allows for the creation of an income level *Y*. In the figure, the changes in income are higher than the changes in capitalist expenditure because, given profits, wages will also increase (the angle of the straight line "*OE*" is lower than 1). That is to say

$$\Delta Y = \Delta P + \Delta W$$

or $\Delta Y = \Delta I + \Delta C_w$

3
Genesis and Originality of Kalecki's Theory

As mentioned in Chapter I, Kalecki set up for the first time the essential of his formulation of the principle of effective demand already in 1933 in his booklet *Essay on the Business Cycle Theory*, which was followed by several other publications, where he further developed his theory. The first objective of this chapter is to present the main steps in the development of Kalecki's theory of profits, output and employment; whose final version we presented in the previous chapter. The second objective will be to show the originality of Kalecki's formulation of the principle of effective demand. In this context we will discuss whether or not he anticipated some of the main ideas that Keynes put forward in *The General Theory of Employment, Interest and Money*, as well as some differences between the two authors. Our last objective will be to contrast Kalecki's theory with the neoclassical synthesis into which J.R. Hicks embedded Keynes's theory shortly after the publication of *The General Theory*.

A thesis we put forward is that Kalecki arrived at his final theory of income determination in a four-step process. His 1933 *Essay* forms the first step; his 1934 *Three Systems* paper is the second step; the 1936 review article of *The General Theory* the third one; and his 1939 *Essays in the Theory of Economic Fluctuations* the fourth one. Drawing on this study, we shall be able to deal with the question of the anticipation of *The General Theory*.[1]

Profits, employment and short-period equilibrium

As mentioned in the previous chapter, Kalecki carried out his analysis distinguishing the two main social classes, workers and capitalists, under the simplifying assumption that the former consume their entire wages whereas there is considerable saving out of profits. From this general view of differential savings propensities, Kalecki arrives straightforwardly at the idea that profits are an increasing function of investments. Given the relationship between profits and investment, what Kalecki needed for a simple presentation of the theory of aggregate demand and output determination, was a relationship between profits and national income. He first dealt with this relationship in a perfect competition framework in his 1933 *Essays* and later, from 1936, in an imperfect competition context.

Income determination and the theory of the multiplier

The Essays *(1933)*

The main objective of the Essays was to show that capitalist economies are subject to cyclical fluctuations. We discuss Kalecki's theory of the business cycle in chapter 5 while in the present one we only consider a situation of quasi-equilibrium. Centred on a "free" competitive economy, the 1933 *Essays* resorts to a conceptual frame closely linked to the marginalist approach. In every firm the level of production is determined by the intersection of the curves of marginal cost and marginal revenue. Because firms have no monopoly power, the latter is a horizontal line.[2] Given the capital stock of equipment, the short-term equilibrium is thus reached through the shifting downward or upward of the marginal revenue curves, until these curves do not tend to move any further.

Let us consider, for example, a fall in aggregate demand entailing a downward shift of marginal revenue curves, under condition of rising marginal cost curve. If the price is below the average variable cost curve, the marginal revenue no longer covers even current expenses for variables costs and production is suspended; but otherwise the firm will remain active. In any case, Kalecki shows here how investment and capitalist consumption determine profits; he also shows that the shifts in the marginal revenue curve of each firm cause changes in the same direction of profit and in the degree of capacity utilization.

The Review article of the General Theory *(1936)*

Kalecki referred for the first time to imperfect competition in his 1933 booklet; but he made his analysis more precise in his review article of Keynes's *General Theory* (published in 1936 in *Ekonomista* (Kalecki 1936 [1990]); the leading Polish journal of economics) the main part of which was integrated one year later in his 1937 article on business-cycle theory. The analysis presents a *General Theory* interpreted from a Kaleckian viewpoint. Macroeconomic equilibrium is shown in a diagram presenting microeconomic curves, which are summed up to bring about the macroeconomic aggregates.

Every imperfectly competitive firm produces so as to equate marginal revenue and marginal cost. The intersection of the curve of marginal revenue and marginal cost is thus a representation of profit maximization. Once the costs of material inputs are deducted from both curves, we obtain Kalecki's diagram (Figure 3.1).

The marginal "value added" curve is the marginal revenue curve of any firm and the marginal labour cost curve is simply the marginal cost. The sums of the shaded areas are equal to profits of the firm (entrepreneurs and rentiers) whereas the sums of the non shaded area are equal to worker's wages. The labour market is characterized by an exogenous given money wage, which determines the absolute level of prices, and by the existence of a reserve of unemployed workers.

On scaling up from micro to macro the diagram reconciles micro analysis and macro aggregates. The area OABC is nominal income, expressed in wage units, the corresponding shaded area, global profits, and the residual area, aggregate wages. Macro equilibrium in the goods market implies that nominal income is equal to the value of consumption plus investment. As workers consume all their wages, it follows

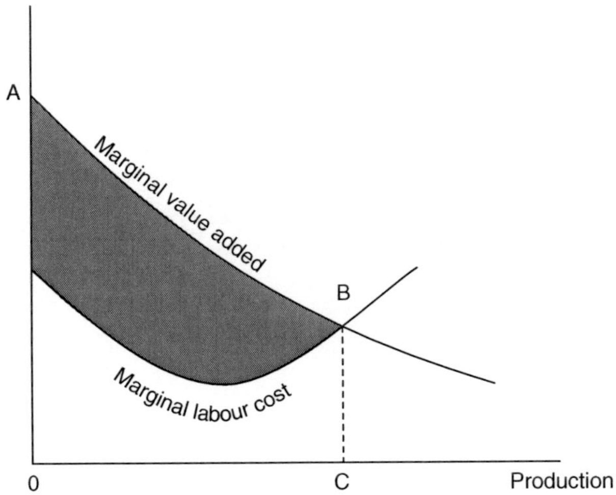

Figure 3.1

Source: Kalecki 1936 [1990].

that the area under the marginal revenue curve to the left of the intersection and above the cost curve is the value of capitalists' consumption and investment and the residual area the value of worker's consumption.

With this figure, Kalecki was thus able to illustrate his theory of profits showing that capitalists earn what they spend. Let us consider a spontaneous change in capitalist expenditure. As aggregate demand increases, the marginal revenue curve shifts to the right up to the point where the shaded areas is just equal to the higher capitalist expenditure. And since, in equilibrium, capitalist expenditures are equal to profits, higher capitalist expenditure generates higher profits of the same amount.

> Therefore we see that the sum of capitalist expenditure determines the position of the value-added curve in such a way that the sum of the shaded areas – that is, of capitalist income – is equal to their expenditure. Thus the level of expenditure (expressed in wage units) is the crucial factor in determining the short-period equilibrium. (Kalecki 1936 [1990]: 227)

Besides, when aggregate demand from capitalists changes, the areas of wages, and hence the value of their consumption (measured in wages units), are also higher than before.

"Naturally, in the new short-period equilibrium, the employment and income of workers, and therefore the value of their consumption (measured in wage units), are higher than before. It follows that the demand for every kind of goods, both for investment as well as for consumption by capitalist and workers, has grown, therefore the shift of the curves of marginal value-added has had take place in all branches of industry." (Kalecki 1936 [1990]: 226)

As in his 1933 *Essay*, to arrive at a precise expression of income determination what Kalecki required was a relationship linking income and profits. Note, when capitalist expenditure changes, not only *total* profits, but also the profit *share* move in the same direction. Graphically, we can see the share of profits is the ratio of shaded area to the area OABC. Its evolution thus depends on both the shape of demand schedules and the shape of cost curves.[3] Since the relationship between investment, profits and national income is non-linear, Kalecki used the general expression $Y = f(I)$, without specifying the precise shape of the function f. It is in fact in his 1939 *Essays* that Kalecki finally proposed a determinate relation between income and investment.

Essays in the Theory of Economic Fluctuations *(1939)*

From 1939, two special assumptions about microeconomic behaviour lead Kalecki to give a precise, and in fact a linear form, to the function linking profits with income. First, supply is elastic and costs are constant up to the full capacity utilization of equipment, beyond which it slopes sharply upward. Second, the degree of monopoly at the level of each firm is assumed constant, provided the fundamental data do not change. With these assumptions, micro-equilibrium of the representative firm is now represented in Figure 3.2.

The area OABC still represents the total value revenue obtained by the firm producing OA. The sums of the non-shaded areas represent the sums of the cost composed of wages and raw materials. The shaded area represents profits. The ratio of the shaded area to the non shaded area is equal to the price/unit cost ratio (what he will later call "degree of monopoly"; see next chapter), divided by one minus the degree of monopoly ($k/(1-k)$).[4]

Drawing on this theory of income distribution, showing the share of profit is equal to the degree of monopoly; Kalecki was now able to establish a constant relation between income and profits, permitting a new expression for the multiplier.

Let us reconsider his model when costs are constant and the degree of monopoly is given. At the equilibrium in the goods markets, we get $Y = C_k + C_w + I$. Workers consume their entire wages; and capitalists consume

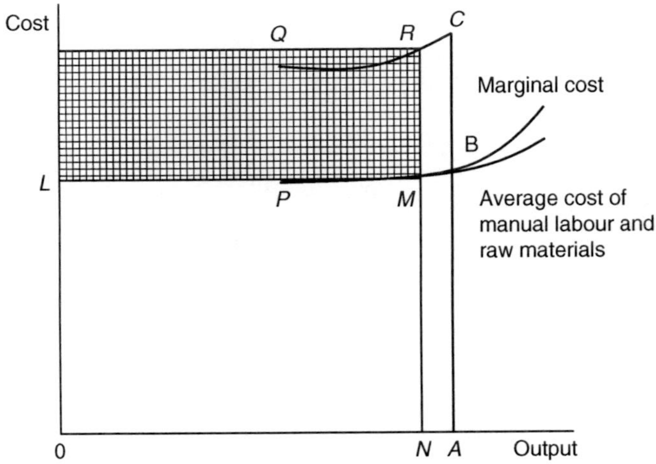

Figure 3.2

a constant amount, A, and a proportion of profits (λP), and equilibrium in the goods market implies $Y = \lambda P + A + C_w + I$. Finally, as the share of wages, ω, is given by the degree of monopoly, the multiplier is now:

$$Y = \frac{A + I}{(1-\lambda)(1-\omega)}$$

The multiplier depends on the marginal propensity to consume of the community, equal to the product of the marginal propensity to save out of profit, $(1-\lambda)$, and the coefficient of the share of profit in the national income $(1-\omega)$.

We should stress that the argument advanced on the determination of national income rests on the assumption of elastic supply (Indeed, the equation for the determination of national income reflects Kalecki's approach to the theory of the firm and the special price–cost relationship postulated). Moreover, this theory of income distribution implies that the multiplier depends mainly on factors determining the distribution of income between classes, in contrast to Keynes's version in which psychological factors play a crucial role.

The money market, the rate of interest, and output determination

Already In his 1933 *Essay*, Kalecki considered the real and monetary aspects of his theory. However, in his 1934 article he presented a more integrated analysis of the commodity and money market, based on his particular vision of liquidity preference (different from Keynes's). In a nutshell, the rate of interest, which is a monetary variable, together with the expected profitability of capital, determines the level of investment, which determines the level of both nominal and real income. These, in turn, influence the rate of interest by their effect on the demand for money. Equilibrium is hence reached through the interactions between money and commodity markets.[5] Here, we will propose an interpretation of the gist of Kalecki's view of the interaction of monetary and real variables, drawing mostly from his 1934 analysis.

"Three Systems" (1934)

Kalecki's (1934a) model describes a perfectly competitive economy whose employed workers consume their entire wages, and he distinguishes two sectors of production. One sector produces consumer goods and the other producer goods.[6] He considers three variants. The first variant of this model – System I – is a classical model founded on Say's law.[7]

Kalecki developed his analysis of System I by considering two shocks: a rise in the labour supply and an exogenous reduction in capitalists' consumption (capitalists' consumption being considered exogenously given). In both cases he showed that the production of investment goods increases.

Kalecki assumes that an excess supply of labour reduces money wages. This, under the assumptions of Say's Law, causes on the one hand a rise in employment and aggregate production, because of the fall in real cost and the rise in profitability. On the other hand it brings about a rise in investment because, according to Say's law and capitalists' consumption assumed given, capitalists invest the profits due to the fall in money wages. Finally, because there is at the same time a rise in demand and in profitable output, a level of macroeconomic equilibrium, characterized by a higher level of employment and of production of investment goods, is reached.

Kalecki envisioned then a second shock: an exogenous fall in capitalists' consumption. By reducing their consumption, capitalists correspondingly increase investment, because of the assumption of Say's law. The price of investment goods rises because demand is greater whereas the price of consumer goods falls because demand is smaller. Finally, employment and production rise in the investment goods sector and shrink in the consumption goods sector (Kalecki (1934a [1990]: 205).

Then, Kalecki concluded, the production of investment goods I is an increasing function of the supply of labour N (assumed inelastic) and a decreasing function of capitalists' consumption C_k[8]:

$$I = f\left(\overline{N}, C_k\right) \tag{3.1}$$

Investment demand is also assumed to depend negatively on the interest rate r, and positively on the current profitability of equipment for which entrepreneurs expect the return of their investment projects:

> The number of investment projects which pass the profitability test depends on the mutual relation at a given moment between prices of consumer goods, prices of investment goods, and wages (which are determinants of the expected gross profitability), and on the rate of interest. (Ibid: 206)

Since the supply of labour and capitalist consumption entirely determine the relation of prices and wages, investment demand can be presented as the function Ψ ($\overline{N}$, C_k, r) (Ibid: 206).

Since the production of investment goods is determined by equation (3.1), and the demand for investment goods is represented by the function $\Psi(\bar{N}, C_k, r)$, we obtain the condition of equilibrium in the investment good market from which Kalecki obtains the equilibrium rate of interest:

$$I = \Psi(\bar{N}, C_k, r) \tag{3.2}$$

The functions f and Ψ thus determine investment goods output and the rate of interest.

Thus, by constructing a model based on Say's law, Kalecki described an economy for which real variables and nominal variables are respectively determined by the real and the monetary parts of the model and in which the market mechanism spontaneously re-establishes full employment.

In order to determine whether this result depends on the absence of hoarding, Kalecki considered in his System II the implications of variations of cash reserves owned by firms. In System II money supply is first assumed given.[9] Money demand is instead assumed to increase with income and to decline with the interest rate. More precisely, Kalecki argued that agents choose between "cash reserves", which they need in order to make transactions – insisting on the transaction motive for financing production – and financial assets, which do not allow making transactions but yield interest.

> In contrast to System I, individual economic agents in System II hold cash reserves which can be increased or decreased. A cash reserve is necessary to run an enterprise at a given turnover smoothly. The volume of this reserve depends not only on the turnover of the enterprise, but also on the rate of interest. The higher the rate of interest, the smaller the cash reserve held by an enterprise at a given turnover. Hence if sales increase while the volume of money in *circulation* remains constant, that is, if the velocity of money circulation increases, the rate of interest rises, since there will be a tendency to increase reserves in the same relation, which must be counteracted by an increase in the rate of interest. The rate of interest [...] is determined in this way by the velocity of money circulation. (Ibid: 207)

Formally, by assuming that the elasticity of money demand with respect to nominal income is equal to 1, the money demand function described by Kalecki – which we denote by M_d – can be written as follows: $M_d = (p_I I + p_C C)L(r)$ where the function L is a decreasing function of the rate of interest, p_I the price of investment goods, p_c the price of consumption goods, I the volume of investment goods produced and C the volume of consumption goods produced. From the condition of equilibrium in the money market, $\overline{M} = (p_I I + p_C C)L(r)$, where $\overline{M}$ is the supply of money supposed as given, we obtain the velocity of money circulation: $V = (p_I I + p_C C)/\overline{M} = (1/L(r))$.

It thus appears that when nominal income rises, the velocity of money circulation increases, and equilibrium in the money market is re-established by a rise of the interest rate. By including this money market conception in his System II, Kalecki showed that the final position of equilibrium in this system is the same as under Say's law.

Kalecki discussed at length the interactions between the monetary and the real sectors by considering the impact of an exogenous decrease in capitalists' consumption, a rise in the inducement to invest, and an increase in the labour supply. Since in the three cases the argument develops along the same lines, here we will only examine his analysis of the impact of a rise in labour supply.[10]

Due to the complete flexibility of money wages, an excess labour supply causes money wages to fall. Under the assumptions of the model, real wages decrease, causing a rise in employment and production. As a result, prices decrease due to the appearance of an excess supply of goods, which results in a rise in the (real) value of money holdings. More real balances are then available to finance production activities, causing the interest rate to fall and stimulating an investment rise.

In his words: "on account of the falling money value of sales the velocity of money circulation declines and with it also the money rate of interest, which encourages entrepreneurs to make investments" (Kalecki 1934a [1990]: 212). A set of real variables identical to the one defined by Kalecki's first model is thus determined. (Kalecki's System II is formally discussed in Appendix 3.1.)

As mentioned, disequilibrium in the labour market entails a variation in money wages, which causes a variation in price. This variation of price modifies the real value of the money supply, which modifies the interest rate and stimulates or slows down investment. This process occurs until income and production reach a level ensuring equilibrium in all markets. As Kalecki stressed, "[T]his is the essence of arriving at equilibrium identical with one which would be established in System I" (Kalecki 1934a [1990]: 214–215).

Summarizing, this adjusting mechanism, through which lower prices and wages could eventually generate a move towards full employment, relies entirely on what came later to be known "the 'Keynes effect'".

We can see, then, that the discovery of this effect can also be credited to Kalecki!

Finally, in model III, Kalecki modifies the conception of the labour market, and shows that the economy could get stuck in a position of "quasi-equilibrium" with unemployment. The central hypothesis is that the *level* of unemployment, as such, is no longer supposed to push money wages down. Kalecki argues as follow:

> [A]s long as it remains unchanged, existing unemployment does not "pressure" the market. Without going into the reasons for this, we shall continue to study System II, except that now it permits the existence of some reserve army of the unemployed. This we call System III." (Kalecki 1934a [1990]: 215)

And he clarified the point as follows:

> Namely, while the *existing* unemployment does not exert any pressure on the market, we postulate that *changes* in unemployment cause a definite increase or fall in money wages, depending on the direction and volume of these changes. (Ibid: 215; emphases in the original)

The first hypothesis according to which money wages do not fall for a given level of unemployment allows the determination of what Kalecki called a position of quasi-equilibrium; it can be defined by a set of equations identical to that of his second model, except that in each equation the level of the supply of labour has been replaced by the level of actual employment. Thus, as soon as actual employment is known, the quasi-equilibrium is determined. Yet if the actual level of employment is unknown, then so are quasi-equilibria. Kalecki's second hypothesis, according to which money wages are related to the variations of unemployment – we shall refer as follows with the equation $W = g(\overline{N} - N)$ where $g < 0$ – allows one to define a quasi-equilibrium (Ibid: 215–216). By introducing the equation $W = g(\overline{N} - N)$, we obtain Kalecki's third model. The endogenous variables remain $N_C, N_I, N, C, I, p_C, p_I, r, W$ and the exogenous ones are $\overline{N}$, $\overline{M}$, C_k. The model still has nine equations (see the appendix). However, contrary to the other model, it is not dichotomic,[11] so that shocks in demand now have an impact on employment. To show this, Kalecki carries out two comparative statics exercises: first, an improvement in the inducement to invest and second, a drop in capitalists' consumption.

Let us consider the effects of an increase in the inducement to invest. This leads to an increase in the price of investment goods. As a result, in the investment sector profitability rises and production and employment expand. In turn this causes increased worker's consumption, which boosts prices and production in the consumption good sector. As capitalists' consumption is given, aggregate production will expand until profits increase by the same amount as the increase in real investment. However, this is not the end result. As Kalecki emphasized, the rise in prices and in money wages due to increases in employment and production, leads to a rise in the "money value of turnover;" this also causes a rise in the transaction demand for money that can only be met by an increase in the rate of interest, which in turn reduces somewhat the volume of investment (see Kalecki 1934a [1990]: 217).

But despite this depressive effect, the new quasi-equilibrium is established at a higher level of employment because of the upward movement of the schedule of marginal profitability of new investment projects: "the increased output and rise in prices in relation to wages in turn increase profitability, which additionally stimulates investment activity" (Ibid).[12]

Hence, monetary variables can affect real variables and real variables can affect monetary ones. The channel of transmission of the monetary sector is through investment. Changes in the level of income lead to changes in the transactions demand for money which, in turn, influences the rate of interest.[13] However, even if falling money wages are followed by price falls, which lower the interest rate, unemployment may persist. The reason is that investment may not be stimulated to a sufficient extent to raise enough effective demand and output.

More on the real-monetary sector interactions

Kalecki further developed his vision of the interaction between the real and the monetary sectors after the publication of *The General Theory*. To some extent he answered to objections put by several authors to Keynes's book from the perspective of his own theory. We shall now look at some of the most important of these developments (see also Chapter 6).

Kalecki's criticism of "the real balance effect"

After the publication of *The General Theory*, Arthur Cecil Pigou, attacked the conclusion of that book arguing that Keynes had neglected the influence of real wealth on consumption; thus came into existence what is known as "The Pigou-effect", or the wealth effect on consumption. The argument was that the lower the nominal wage rate, and thus the lower the price level, the higher the real value of wealth of the community. Money, and other assets denominated in money are part of the public's wealth. At lower prices their purchasing power is greater, while the real value of wealth held in the form of goods is unchanged. People save to accumulate wealth to provide for their future consumption. When the real value of their existing assets is increased, these purposes are more adequately satisfied and they will increase current consumption at the expense of saving.

In the debate with Pigou, Kalecki first of all restricted considerably the generality of Pigou's arguments, observing that the largest part of private holdings of monetary assets, including bank deposits counted as money, had direct or indirect counterpart in private debt. Deflation is thus likely to raise the burden of the debts as much as the real value of assets. According to Kalecki, the gross amount of the "inside" assets corresponding to private debts and credits, are orders of magnitude larger than the net amount of the base.[14]

But Kalecki went further in his criticism of Pigou. If the spending propensity is systematically greater for debtors, the Pigou effect would not only be nullified, but it may make matters worse, because it may bring about generalized bankruptcy and a resulting crisis of confidence.[15] Lower prices impose an increased burden on debtors which can generate debt squeezes, default and bankruptcies which are likely to intensify and spread the slump in economic activity. In his words:

> If in the initial position the stock of gold is small as compared with the national wealth, it will take an enormous fall in wage rates and prices to reach the point when saving out of the full employment income is zero. The adjustments required would increase catastrophically the real value of debts, and would consequently lead to wholesale bankruptcy and "confidence crisis". The adjustment would probably never be carried to the end: if workers persisted in their game of unrestricted competition, the government would introduce a wage stop under the pressure from employers. (Kalecki 1944b [1990]: 343)[16]

Using contemporary language, Kalecki was calling attention to the fact that if nominal wages fall too much, a bifurcation point in the dynamics of the system may be reached. Beyond that point the economy would no longer exhibit cyclical fluctuations, but rather would tend to collapse. But, of course, state intervention could prevent this from happening.

Final remarks on the real-monetary interactions

Kalecki gave a final consideration to the issue of the relation between the real and the monetary sectors in his *Theory of Economic Dynamics*. There he concluded:

> A long-run fall in money wages causes a fall in the money volume of transactions. If the supply of cash by banks is not proportionally reduced, this leads in turn to a fall of the long-term rate of interest. Such a fall ... would cause an upward trend movement. ...
>
> It is, however, highly doubtful whether the mechanism described will be effective in increasing output at all. The connection between the fall in turnover and the fall in the short-term rate of interest is in fact fairly uncertain in the long run. If the fall in turnover continues over a long period, the banking policy may easily adapt itself to this secular fall in such a way as to reduce the supply of balances *pari passu* with turnover and thus to sustain the sort-term interest rate. (Kalecki 1954a [1991]: 336)

Reconsidering Kalecki's principle of effective demand

Kalecki's originality

We have already described the main steps taken by Kalecki to elaborate his theory. With these antecedents in mind, we may now summarize how Kalecki originally formulated the principle of effective demand. In this context, we may attempt a first comparison between Kalecki and Keynes's theories; as they stood at the moment of the publication of *The General Theory*.[17]

Let us first mention the ideas the two authors shared, which can be simply put as follows: i) In a capitalist economy the level of output and employment are, under normal conditions, determined by demand and not by supply. ii) The level of investment is a central factor that determines the level of demand. iii) There is nothing in a capitalist economy that guarantees investment will reach such a level that full utilization of the productive capacity and full employment of the workforce will be attained. In particular, a fall in the interest rate may not be sufficient to stimulate enough investment. In Kalecki's words:

> our analysis of the money market ... has shown that the rate of interest does indeed rise during the upswing and falls during the downswing.

> Expressing i [the rate of interest – JL, MA] as a function of P/K [the profit rate; namely total profits divided by the capital stock – JL, MA], in order to show the link between the interest rate and the business cycle, is only a crude approximation, of course. Nevertheless, the arbitrariness involved has little effect…, since ***the rate of interest is of secondary importance for the will to invest, the factor of prime importance being unquestionably the gross profitability of existing plants***. (Kalecki 1933a [1990]: 97–98; emphasis added)

In other words, Kalecki recognized that the interest rate may decline during the business downswing (or may rise during the upswing). However, he emphasized that this, in itself, would not necessarily bring about a re-absorption of unemployment. The recovery of investment, which is indispensable for this, necessitates above all a rise in profits, the fundamental factor determining investment decisions.[18]

Let us now look at how Keynes considered this issue in *The General Theory*. Briefly stated, he thought that demand would be insufficient to absorb full-employment output if part of it is directed to non-reproducible objects, such as Old Masters' paintings, rare stamps or, more notably, money. Income used to buy these non-reproducibles would "leak" out of the commodity circuit, breaking the equivalence between distributed income and total value of commodities produced in the period. The central aim of *The General Theory* was to show that these leakages are more frequent than classical economic theory was prepared to acknowledge. The point is established by reference to the concept of uncertainty. In a nutshell, according to Keynes, acquiring job-creating reproducibles like capital goods involves firms and wealth holders in a risky bet against the future. If uncertainty surrounding this future is overwhelming, as it is in times of crises, these potential buyers may prefer some alternative, safer asset, such as money. When wealth holders prefer to hold money instead of buying capital goods, jobs are destroyed in the capital goods producing sectors but this loss is not compensated by higher levels of output and employment in the production of money, causing aggregate demand to fall below full employment output.

It is not easy to summarize, in a few words, what were the main differences between the two authors regarding the essential explanation for unemployment. But in the light of what we have discussed up to now, and referring exclusively to the situation as it stood at the moment of the publication of *The General Theory*, we can make an attempt. Perhaps we could say simply that Keynes explained unemployment within the framework of a short-period analysis, on the basis of the community's desire for liquidity, due to fundamental uncertainty. By contrast, Kalecki, in his early formulation of theory of output and employment, explained unemployment in the context of his business-cycle theory, on the basis of capitalists' lack of adequate incentives to invest, due to an insufficient profit rate. Later he would refine his theory of business cycles and also his explanation of unemployment.

Anticipation of *The General Theory* or Alternative Formulation of the Principle of Effective Demand?

The question of Kalecki's coincidental discovery of the Principle of Effective Demand was raised shortly after the appearance of *The General Theory*, and it received support by some members of the economics profession; including two prominent associates of Keynes's Circus.[19] In 1982, however, Patinkin (1982) concluded in his influential book *"Anticipations of the* General Theory*?"* that Kalecki did not anticipate Keynes's central message. Several works appeared to rebut Patinkin's statement (Laski (1987), Osiatynski (1989) and S. Chapple (1995)). However, these statements have not yet succeeded in altering the balance of opinion in favour of Kalecki's independent and previous discovery of the Principle of Effective Demand.

In the following we will take issue with Patinkin's conclusion. We discuss the three main arguments developed by this author with reference to his interpretation of Keynes's *General Theory*. We argue contrary to Patinkin: i) Kalecki set out a static (or, better, short-period) unemployment model; ii) this model provides an integrated general equilibrium treatment of goods and money markets[20]; iii) Kalecki developed an original analysis of the relative movements of wages and prices. Thus, drawing on these three arguments, we conclude that we must give Kalecki credit for anticipating part of the essential ideas of *The General Theory*.

Patinkin suggests that to deal with the issue of the anticipation of the *General Theory*, one must before specify its major innovation, or what he calls his central message. To him, Keynes's major contribution was his explanation of unemployment equilibrium as presented in chapter 3 of the *General Theory*.

> This is the major novel feature of the *General Theory* and its central message: the theory of effective demand as a theory which depends on the equilibrating effect of the decline in output itself to explain why "the economic system may find itself in stable equilibrium with

> N [employment] at a level below full employment, namely at the level given by the intersection of the aggregate demand function with the aggregate supply function". (Patinkin 1982:16)

Drawing on his interpretation of Keynes's central message, Patinkin comes to reject the claim that Kalecki anticipated *The General Theory*. After examining Kalecki's pre-General Theory writings, he concludes:

> Kalecki's central message has not to do with the forces that generate equilibrium at a low level of output, but with the forces that generate cycles of investments: more specifically, not with the feedback mechanism that equilibrates planned saving and investment via declines in output, but with the cyclical behaviour of investment on the implicit assumption that there always exists equality between planned savings and investments. (Patinkin 1982: 77–78)

We have given enough evidence, we hope, to demonstrate that Patinkin's conclusion is unwarranted. The key features of Kalecki's 1933 *Essay* and his 1934 "Three Systems" are at least twofold. First, Kalecki succeeded in defining a model allowing to deal with the mechanism by which the economy can reach a stable position of unemployment he labelled "quasi-equilibrium". Second, Kalecki conceived economic fluctuations as a chain of quasi-equilibrium, underlining therefore clearly that these equilibrating changes in output play a role in dynamics whereas the economy during the business cycle go through unemployment positions, reaching only barely a full employment position at the top of the boom.

We stress again that Kalecki's approach was not identical to Keynes's model. For example, Keynes succeeded in establishing a simple, linear relationship between consumption and income, partly because he made no distinction between workers and capitalists. In the first versions of Kalecki's formulation that relationship was non-linear, but his model also allows dealing in depth with the issue of the stability of unemployment equilibrium. For, even if the propensity to consume of both workers and capitalists vary with output changes, insofar it remains always below one the economy tends to a stable position of quasi-equilibrium.

Let us now focus on the second point of Patinkin's analysis. In his words:

> Kalecki's theory lacks the integrated character of Keynes' *General Theory*. It fails to integrate value theory with monetary theory and is

> indeed devoid of the marginal analysis on which the former is based. And though Kalecki's theory adverts to the simultaneous developments in the money market, fails to present a systematic analysis of the latter and accordingly fails to present an integrated analysis of the commodity and money markets. (Patinkin 1982 : 77)

As we have shown while presenting Kalecki's 1934 short-period analysis, one cannot subscribe to this second Patinkin argument. As we emphasized, it is precisely by introducing the rate of interest in the money demand function in his System II that Kalecki succeeds in defining new adjustment mechanisms between goods, labour and money markets. It is especially when he firstly explained what is nowadays called the "Keynes effect", that Kalecki showed how any excess supply of labour, through the fall in wages and prices, by causing the rate of interest to fall, stimulates investment, may lead the economy to reach a position of full employment equilibrium. Moreover, it is still with reference to this effect that, in his System III where Kalecki can deal with the effect of the wages changes induced by employment variation on the interest rate and aggregate demand.

For all that, are the systems defined by Keynes and Kalecki similar? We already gave arguments to show that they are in fact dissimilar. We add an additional one.

As Patinkin underlines, in Chapter 18 of *The General Theory* where Keynes sums up his theory, he takes as given on the one hand the usual fundamentals of the economy and the capital stock, and on the other hand the nominal quantity of money, the money wage rate bargained between workers and employers, and the state of long term expectations. If one of these classes of variables remains unknown, then the general equilibrium, in the meaning of a temporary equilibrium, is indeterminate.

Kalecki's quasi-equilibrium is also a temporary equilibrium. However, contrary to Keynes, Kalecki does not assume that money wages are given, for a given quantity of nominal money and a given state of the marginal efficiency of capital. Instead, under the assumption that, on the one hand the existing *level* of unemployment does not exert any pressure on the market; and on the other that *changes* in unemployment do cause changes in money wages, Kalecki obtains a functional relation between employment and money wage $N \to W$ allowing him to determine the equilibrium.

As regards Patinkin's interpretation of *The General Theory*, this difference between the two authors is also very important. Patinkin emphasized that a relevant point of Keynes's argument for unemployment equilibrium, was an explanation why the money wage rate, though slowly, falls in the face of excess labour supply. Keynes's most important contribution would thus have been to demonstrate that if money wages decline, instead of leading to an increase in employment, this would on the contrary conduct the economy in a destabilizing disequilibrium process.

Kalecki knew that money wages variations can in fact be induced by the situation of the labour market; but he did not put the emphasis there for his explanation of the dynamics of the economy. Rather, as he shows in his 1933 *Essay*, the really important factor is the profitability of actual equipment, generated by the variations in profits and in the capital stock. In other words, the temporary feature of Kalecki's "quasi-equilibrium" is based principally on the assumption that the profit rate *which was achieved in the previous period*, is given. So, though both Keynes and Kalecki's unemployment analysis are dynamic, they are not the same. In one case, the economy enters in a dynamic process due to the fall in money wages whereas in the other case, it enters in a dynamic process due to the evolution of the profit rate.

Patinkin goes on to argue that Kalecki's analysis of money wage flexibility is really inferior to that Keynes:

> Kalecki's analysis of the impact of a wage decline on the level of output is actually inferior to the detailed analysis of the effect of such a decline (via expectations, possible effect on the balance of trade, interactions with the liquidity-preference function and hence the rate of interest) which Keynes provides in the chapter of the General Theory which he devotes to "Changes in Money wages". (Patinkin 1982: 76–77)

We do not deny Patinkin's point; but we think that it should be put in a proper context. Keynes stressed the effect of money wages changes on the marginal efficiency of capital through long term expectations. It is especially thanks to this argument, absent from Kalecki's works, that Keynes came to the conclusion that, despite the fall in the rate of interest, the fall in money wages is likely to destabilize the economy and may even reduce employment. We have emphasized that by assuming money wages are endogenous in his 1934 model of unemployment, Kalecki also considered changes in money wages induced by variations in capitalist expenditures. But certainly Kalecki did not find wage rigidity central for his explanation of the business cycle, or for long-lasting unemployment in capitalism.

Kalecki and the Neoclassical Synthesis

In this final section of the present chapter, we shall analyse the differences between Kalecki's (1934) unemployment model and the Hicks (1937) IS-LM model. We will show that Kalecki's model differs from the classical models (based on Say's law) and from the types of models which were later to be called Keynesian models. We argue that the validity of his analysis does not depend on the existence of the special assumptions of the liquidity trap (Hicks).

Kalecki's employment model versus Hicks's IS-LM model

Hicks (1937) constructed three models to draw a contrast between the classical and the Keynesian perspectives. The first model he qualified as being classical; the second Keynesian; and the third a synthesis. Given the importance of Hicks's paper, we shall give a somewhat detailed account of his three models.

Hicks's first system is a classical system in which money demand, in accordance with the quantitative theory of money, does not depend on the interest rate. Hicks presented it as follow:

$$\overline{M} = kY^n, I^n = I^n(r), I^n = S^n(r, Y^n)$$

Y^n, is nominal income, I^n is nominal investment, r is the interest rate, $\overline{M}$ the quantity of money in circulation supposed given and k a constant corresponding to the inverse of the velocity of money circulation. Hicks showed how a rise in the inducement to invest in this model affects only the interest rate and leaves nominal income the same. Consequently, employment will vary only if the supply elasticity of each sector is not equal. Hence, as he pointed out: "labour will be employed more in the investment trades, less in the consumption trades; this will increase total employment if elasticity of supply in the investment trades is greater than that in the consumption-goods trades – diminish it if vice versa" (Hicks 1937: 149).[21]

A second, Keynesian model, differs from the previous one in that, on the one hand, the demand for money depends on the interest rate. Besides, nominal savings, in accordance with the multiplier, depend only on nominal income. Hicks wrote it as follows:

$$\overline{M} = L(r), I^n = I^n(r), I^n = S^n(Y^n)$$

The singularity of this specification is that it is the interest rate, and not nominal income, that is determined by the quantity of money: the interest rate determines nominal investment, which, via the multiplier, determines nominal income. It results in a rise in the inducement to invest, which increases national income without affecting interest rate. Obviously a rise in the quantity of money, by reducing the interest rate, increases nominal investment and employment. According to Hicks, Keynes's essential contribution is therefore his liquidity preference analysis, because without it the multiplier would have no role.

However, Hicks thought the economy described by Keynes corresponds more closely to the following Keynesian model:

$$\overline{M} = L(Y^n, r), I^n = I^n(r), I^n = S^n(Y^n)$$

In the previous model, nominal income has been introduced in the function of the demand for money. For Hicks, this modification restricts considerably the opposition between Keynesian theory and classical theory. Indeed, a rise in the inducement to invest triggers an increase in nominal income as well as in the interest rate, whereas a rise in the quantity of money reduces the interest rate and increases employment. Graphically this result appears clearly. If *LL*,[22] the curve representing equilibrium of the money market in the plane (r, Y^n) is increasing, a rise in the inducement to invest shifts the *IS* curve to the right and generates a rise of national income and of the interest rate. It is only if *LL* is horizontal in the case of the liquidity trap that a rise in the inducement to invest causes only a rise of national income.

Last, aiming to show that it is possible to realise a complete synthesis between the classical tradition and the Keynesian theory, Hicks built a variant of the latter, where the nominal income and the interest rate are the arguments for the demand functions of money, investment, and savings, the model of generalized *General Theory*, which he wrote as such:

$$\overline{M} = L(Y^n, r) \quad I^n = I^n(Y^n, r) \; I^n = S^n(Y^n, r)$$

Thanks to this, Hicks can also show that a rise in the inducement to invest causes an increase in nominal income and in the interest rate, whereas a decrease in the quantity of money reduces the interest rate and raises the nominal income.

Hicks then stressed that the opposition between Keynes and the classical authors is neither a conflict between rigidity and flexibility of money wages nor a conflict between unemployment and full employment, but originates in liquidity preference theory.

As can be easily seen, the conception of the classical theory of the labour market put forward by Hicks and by Kalecki, are radically different from one another. Thus, Hicks assumed that the "rate of money wages per head can be taken as given" (Hicks 1937: 148); whereas Kalecki recognized, on the contrary, that for the classics the money wage rate decreases with an excess supply of labour. Moreover, while Hicks's article lacked an explicit account of how the labour market works and in which state it happens to end up, Kalecki insisted on the idea that for a system to be accepted by classical economists it must display full-employment equilibrium (Kalecki 1934a [1990]: 201). As a result, the impact of a rise in the inducement to invest and in the quantity of money differs significantly in Hicks's and Kalecki's classical models.

Let us focus now on the way Hicks and Kalecki, respectively, envisioned the effects of a rise in the inducement to invest in their classical models. Hicks argued that in his system of two production sectors, such a rise modifies the structure of production. Thus, because total employment depends on how production is divided between sectors, it will not necessarily remain unchanged. Only if sectoral supply elasticities are identical will there be no change in employment. On this point, in both of Kalecki's classical models (Systems I and II), an increase in the inducement to invest (i.e., a rightward movement of the schedule of marginal profitability of new investment projects) always elicits a rise in the rate of interest, which results in unchanged total employment.[23] In the same way, an exogenous decrease in capitalists' consumption will not affect total employment. Indeed, according to Say's Law, if saving rises, investment spending rises to the same extent. Thus, whatever the differences of supply elasticity between production sectors are, workers unemployed in the sector of consumption goods are hired in the investment sector. Because, as long as they are still unemployed, money wages will fall, inciting capitalists to increase their spending until full employment is reached. And this result is not modified when the demand for money depends on the interest rate as in Kalecki's System II.

With regard to the effects of monetary expansion in their classical models, the differences between Kalecki's and Hicks's analysis also have their roots in the treatment of the labour market. In Hicks's model, an increase in the supply of money causes a rise in employment, due to the rigidity of money wages, whereas for Kalecki, money is neutral due to the flexibility of money wages. Indeed, whether it is in his System I founded on the quantity theory or in his System II in which nominal income and the interest rate are the two arguments of the money demand function, any rise in the supply of money entails only a change in nominal variables. Contrary to Hicks, Kalecki claimed that introducing the interest rate in the money demand function alone is not sufficient to get a system that leads to non-classical conclusions. What is needed is to add a particular conception of the labour market.

Let us now turn to the differences between Kalecki's unemployment model and Hicks's Keynesian model. As we previously explained, in Kalecki's vision, the most important element in the inducement to invest is the profit rate; which is absent in Hick's Keynesian model. But let us abstract from that difference for the moment; to concentrate on the labour market. In order to build a model with unemployment Kalecki developed a very peculiar conception of the labour market, very different from Hicks's. The central hypothesis of Kalecki's conception is that unemployment, as long as it remains unchanged, is not supposed to pressure money wages downwards. However, Kalecki did not assume that wages are completely rigid. On the contrary, he believed that money wages respond to variations in unemployment. For Hicks, on the one hand, money wages are given, and on the other hand the supply of labour is not specified, making it difficult to say whether or not unemployment exists (see De Vroey 2000).

Despite this difference, Kalecki's model with unemployment behaves somewhat similarly than Hicks's. Both models react likewise in the face of a rise in the inducement to invest and the supply of money. But the similarity ends here, because Hicks introduced the notion of a liquidity trap.[24] Kalecki did not refer to a situation in which the liquidity preference schedule is interest inelastic. Consequently, whereas in Hicks's model, a rise in the inducement to invest can trigger a rise in employment without affecting the interest rate, such a shock in Kalecki's model obviously creates a rise in employment and in the interest rate.

Appendix 3.1

Kalecki's SYSTEM II

The formal model underlying Kalecki's System I can be represented as follows:

$$C = f_C(N_C) \tag{A3.1}$$

$$I = f_I(N_I) \tag{A3.2}$$

$$W = p_C f_C'(N_C) \tag{A3.3}$$

$$W = p_I f_I'(N_I) \tag{A3.4}$$

$$N_I + N_C = N \tag{A3.5}$$

$$I = I\left[\frac{p_C}{W}, \frac{p_I}{W}, r, \gamma\right] \tag{A3.6}$$

$$C = \overline{C_\pi} + \frac{WN}{p_C} \tag{A3.7}$$

$$\overline{M} = k(p_I I + p_C C) \tag{A3.8}$$

$$N = \overline{N} \tag{A3.9}$$

Equations (A3.1) and (A3.2) represent the sectoral production functions where *C* is the output of consumer goods and *I* is the output of investment goods. N_c, N_I is employment in the consumer-good (investment-good) sector. The marginal productivities in both sectors are equal to product wages (equations (A3.3) and (A3.4)). N_I plus N_c results in aggregate employment demanded (equation (A3.5)). Real investment depends on the inverse of the product wages of the two production sectors[25] and on the rate of interest (equation (A3.6)). We have added the parameter γ to represent explicitly a propensity to invest.[26] The level of consumption demand is equal to the demand of capitalists and the demand of workers who consume their entire wages (equation (A3.7)). Nominal money demand function is written, in accordance with the quantity theory, as a function of nominal income. By equating this demand function with the quantity of money, $\overline{M}$, we get the equilibrium condition of the money market (equation (A3.8)). Finally, because the labour market is balanced, employment is equal to labour supply (equation (A3.9)). The endogenous variables are $N_C, N_I, N, C, I, p_C, p_I, r, W$. The exogenous variables are $\overline{N}$, $\overline{M}$, $\overline{C_\pi}$. Equations (A3.1), (A3.2), (A3.3), (A3.7) and (A3.9) result in Kalecki's equation (1). Equations (A3.1), (A3.3), (A3.4), (A4.5), (A3.6), (A3.7) and (A3.9) result in Kalecki's equation (2).

First of all, we determine real variables. With (1.1), (1.3), and (1.7) we determine real wages in the consumption goods sector as an implicit function of aggregate employment and capitalists' consumption:

$$C = f_C\left(f_C'^{-1}\left(\frac{W}{p_C}\right)\right) = \frac{\overline{N}W}{p_C} + \overline{C_\pi}$$

Knowing W/p_c, we may determine the employment in the consumption goods sector. Because employment in the two sectors of production is equal to the supply of labour, we can then deduce the employment in the investment goods sector. The quantities of consumption goods and investment goods are then given by (A3.1) and (A3.2). From (A3.4) we can determine W/p_I, from which the value of interest rate can be deduced. Indeed, the equilibrium condition is $f_I(N_I) = I(p_C/W, p_I/W, r, \gamma)$ which implies that the rate of interest is an implicit function of N_I, W/p_c and W/p_I. With these variables now determined, the value of the equilibrium interest rate can be deduced. The money variables are determined by (A3.8). Knowing W/p_I and W/p_c, W is given by:

$$\overline{M} = Wk\left(\frac{C}{f_C'(N_C)} + \frac{I}{f_I'(N_I)}\right)$$

Then, p_I and p_c are determined by (A3.3) and (A3.4).

Kalecki's SYSTEM II

Its resolution reveals that its real solutions are identical to those of System I. Indeed, the real wages in the consumption goods sector is still defined as an implicit function of aggregate employment and capitalists' consumption. Thus:

$$C = f_C\left(f_C'^{-1}\left(\frac{W}{p_C}\right)\right) = \frac{\overline{N}W}{p_C} + \overline{C_\pi}$$

Knowing W/p_c, employment in the consumption goods sector can be determined. Because employment in the two sectors of production, according to (A3.5), is equal to the supply of labour, employment in the investment goods sector can also be determined. (A3.1) and (A3.2) give the quantities of consumption and investment goods. (A3.4) helps to determine real wages in the investment goods sector, W/p_I, from which the value of interest rate can be determined. Thus, in equilibrium, $f_I(N_I) = I(p_C/W, p_I/W, r, \gamma)$, which means that the interest rate is an implicit function of N_I, W/p_I and W/p_c. These variables being determined, the equilibrium interest rate and nominal variables can also be deduced. When $W = p_I f_I'(N_I)$ and $W = p_C f_C'(N_C)$, by considering the new equilibrium relation in the money market, we reach the value of the nominal wage. Thus:

$$\overline{M} = W\left(\frac{C}{f_C'(N_C)} + \frac{I}{f_I'(N_C)}\right)L(r)$$

Through (A3.3) and (A3.4) we determine p_c and p_I. System II, like System I, is therefore also dichotomic.

Kalecki's SYSTEM III

Recalling that the function of money balance is homogenous of degree one in prices, it can be written down in the following way:

$$f_C(N_C) = \overline{C_\pi} + (N_I + N_C) f_C'(N_C)$$

$$\overline{M} = W\left(\frac{f_I(N_I)}{f_I'(N_I)} + \frac{f_C(N_c)}{f_C'(N_c)}\right)\mathrm{L}(\mathrm{r})$$

$$f_I(N_I) = I\left(\frac{p_C}{W}, \frac{p_I}{W}, r, \gamma\right)$$

$$W = g(\overline{N} - N)$$

or

$$f_C(N_C) = \overline{C_\pi} + (N_I + N_C) f_C'(N_C),$$

$$\overline{M} = g(\overline{N} - N_I - N_C)\left(\frac{f_I(N_I)}{f_I'(N_I)} + \frac{f_C(N_c)}{f_C'(N_c)}\right)\mathrm{L}\left[\phi\left(f_I(N_I), f_C'(N_C) f_I'(N_I)\right)\right]$$

where the interest rate is an implicit function of N_I and N_C. The endogenous variables are N_C and N_I. The exogenous variables are, $\overline{N}$, $\overline{M}$ and $\overline{C_\pi}$. Thus, employment in the two sectors is an implicit function of capitalists' consumption, of the quantity of money, and of the supply of labour. Kalecki's second system is therefore no longer dichotomic.

4
The Theory of Prices and Income Distribution

Introduction

In chapter 2 we argued that in Kalecki's theory output and employment depend on capitalist expenditure, and on the distribution of income; and more precisely on the share of profits in the national income. We will now present Kalecki's theory of income distribution, which is closely related to his theory of price determination. The latter, in turn, is related to his view that modern capitalism is characterized by market imperfections, both on the labour market and product market. By focusing on these imperfections, Kalecki took into account two important differences between perfect and imperfect competition.

The first difference is that under perfect competition, for any particular firm production is not limited by demand, but by costs and prices. Since individual firms face a horizontal demand curve, they can sell whatever quantity they want as long as marginal cost is below the market price. In contrast, in case of imperfect competition firms are demand-constrained, because they would willingly produce more if only they could sell at the prevailing, or a slightly lower, price; but they cannot (or think they cannot) because their own supply has an impact on the market price. In consequence, while changes in the level of aggregate demand cause price variation when competition is perfect, they also entail a quantity variation when competition is imperfect.

The second (and related) difference is that firms in perfect competition operate necessarily on the increasing part of their marginal cost curves. In contrast, the theory of imperfect competition predicts excess capacity as a long-term feature. An important aspect of this proposition is that firms can now operate on the constant part of their marginal cost curves.

Together, both propositions mean, on one hand, that prices remain relatively constant in the face of variations in demand. On the other hand, as regards income distribution, they imply that when demand changes this need not involve a change in income shares, as long as the degree of market imperfection does not change. This led Kalecki to posit that the distribution of income is determined by the price/unit cost ratio, or degree of monopoly, a term summarizing a variety of oligopolistic and monopolistic features.

It is worth emphasizing that Kalecki's model does not involve price rigidity. In a situation of perfect competition, price inflexibility arises generally as an approximation to incomplete price adjustment. In contrast, under imperfect competition prices are assumed to adjust as speedily as required; producers supply whatever is demanded at the price which they have set in their best interests. This remark can help understanding the basic distinction made by Kalecki between prices whose changes, in a perfectly competitive market, are largely determined by changes in the costs of production and those prices whose changes, in an imperfectly competitive market, are determined largely by changes in demand, revealing especially this distinction is not based on differences in the speed of price adjustment but on differences in industrial structure and cost conditions. Kalecki (1954a [1991]: 209) posited: "Generally speaking, changes in the prices of finished goods are 'cost-determined', while changes in the prices of raw materials inclusive of primary foodstuffs are 'demand-determined'".

With his theory of income distribution, Kalecki further developed his theory of effective demand. He had already shown that, *for a given distribution of income between profits and wages* (or our coefficient e from Chapter 2), changes in profits would bring about changes in the same direction as output and employment. Now he added that *for a given level of capitalist expenditure* – and therefore for a given level of profits – income redistribution between workers and capitalists, will provoke a change in aggregate demand and with it in the level of output and employment. The underlying reason is the different propensity to consume between workers and capitalists.

In fact, as we already discussed, one strand of Kalecki's development of the effect of a fall in wages on output and employment was to demonstrate that the alleged positive effects of wage adjustments, giving rise to the so-called Keynes and Pigou effects, may be neutralized. Moreover, he claimed that these adjustments can reduce employment and produce a destabilizing effect, by generating a crisis of confidence caused by the increase in the burden of debts of firms. But Kalecki gave an additional and very important reason why a wage fall may fail to raise employment, and in fact may result in higher unemployment. This reason is the reduced consumption caused by a shift from wages to profits.

There is a strong complementarity between income distribution and income determination, which found expression in the idea that even though the *profit share* depends on the degree of monopoly, the *profit level* remains uniquely determined by the level of capitalist expenditure. This proposition is crucial. On the one hand, it emphasizes that variations in the degree of monopoly affect output and employment only by affecting effective demand through workers' expenditure. On the other hand, it shows that if wages fall (rise), profits will not get higher (go down) because they are entirely determined by capitalist investment and consumption, which are unlikely to change either in the current period or in the following period simply because wages (or the wage share) changed.

Finally, Kalecki's theory of income distribution permits a new analysis of the wages–employment relationship, by taking into account imperfections in the product market.

In the coming section we discuss Kalecki's theory of income distribution. Then we present Kalecki's theory of price determination, in its final version given by him. It is followed by a section on the relationship between wages and employment. Then we move on to present the "marginalist" version of Kalecki's theory. In the final section we add some further comments on the relationship between wages and employment, and we deal in particular with the debate on the wages-prices-employment nexus after *The General Theory*.

Kalecki's theory of income distribution

To grasp the gist of Kalecki's theory of income distribution, let us consider the case of a vertically integrated industry. To simplify the analysis, we assume that all workers are productive and that the productivity of labour is a given constant. Also, we define gross profits as the difference between the total value of production and total prime costs, which are exclusively made up of wages in this simplified case. It can be easily seen that income distribution in an industry is entirely determined by the ability of firms to fix their prices in relation to prime unit costs. More concretely, the higher (lower) the price/unit costs ratio, the higher (lower) the *share* of profits in respect to gross value added will be. Indeed, let us suppose that the wage rate and productivity per worker are given. Then, if firms raise prices, the price cost ratio, and the unit profit margin will rise. But now workers will be able to buy a smaller share of the output (or the value added) of the industry than before, while capitalists will be able to buy a higher share of the value added.

Moreover, we may accept that in any given industry, the higher the monopolistic control of firms on the market, the higher their capacity to fix high prices (in relation to their costs). Therefore, the higher the monopolistic power of firms, the higher the relative share of profits in income in the industry tends to be. This is probably the reason why Kalecki defined "degree of monopoly" as the price cost ratio of the industry. Indeed, the latter is likely to be influenced by the intensity of the monopolization prevailing in the industry. But the "degree of monopoly" is a different and very specific term in Kalecki's theory, since it refers solely to the price cost ratio, and is determined by several factors. One, but only one, of these factors is the intensity of the monopolization of the market.[1]

We will now consider the more complex case of an industry that is not vertically integrated, that is to say, which buys from other firms some of the raw materials it uses. We maintain our assumption that the only labour costs are those of directly productive workers, and we suppose that there are no overhead costs (other than depreciation).

Let us denote by k the ratio between unit price and unit prime cost (in this case, made up of unit wage costs, and unit material input costs); that is, k is Kalecki's "degree of monopoly". If we assume that the prime costs are constant (within the limits of productive capacities), and that everything produced in one period will be sold in this period, then k will also equal the relation between total sales (or total gross income) and total prime costs. We can therefore specify the following equation:

$$P = (k-1)\,(W + MP) \qquad (4.1)$$

In which MP is the total cost of materials.

From our previous assumptions it follows that domestic income equals the total of paid wages plus (gross) total profits ($Y = P + W$). We can now express the share of wages in aggregate value as follows:

$$\omega = \frac{W}{W + (k-1)(W + MP)}\,, \qquad (4.2)$$

or, when dividing everything by *W*, we get:

$$\omega = \frac{1}{1+(k-1)(j+1)}, k > 1 \tag{4.3}$$

where ω is the relative share of wages in the value added (or output), so that (under our simplifying assumptions that all workers are productive workers, and that overheads are negligible) $1-\omega$ is the share of profits in output; what we labeled in Chapter 2 the coefficient *e*. As said, *k* is the "degree of monopoly", or the ratio of aggregate proceeds to aggregate prime costs, (which is also equal to the ratio of average prices to average prime costs). *j* is the ratio of aggregate cost of materials to the wage bill. A rise in *k* or *j* or both will bring about a fall in the relative share of wages in value added.

We can now explain in words what the previous equations convey. In any given industry, the share of wages in aggregate value is entirely determined by the degree of monopoly, as well as by the relationship between prime material costs and wages. For example, let us assume that the costs of prime materials rise and wages do not rise. Then, if the degree of monopoly remains constant, ω will fall. The explanation is simple. On the one hand, a larger share of the industry's value added will have to be used to buy the necessary prime materials. Also, capitalists can "protect" themselves from the increase in their material costs by increasing the prices (the degree of monopoly is constant, the increase in costs is entirely transferred to prices). Since what is left to distribute to the productive factors has fallen, it follows that the wage earners can now buy only a smaller part of the product they produced.

This theory can be extended to the private sector as a whole. But then we will have a third factor, besides the degree of monopoly and the ratio of aggregate cost of materials to the wage bill, that will determine the distribution of income. This third factor is the structure of the industry. In effect, the share of wages in value added will rise, if the relative weight of the industries in which this share is above the average rises.

Thus, income distribution is the result of the clash between the two opposite classes. To quote Kalecki's words used in the title of his last paper on the subject, the "Class Struggle [determines the] Distribution of National Income" (Kalecki 1971 [1991]). But the class struggle manifests itself both in the labour market and in the market for commodities in general. The degree of monopoly reflects the relative force of capitalists and workers *in these two markets*.

Prices and costs in Kalecki's theory

Given the fundamental role played by the price cost ratio in his theory of income distribution, and also in his theory of effective demand, Kalecki found it necessary to formulate a theory of price determination. As mentioned, he accepted that certain prices, and more precisely prices of raw materials and of agricultural goods, are demand-determined. However, prices of finished goods are cost-determined.

Kalecki's price theory underwent several important modifications, until he arrived at a final version in his *Theory of Economic Dynamics* (Kalecki 1954a [1991]). We will discuss first his final version, and afterwards put forward a hypothesis of why, in our view, this was Kalecki's preferred option. In another section of this chapter we will describe the previous "marginalist" version of his theory.

In this final specification the only factors influencing the pricing decisions are the firm's average prime costs and the average price of the industry. On the one hand, "the firm must make sure that the price does not become too high in relation to prices of other firms, for this would drastically reduce sales". On the other hand, the firm must make sure "that the price does not become too low in relation to its average prime cost, for this would drastically reduce the profit margin." (Kalecki 1954a [1991]: 210). This reasoning is formalized with the following pricing equation:

$$p = mu + n\bar{p} \tag{4.4}$$

Where p is the price charged by the firm in question, u is unit prime costs, $\bar{p}$ a weighted average of the prices charged by the firm belonging to the same industry and producing "similar" products (weighted by the respective outputs and inclusive of the firm in question) and m and n are two positive coefficients representing the decisional parameters of the firm.

Summing over all firms in the industry, Kalecki thus deduces the following equation:

$$\bar{p} = \frac{\bar{m}}{1-\bar{n}}\bar{u} \tag{4.5}$$

Here, $\bar{m}$, $\bar{n}$, and $\bar{u}$ are weighted average of the respective variables appearing in the price equations of each of the *i*'s firms. From the characteristics of the price system, it follows that prices in an industry depend on $\bar{m}$ and $\bar{n}$: an increase in $\bar{m}$ and $\bar{n}$ entailing a corresponding increase in $\bar{p}$: "The coefficients m and n characterising the price fixing policy of the firm reflect what may be called the degree of monopoly of a firm's position" (Kalecki 1954a [1991]: 211). Introducing a representative firm for which the coefficients m and n are equal to $\overline{m}$ and $\overline{n}$ for the industry and where degree of monopoly is equivalent to the average of the industry, the relationship between average price and average prime costs is rewritten as $\overline{p} = k\overline{u}$, where $k = m/(1-n)$ determined what Kalecki called the degree of monopoly.[2]

As the reader may have noticed, the pricing policy of the firms, as encapsulated in this equation, does not appear to be the outcome of an optimization procedure. Why did Kalecki choose precisely this equation?

The prevailing interpretation is that within the development of his thought, there was an early marginalist phase followed by a non-marginalist one. Having first linked his initial pricing theory to Robinson (1933) and Chamberlin's (1933) theory of imperfect competition, Kalecki would have subsequently abandoned it in his last formulation (Kalecki 1954a [1991], 1971 [1991]). We will suggest here that there are two possible explanations for Kalecki's evolution of ideas, not necessarily contradictory among themselves. One is related to the methodological preference of the author. The second is that this equation can be made compatible with an optimizing behaviour of firms under certain very specific assumptions. In this chapter we will deal with Kalecki's methodological approach; and we will discuss Kalecki's relationship to the marginalist school of thought later in this chapter.

Kalecki argued "In view of the uncertainties faced in the process of price-fixing, it will not be assumed that the firm attempts to maximize its profits in any precise sort of manner" (Kalecki 1954a [1991]: 210). Now, in an uncertain environment, firms lack the necessary information to optimize an objective function. Under these conditions, we may assume that they try to use as best as possible such information as they may have. The information they know with the greatest (though not absolute) precision is their own prime costs, the price of competitors, and how any change in their own price will affect the average price of the industry.[3] Thus, the supposition that the price of the firm will be a function of its prime cost and of the average price of the industry seems a natural one. Furthermore, if we assume that the firm will use a very simple and straightforward rule to make its decision, then the equation $p = mu + n\overline{p}$, which is linear in its two arguments, seems also a very sensible and natural option.

Therefore, we may propose that with his pricing formula, Kalecki decided to make a radical *departure* with the extant price theory, and to give an altogether *different microeconomic foundation* to his macroeconomic analysis. As we already argued, this different microeconomic foundation is not based on an optimizing behavior, simply because *under uncertain conditions firms do not have the requisite information to follow an optimizing procedure.* With his microeconomic proposal, Kalecki also opened a new line of research for a non-conventional microeconomics.[4] Finally, note that it can be proved that this pricing equation is also an optimal one under conditions of uncertainty (Bhaduri and Falkinger 1990).

Money wage flexibility, output and employment

One important factor shaping the distribution of income is the level of money wages. But changes in money wages are also important because, by affecting distribution, they have an impact on other macroeconomic variables, and especially on output and employment. The reader may recall that all classical economists, including Marx, had argued that if money wages decline, profits, output and employment would increase. As we mentioned in the introduction to this book, money wage flexibility was, and still is, the basic mechanism through which, in conventional analysis, a capitalist economy is supposed to ensure full employment.

This idea links what happens in a private firm with what happens in the whole economy. Let us consider a firm in isolation. Since its (gross) profits are the surplus of total income, once wages are subtracted, the drop in wages would mean an increase in profits. This may then bring forth, with a certain time delay, an increase in the firm's output, employment and investment. Extending the argument to the whole economy, it would appear that lower nominal wages would bring about an increase in output and employment. But the following question should be asked: Can we extend this analysis to the whole economy by simply adding up what happens to a particular firm?

Kalecki rejected the view that macroeconomic results can be reached by simply adding up what is valid at the level of a particular firm. To start with, he acknowledged that firms operate in imperfect markets and possess a monopolistic power, due to the differentiation of their products, which allows them to fix their price by marking up prime unit costs. The existence of a markup implies that the marginal productivity of labour exceeds the real wage per worker, and that no univocal association (much less a negative one) exists between employment and wages. Let us therefore see how he envisaged the whole issue. In this chapter we will discuss the point considering a closed economy. In Chapter 7 we extend the analysis to an open economy.

At an early stage of the development of his theory, Kalecki put forward the following intuition: "We can say, therefore, that during a crisis ... a reduction of wages causes a reduction of prices, but the interval between these events does not permit workers to benefit immediately, while further reductions of wages eliminate altogether the possibility of their being able to do so. As a result, the standard of living of the working class and its share in social income fall, but at the same time the increased share of the capitalists in the social income flows more and more into unsold stocks" (Kalecki 1932a [1990]: 43–44).

Somewhat later he expanded on his intuition:

> Let us assume that wages have been in fact generally reduced, and likewise taxes as a counterpart of cuts in civil servant salaries. Now the entrepreneurs, owing to the "improved" price-wage relation, utilize their equipment up to capacity level and in consequence unemployment vanishes. Has depression thus been overcome? By no means, as the goods produced have still to be sold. Now, production has risen considerably and as a result of an increase in the price-wage relation the part of production equivalent to profits (including depreciation) of the capitalists (entrepreneurs and rentiers) has grown even more. A precondition for an equilibrium at this new higher level is that this part of production which is not consumed by workers or by civil servants should be acquired by capitalists for their increased profits; in other words, the capitalists must spend immediately all their additional profits on consumption or investment. It, is however, most unlikely that this should in fact happen.
>
> Capitalist consumption changes in general but little in the course of the business cycle. It is true that increased profitability stimulates investment but this stimulus will not work right away, since the entrepreneurs will temporize until they are convinced that the higher profitability is going to last; therefore the immediate effect of increased profits will be an accumulation of money reserves in the hands of entrepreneurs and in the banks. Then, however, the goods which are the equivalent of the increased profits will remain unsold. The accumulating stocks will sound the alarm for a new price reduction of goods which do not find any outlet. Thus the effect of the cost reduction will be cancelled. On balance only a price reduction will have occurred, offsetting the advantage of the cost reduction to the

> entrepreneurs, since unemployment going hand in hand with under-utilization of equipment will reappear. (Kalecki 1935c [1990]:188)

Finally, in Kalecki (1938a [1990]), he was able to transform his intuition into a rigorous theoretical argument. To carry out the discussion, let us assume that in any given short period, capitalist expenditure on investment and consumption is predetermined in real terms. That is to say, it has been decided in previous periods and will not change significantly; unless the economic situation changed drastically. This assumption was justified in Chapter 2 and we need not rationalize it further here. Second, we assume that unit prime costs are constant (this assumption is not essential, but simplifies the reasoning).

Now, if money wages decrease, for example due to a lower bargaining power of workers because of high unemployment, two things can happen. One possibility is that prices are flexible and that they will decrease to the same extent as money wages. If this is the case, real wages will not change, because they are equal to money wages deflated by the price index. Total real profits will not change either, since the real expenditure of the capitalists has not changed. We have assumed that this expenditure is constant in real terms in the short run.

In other words, when we assume that the decrease in prices stands in proportion to the decrease in wages, the real wage and income distribution (coefficient *e*) will be constant.[5] Since the profits from this period are not affected by the decrease in nominal wage, they will also be constant. If capitalists do not immediately raise their consumption and investment after the fall in nominal wages, the benefits of firms will not rise either. But then, real income, which depends on profits and on the share of profits in output, will also remain unchanged.

We will now consider a second possibility; namely, that the decrease in money wages will not be completely transferred to prices because of imperfect competition. Kalecki argued about this possibility as follows: "there is a divergence between the prices and the marginal costs due to cartelization or imperfect competition. Moreover, the reduction of wages will tend to cause a rise in this divergence because most likely some prices will prove to be 'rigid' and thus will fail to decline in the same proportion as wages. Consequently the real purchasing power of the workers will decline... As a result, the demand for wage goods will fall and in consequence the employment in the corresponding department as well" (Kalecki 1939c [1991]: 35–36).

Let us consider the chain of events in detail. In this case real capitalist expenditure will not change either. But workers consumption decreases. Then, as a result, real profits will not change but effective demand, and therefore income, will change. That is to say, capitalists will now get a greater relative *share* of a lower *total* income. In fact, the decrease in real wages triggers a decrease in the consumption of wage earners, which – under our supposition that workers do not save – equals the decrease in wages. In other words, when the demand directed to the sector producing wage-goods decreases, then production and employment will decrease too.

From another angle, the constancy of real profits can easily be deduced from their definition as the difference between total sales and total prime costs. Upon a decrease in wages, total sales fall by an amount equal to the decrease in the consumption of wage earners (plus the decrease in sales of inputs, if we drop our assumption that firms are vertically integrated). Costs will drop by an amount equal to the decrease in wages (plus the decrease in costs of intermediary inputs). If wage earners do not save, the decrease in sales equals the decrease in costs, and gross profits remains constant (if workers do save, sales decrease less than costs and profits will rise). Profits do not only need to be produced, they also need to be realized. This will only occur when there is a similar amount of higher capitalist expenditure. If capitalist expenditure remains unchanged, profits will remain constant too.

On the contrary, given the constancy of capitalist expenditure, the decrease in the consumption of wage earners triggers a decrease in effective demand and total income. Or, looking at it from another angle, given capitalist expenditure (and therefore gross profits), the decrease in wages and the relative share of wages in gross value added leads to a decrease in income. This occurs because a change in income distribution negatively affects effective demand. This can be easily seen if we look at the final specification of Kalecki's theories of effective demand, and of income distribution:

$$Y = \frac{P}{e} = \frac{I + Ck}{1 - \omega}$$

$$\omega = \frac{1}{1 + (k - 1)(j + 1)}$$

The wage reduction brings about a fall in coefficients k, the price cost ratio, and j, the ratio of aggregate cost of materials to the wage bill. Therefore, ω, the relative share of wages in value added, will fall. Since capitalist expenditure is given, demand and output Y will decline.[6]

Clearly, the deflationary process derived from this type of income redistribution is accompanied by a decrease in employment. But it is also accompanied by a decrease in the wage-goods-sector's utilization of productive capacity, and by a change in the distribution of profits.

Simplifying, we suppose that prices do not decrease when wages fall. In those sectors producing investment goods (sector I) and consumer goods for capitalists (sector II) sales do not fall, but wages decrease. Thus profits rise in both sectors. However, in the sector producing wage goods (sector III) sales decrease more than wages. In this sector profits decrease by the same amount as they rise in the other two sectors. In effect, given that the sales are constant and that wages decrease by an amount equal to (in an obvious notation) $\Delta W_1 + \Delta W_2$, profits in sectors I and II will rise by an amount equal to $\Delta W_1 + \Delta W_2$. In sector III, however, sales decrease by an amount equal to $\Delta W_1 + \Delta W_2 + \Delta W_3$. That is to say, by an amount equal to the total decrease in wages, whereas costs decrease with an amount equal to ΔW_3. Therefore, the decrease in profits of sector III, equal to $\Delta W_1 + \Delta W_2$, equals the increase in profits of sectors I and II.

Kalecki summarized the whole process as,

> A reduction in money wages is usually accompanied as a result of "price rigidity" by an increase in "the degree of monopoly", and consequently leads to a reduction in real wages as well. However, this decline is accompanied by a fall rather than a rise in employment. The slump of employment in question affects the wage good industries, while employment in industries producing investment and capitalist consumer goods remains unchanged. The real income of the capitalists does not rise, but the real income of the workers declines. (Kalecki 1939c [1991]: 36)

The "marginalistic" version of the theory

The most detailed discussion of prices in Kalecki's early marginalist writings is to be found in his article "The Supply Curve of an Industry under Imperfect Competition" (Kalecki 1940a [1991]). This article was a summary of his work for the "Profit Margins Inquiry", also known as the "Cambridge Research Scheme" of the National Institute of Economic and Social Research (see chapter 2).

Following Chamberlin (1933), Kalecki proceeded in two steps, analysing first the equilibrium of the industry composed of a large number of firms producing heterogeneous goods, a situation he termed "pure imperfect competition"; and second, examining the equilibrium of the industry composed of a small number of firms producing heterogeneous goods, a situation he termed "imperfect competition". In modern terminology, Kalecki envisaged successively the equilibrium in the presence of monopolistic competition and then oligopoly with differentiated goods. In both cases, the shape of the elasticity function (depending on the relative price of the firm) is assumed to represent the state of market imperfection: the less elastic is the demand for any given value of relative prices, the more imperfect is the market.[7]

Let us see how Kalecki deals with the situation of "pure imperfect competition". In such case, the demand function facing each producer is proportional to aggregate demand and a decreasing function of the relative price.[8] In equilibrium, when the equality between marginal cost and marginal revenue is fulfilled, the following condition is obtained:

$$MC_i = p_i\left[1 - \frac{1}{\varepsilon_i}\right]$$

or

$$p_i = \left[1 + \frac{1}{\varepsilon_i - 1}\right]MC_i$$

where MC_i is the marginal cost of firm i, p_i its price and ε_i the demand elasticity. The elasticity of demand of each firm determines the mark-up (equal to $1/(\varepsilon - 1)$) on the marginal cost. It is easy to give a characterization of the equilibrium. Let us consider the case where there is symmetry across firms: each firm *i* has the same technology and faces the same demand curve. For a given level of aggregate demand, we can draw the marginal revenue and the marginal cost functions faced by a producer. The profit-maximizing level of output is at the intersection of marginal revenue and marginal cost with the associated price given by the demand curve.

The equilibrium is characterized graphically in Figure 4.1 where the price is measured on the vertical axis and the output of the firm on the horizontal axis. When costs are increasing, the marginal cost curve (MC) is upward sloping, while both the marginal revenue (MR) and individual demand curve (D) are downward sloping.

Let us now describe informally the process of adjustment through which equilibrium may be reached in response to, say, a decrease in marginal cost. The economy begins in equilibrium: thus the firm is producing at the point where marginal cost equals marginal revenue (point A in the diagram). At the existing average price for the industry, marginal revenue exceeds marginal cost, and so the firm has some incentive to lower its price and to produce at the point where the new marginal cost curve and the initial marginal revenue curve are equal. However, as all firms behave in the same way, the average price does not stay constant but falls in the same proportion so that the demand and

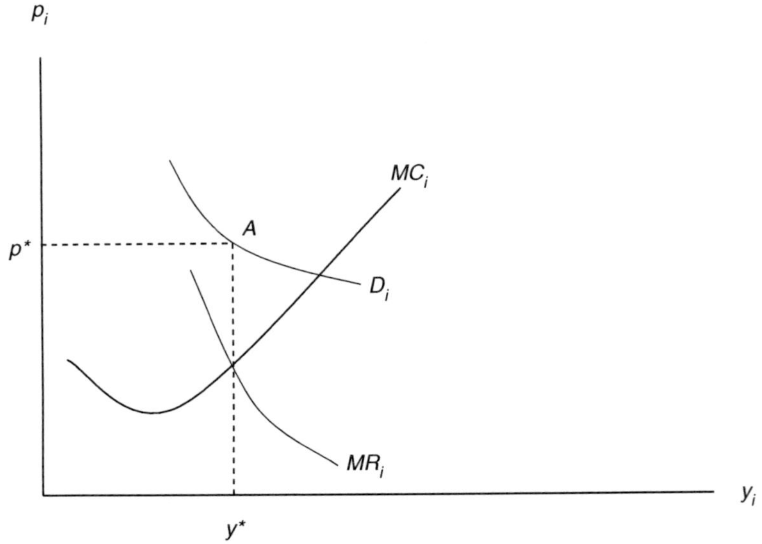

Figure 4.1

marginal revenue curves shift leftwards. Finally, insofar as the price level falls in the same proportion as individual prices, it follows that neither the elasticity of demand nor the level of demand changes for any firm. Proportionate changes in marginal costs for all firms thus lead to a fall in all prices in the same proportion, entailing an "iso-elastic downward shift" of the individual demand curve reducing their ordinates in the proportion in which the unit prime costs have fallen. Pressure on the price level thus continues until demand is back to normal.

Up to this point, we have gained only a few insights on the micro – macro articulation issue in Kalecki's early works. To deal with this problem, we already referred to his 1936 review of *The General Theory* (see Chapter 3). An analogous presentation is given in his famous 1938 article on the distribution of the National Income.[9] As Marris (1991) shows it, basing our analysis on these articles, one can reconstruct Kalecki's reasoning. In the lower sector, the intersection of the aggregate-demand curve with the 45° line determine macro equilibrium real output. The upper sector represents micro foundations. As we see it, under the hypothesis of monopolistic competition, individual demand curves are an increasing function of the aggregate demand and a decreasing function of the relative price. It results as long as relative price remain unchanged, a change in aggregate demand, due to an increase in investment for instance, materialize only as income effects, shifting individual demand curve rightwards, giving successively higher micro equilibrium. Two assumptions made by Kalecki are hence required to move easily from the micro to macro equilibrium: i) in the short period, the number of firms is unchangeable, ii) variations in aggregate demand are shown through horizontal shifts of individual demand curve; which means that aggregate demand is uniformly distributed between firms and aggregate demand changes leave unchanged the demand elasticity of firms.

The reasoning can be easily followed with the aid of Figure 4.2. The upper half is micro, the lower macro. The upper sector represents the condition for micro-equilibrium, the lower sector the corresponding

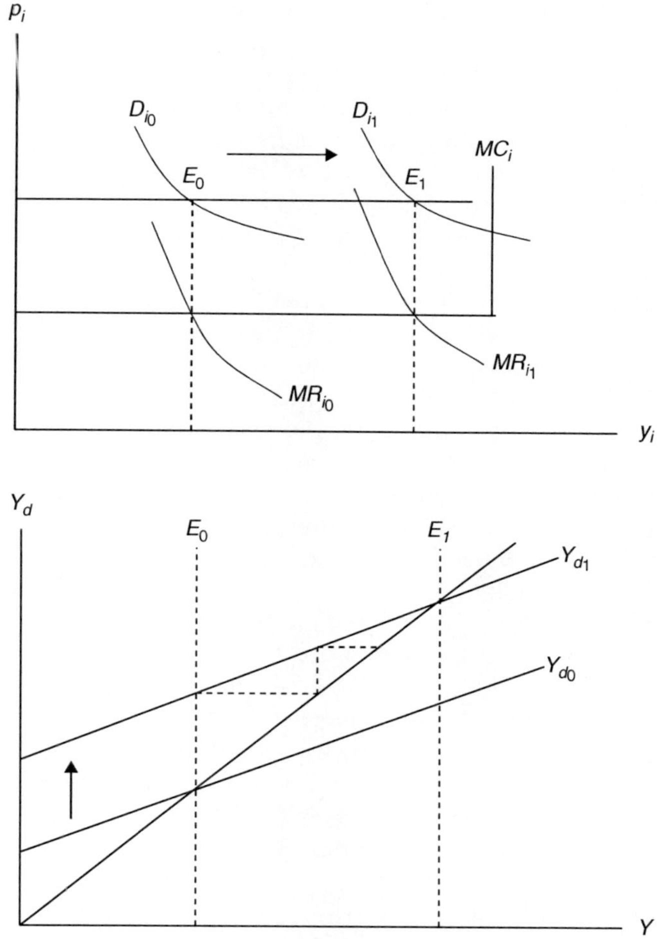

Figure 4.2

macro condition. The lower sector is the macro model, the upper its micro foundations. For stationarity, the solutions in both halves of the diagram must coincide in the horizontal plane. The micro demand curves are a family of equations $y_i = a_i f_i\,(p_i/P)$ where y_i is micro quantity, a_i an income effect which will vary with the location of the aggregate demand curve in the lower sector. To map between the two sectors we require two steps, first a scale factor and second a connection between the locations of micro demand curves on the one hand and the intersection of the aggregate demand curve with the 45 degree line on the other. The first step is accomplished by assuming a fixed-structure economy with a constant number of firms (i.e., no entry or exit of firms), the second by assuming that shifts in the aggregate demand curve, due to an increase in investment for instance, materialize as income effects on the scale factor a_i, in the micro demand curve, shifting it outward horizontally, giving successively higher micro equilibrium.

The policy of the individual firm is depicted below where we have admitted, as Kalecki in 1938 and 1939, that the marginal cost curve is horizontal. The price is equal to $p_i = \left(1 + 1/(\varepsilon - 1)\right) MC_i$. It remains constant because of constant returns and decreases with the elasticity ε of demand faced by each firm.

When aggregate demand from capitalists changes, the area of profits change correspondingly. At the new equilibrium point, the shift of the marginal revenue curve is precisely such that the sum of shaded areas is just equal to aggregate profits, corresponding, via the multiplier of capitalist autonomous expenditure, to investment, and what is left is made up of wages, which bring about a demand for consumption goods equal to their amount. We confirm therefore, on the basis of our microeconomic reasoning, what we previously argued with purely macroeconomic arguments. We see namely that, when workers spend what they earn, capitalists earn what they spend. Moreover, the share of wages and the level of national income are determined again by the microeconomic conditions of the equilibrium of firms.

It is also worth emphasizing that the global profits are still only determined by capitalist autonomous expenditure. As a consequence, since the relative shares of income depend on the degree of monopoly in a monopolistic competition framework, this means that if the degree of monopoly rises, and capitalist's expenses are unchanged, global profits will not be modified. As Kalecki remarked:

> Percentage gross margins increase, but the national output falls just so much that, as a result, the real total profits remain the same.

> However great the margin of profit on a unit of output, the capitalists cannot make more in total profits than they consume and invest (including accumulation of unsold goods). (1943c [1991]: 153–154)

An increase in the degree of monopoly shifts the demand curve upwards and to the right. The profits of each firm, for a lower production, doesn't

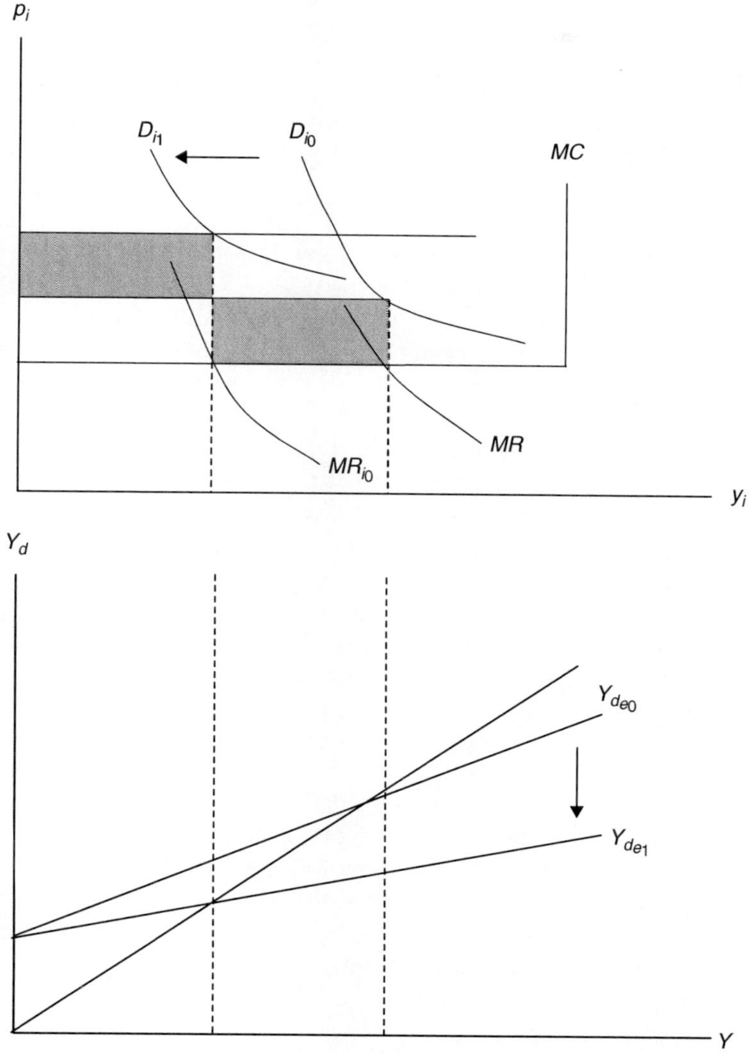

Figure 4.3

vary (which is illustrated by the equality between the shaded areas). At a macroeconomic level, this rise reduces the global propensity to consume and therefore depresses effective demand by reducing workers expenditures. Graphically (from Figure 4.3), we see the slope of aggregate demand curve decreases which entails a decrease in production and employment.

Further comments on the relationship between wages and employment

An important feature of Kalecki's first theoretical works was his view whereby there exists an inverse relation between money and real wages; a view similar to Keynes's in *The General Theory*, but which Kalecki would later modify.

Both author's argument for this association was similar and had two strands. The first, concerning the labour market, was an explanation of the relation between money wages and employment. The second, concerning the product market, was an explanation of the relation between real wages and output. Real wages should be increasing and money-wages decreasing, when output and employment fall. The argument goes as follows. Money wages are supposed to decrease in the face of greater excess of labour supply; workers being readier, because of a decrease in their bargaining power, to accept wage-cuts when unemployment is rising. As for the second point, the argument was that, due to diminishing returns and the associated shape of the short run-run marginal product of labour, real wages have to increase when effective demand decreases. Then, at a short period equilibrium, we get a negative correlation between real and money wages.

In *The General Theory* Keynes had stated the following conjecture:

> It would be interesting to see the results of a statistical enquiry into the actual relationship between changes in money-wages and changes in real wage. [...] When money wages are rising, that is to say, it will be found that real wages are rising. This is because, in the short period, falling money wages and rising real wages are each, for independent reasons, likely to accompany decreasing employment; labour being readier to accept wage cuts when employment is falling off, yet real wages inevitably rising in the same circumstances on account of the increasing marginal return to a given capital equipment when output is diminished. (Keynes 1964: 9–10)

In two articles, Dunlop (1938) and Tarshis (1939) rejected, on empirical grounds, Keynes's conjecture. Dunlop, examining the question using British data for the period 1860–1937, concluded "increase in wage rates have usually been associated with increased real wage rates, while decreases in wage rates have equally often been associated with a rise or fall in real wage rates." (1938: 432). In an article based on US monthly data for the period 1932–1938, Tarshis concluded for his part that empirically there is a rather high direct or positive association between changes in money wages and changes in real wages.[10]

Before Dunlop and Tarshis published their results questioning Keynes conjecture, Kalecki had tried to reconcile his theory of effective demand with statistical data, which showed that his original hypothesis concerning the negative association between employment and the real wage was wrong. Centering his efforts on the relationship between real wages and employment, Kalecki (1938 [1990]) resorts almost exclusively to imperfect competition in the product market to match his theory with facts. Among all the reasons that can be set forth against the conjecture of a positive association between real and money wages, he thought from the beginning that the main one was the unrealistic character of the perfect competition assumption in the product market. In that respect, imperfect competition allowed modifying some assumptions of his original reasoning. One modification is to assume firms can operate, due to excess capacity, on the horizontal part of their marginal cost curve.

Following Harrod (1936), Kalecki considered that marginal cost is constant and equal to average cost up to the point of full capacity utilization. After this point, marginal cost and average cost are no more equal and the divergence between them increases. On the basis of realism, Kalecki stresses that most firms operate below the point of "normal use" of equipment. The explanation is imperfect competition.

> Such a state of affairs is possible only with the existence of monopoly or imperfect competition. If free competition prevails [...] enterprises must close down or maintain such a degree of employment that the marginal cost is higher than the average cost. (Kalecki 1938a [1990]: 241)

Besides this discussion about the shape of the marginal real cost curve, there is another line of reasoning related to imperfect competition concerning the analysis of the determinants of the mark-up and its possible variability during the cycle.

Drawing on Chamberlin's (1933) monopolistic competition framework, Harrod (1936) addressed for the first time the question of the causes of changes in the degree of monopoly during the business cycle. As we know, the necessary condition for profit maximization is the equality between marginal cost and marginal revenue. Now, under imperfect competition, the difference between price and marginal cost, divided by price, is equal to the elasticity of demand. It may therefore be considered[11] as a measure of the degree of monopoly. In the case of constant marginal costs, given that under perfect competition price equals marginal cost, the degree of monopoly measures the share of monopoly revenue (arising from the equality of price and marginal cost) in total receipts. Assuming that "as income rises the elasticity of demand becomes less", Harrod (1936: 86) arrived at the conclusion that the degree of market imperfection decreases on the upswing and increases on downswing. He rationalized this hypothesis with the notion that the greater income is, the less the expected value for searching for better opportunities among close substitutes will be. Chamberlin's reasoning led Harrod to conclude that markups are procyclical, a feature which according to him can "be taken for granted as established by wide observation" (Harrod 1936: 84).

However, Harrod's claim would entail that the counter cyclicality of the real wage would be reinforced; which was not supported by the available information. This is why Harrod's conclusion was rejected, first by J. Robinson (1936) in her review of Harrod and then by Kalecki (1938). As sharply put by Kalecki:

> Mr Harrod was rightly criticised in that there exist other factors which influence the degree of monopoly in the opposite direction. (Kalecki 1938a [1990]: 249)

Among different factors that would invalidate Harrod's conclusion, Robinson (1936) argued that, due to the variability of the number of active firms over the cycle, the tendency is just the opposite:

> The degree of monopoly does not depend only on the imperfection of the market for a commodity, but also on the number of separate units of control engaged in selling it. (Robinson 1936: 59)

This argument can be developed under a Cournot-type model. It is related to oligopolistic factors showing how the entry and exit of firms over the business cycle and the influence of the number of firms can react on the degree of monopoly and hence countervail the influence of Harrod's conjecture, and bring about counter cyclicality of mark-ups. Drawing from another important argument from Joan Robinson,[12] Kalecki arrived at a similar conclusion. According to him, the counter cyclicality of the mark-up relies on the fact firms are reluctant to reduce prices for fear that competitors will be pushed to emulation.

> [...] there exist other factors which influence the degree of monopoly in the opposite direction. For instance, in the slump, cartels are created to save profits and this of course increases the degree of monopoly, while they are afterwards dissolved in the boom because of improving prospects of independent activity and the emergence of outsiders. It must be added that the fall in price of raw materials in the slump creates among the entrepreneurs a reluctance "to pass it on to the buyer", and this too, of course, increases the degree of monopoly. And it can be stated, on the basis of data quoted above, that the influence of these factors in raising the degree of monopoly during the slump is stronger than that of the diminishing imperfection of the market. (Kalecki 1938a [1990]: 249)

Different authors have tried to represent such an oligopolistic coordination, which stimulates competitors to cooperate (reducing their incentives to compete), despite their partly divergent interests. It may be interesting to make a digression here and briefly consider one of the pioneering works on this subject. At the time Kalecki wrote, a line of thought was developed whereby it was assumed that the oligopolist sets his price on the belief that rivals would not follow the price increase, but would match the price decrease. This behaviour would result in a kink in each firm's demand curve (the demand becoming inelastic for price reductions and elastic for price increases). Hall and Hitch (1939), together with Sweezy (1939), are the founders of the kinked demand curve approach. The analysis of Sweezy (1939), based on the notion of an "imagined demand curve", is probably the most interesting. It is based on the assumption that oligopolistic firms have asymmetric conjectures concerning the effects of their price choice on their rivals' reactions. It is the demand perceived by the firm which is kinked at the current price:

> From the point of view of any particular producer this means simply that if he raises his price he must expect to lose business to his rivals

> (his demand curve tends to be elastic going up), while if he cuts his price he has no reason to believe he will succeed in taking business away from his rivals (his demand curve tends to be inelastic going down). (Sweezy 1939: 405)

Since the corresponding marginal revenue curve has a discontinuity at the quantity corresponding to the kink, and the marginal cost curve passes between the two segments of the marginal revenue curve, a movement of the former need not affect the short-run equilibrium price and output. From a macroeconomic point of view, it is important to analyse the effect, in such a model, of a shift in demand. Sweezy proposed:

> It may be suggested that an increase in demand leading to a fuller use of capacity, more difficulty in getting quick delivery, etc; will make the imagined demand curve less elastic for upwards movements in price. For downward movements in price the result is likely to be a more elastic curve, since it may be assumed that rivals are less worried about losses in business and hence less ready to retaliate against a price cut. (Sweezy 1939: 407)

The opposite can be expected in case of a decrease in demand; thus, contrary to what happens in the case of an increase, the gap between the two segments of the marginal revenue curve will widen. In Sweezy's words:

> The result will be that the producer will be more anxious than ever to hold his price where it is. [...] as far as the cyclical behaviour of oligopoly prices is concerned we might expect to find (1) that prices go up easily and openly in time of upswing; (2) that prices resist downward pressure in times of recession and depression; and (3) that list prices become less trustworthy guides to real prices the longer bad times last. (Sweezy 1939: 408)

Let us now return to Kalecki's theory. Assuming that the influence of factors related to the imperfection of the market, represented by the elasticity of demand, are weaker than the factors related to collusive behaviour between firms, he proposed that the degree of monopoly evolves counter cyclically within the cycle. However, this does not imply the pro cyclicality of the real wage. As his formula of income distribution points out, the relative share of labour in national income depends on both the degree of monopoly and the ratio between unit wage costs and prices of basic raw materials. If both factors are stable, the relative share of labour will also necessary be stable. It can also be stable if both factors offset each other. And it is this explanation Kalecki defended: "The apparent stability of relative shares in the cycle is in reality the effect of the opposite changes of μ (the degree of monopoly) and T/Y (the ratio of turnover, including expenses in raw materials, to income)" (Kalecki 1938a [1990]: 249).

As we saw, factors determining the evolution of the degree of monopoly ought to be found in the various sources of price rigidities in the product market, and in the cooperative behaviour among firms, which tend to protect profits during the business cycle by reinforcing their market power in the slump and reducing it in the boom. Factors relating to the shape of cost curves in raw material sectors act in the opposite direction, reducing the wage share during booms, and decreasing during slumps.

> This is due to the fact that marginal-cost curves in agriculture and mining, as distinct from other sectors of the economy, slope steeply upwards. In addition, wages in agriculture fluctuate much more strongly during the business cycle than in other branches of the economy. The rise (or fall) in the price of basic raw materials relative to labour costs causes, as was shown above, an increase (or decrease) in value of T/Y. Thus the value of T/Y must rise in the boom and fall in the slump. (Kalecki 1938a [1990]: 248)

Keynes recognized the originality of Kalecki's explanation of the considerable stability of the relative share of wages in national income. However, he did not consider it totally satisfactory.

> Kalecki makes, to the best of my understanding, no definite progress toward explaining why, when there is a change in the ratio of actual to capacity output, the corresponding changes in the degree of the imperfection of competition should *so exactly* offset other changes. (Keynes 1939: 49)

We think that Keynes missed the point, and in our opinion he also was asking too much from Kalecki. The latter never asserted that changes in the degree of use of capacity should bring about changes in the imperfection of competition that exactly offset other changes.

Anyway, some years after Kalecki gave an indirect answer to Keynes's observation, stating:

> the interpretation of the movement of the ratio of proceeds to prime costs in terms of changes in the degree of monopoly is really the task of the economic historian, who can contribute to such a study a more thorough knowledge of changing in industrial conditions. (Kalecki 1954a [1991]: 220)

5

Kalecki's Long-Run Theory of Effective Demand: The Trend and Business Cycles

In 1933, when constructing a macrodynamic business-cycle model, Kalecki's purpose was to explain observed cycles with a macroeconomic theory capable of mathematical expression, leading to a dynamic system whose solutions are endogenous, deterministic cycles of constant amplitude. In substance, the demonstration of the intrinsic instability of capitalist economies was at stake. With this purpose in mind, using a linear mixed difference and differential equation, Kalecki tried to show at the 1933 Leyden meeting of the *Econometric Society* that this aim had been reached, showing in particular that his system gave rise to a cyclical solution of constant amplitude for a special value of the parameters. But,

> Alas, Frisch was there to point out that since the Greeks it has been accepted that one can never say an empirical quantity is exactly equal to a precise number. Given his aim, this was a deadly blow to Kalecki [...]. (Goodwin 1989, in Sebastiani 1989: 249–250)

Owing to the remarks he received, Kalecki afterwards temporarily accepted Frisch's Swinging System approach whereby the economy has a natural tendency to reach a stationary equilibrium and cycles occur due to exogenous shocks. Pushing momentarily into the background the demonstration of the intrinsic instability of capitalist economies, he thus centred his efforts on the explanation outlined in the conclusion of his 1934 article "Three Systems" (Kalecki 1934a [1990]). In this paper, taking into account a gestation period of investment, Kalecki described cycles as a succession of temporary equilibrium, each one characterized by both a given level of investment expenditures and capital stock; resulting respectively from decisions taken in the past. The case corresponding to undamped oscillations appears thus as a special configuration in which the economy, passing from one quasi-equilibrium to another, never reaches a stationary equilibrium (two equilibria being then crucial: the quasi-equilibrium "high" and the quasi-equilibrium "low", respectively perturbed by variations in the capital stock).

Somewhat later, still unsatisfied with his previous model, Kalecki outlined a new business-cycle theory, whose main innovation found its root in a critic he had addressed to Keynes (Kalecki (1937 [1990]). In this model, Kalecki aimed at generalizing Keynes's analysis of investment to situations in which i) long-term expectations are not exogenous but endogenous and related to the current situation and ii) returns on capital equipment are not decreasing but constant. Regarding the first point, Kalecki suggested capturing the sensitivity of long-term expectations to the current situation by introducing a non-linear function of investment decisions, aiming at showing that these are affected by waves of optimism and pessimism occurring at particular moments of the cycle. Regarding the second point, Kalecki introduced one of his most important considerations, namely the principle of increasing risk, on which he built a new analysis of the decision to invest.

In 1943, however, in his *Studies in Economic Dynamics* he developed a new model and introduced two important innovations to his previous version. In the first place, he followed a remark of Kaldor (1940) who, relying on Kalecki's (1939a) model,[1] showed that what was logically required for constructing a mathematically robust endogenous explanation of fluctuations is that the stationary equilibrium must be unstable, so that the system will never reach it. Thus, abandoning the reference to random shocks, he developed a new explanation fundamentally endogenous in which fluctuations result mainly from waves of optimism and pessimism. In the second place, he enlarged the scope of his model, with the aim of formulating a dynamic system whose solution would encompass both the cycle and the long-run development of the capitalist economy.

However, he came again, in a new form, to deal with the factors explaining the cycle and long-term growth in the *Theory of Economic Dynamics (*Kalecki 1954a [1991]). In this book he admitted the damped nature of fluctuations and explained the constant amplitude of the cycle by shocks; however, apart from this, the 1954 version of the cycle is not radically different from the 1943 one. Finally, in 1968, in the last version of his theory, he introduced some important modifications, which have to do with the influence of technical progress on profits achieved by firms having invested in the recent past.[2]

In this presentation, we will attempt to describe the different steps in Kalecki's works on growth and cycles in the capitalist economy. In the text we will not deal extensively with his last attempt of 1968, because in the Appendix we reproduce Kalecki's lectures on his 1968 paper, based on the notes taken by one of us (JL) who had the opportunity to attend these lectures.[3]

Kalecki's 1933 model

Kalecki's business-cycle theory can be considered as one of the first results, together with Frisch's (1933 [1990]) "Swinging System", of a mathematical theory of the business cycle. Each one combines two essential elements. A set of carefully chosen and empirically observable facts is formalized, and then a soluble mathematical model is deduced. As Tinbergen emphasized: "the exact form in which it is presented [Kalecki's theory] creates the possibility of a clear and fruitful discussion" (Tinbergen 1935: 270). Furthermore, Kalecki presented his business-cycle theory in the form of a linear mixed difference and differential equation so that the properties of his approach become obvious.

The model concerns a two-class society in which income distribution and profitability variables are of primary importance. National income is equal to wages plus profits; spending by capitalists depends on profits, whereas workers' spending is equal to total wages.

As regards consumption, capitalists are assumed to spend their profits either on consumption (C_k) or investment goods. Let P stand for total real income of capitalists, W for total wages and C_w workers's consumption. Kalecki uses the following relations:

$$C_k = \lambda P + B$$

$$C_w = wN$$

Where C_k and C_w are respectively real purchases of consumer goods by capitalists and by workers, and N is total employment. The consumption function of capitalists is very similar to the Keynesian consumption function, with $0<\lambda<1$ and $B>0$, the main difference being that it applies only to capitalists and not to all consumers.

There are two main determinants of investment: the gross rate of profit P/K and the money rate of interest denoted by ρ. However, such variables, in Kalecki's opinion, do not influence the investment orders D but rather their level relative to the capital stock, that is the ratio

D/K: when P and K increase in the same proportion, so that the ratio D/K remains unchanged, D probably rises (Kalecki 1933 [1990]: 74). Thus we have the equation:

$$\frac{D}{K} = f\left(\frac{P}{K}, \rho\right)$$

In the absence of external shocks and except for situations of "financial panic", the money rate of interest usually varies according to the general business conditions, which are represented by P/K. Being thus directly related to the current profitability of the equipment in use, the money rate ρ is discarded, and consequently f is a function of P/K only. In a linear form, the investment function can be written as follows:

$$D = mP - nK \tag{5.1}$$

P denotes gross profits (inclusive of depreciation), D investment orders, K, capital stock and m and n two parameters assumed to remain constant.

The cyclical nature of the solution of this model is due primarily to the gestation period of investment, from which results two lags: one between investment orders D and actual expenditures of investment I and another between investment orders and the deliveries of equipment. Three stages must thus be distinguished for each investment: investment orders D, the production of investment goods I and their deliveries L.

Let ϑ be the average gestation period of investment so that deliveries of equipment at time t are equal to orders of investment at time $t-\vartheta$. We thus have:

$$L_t = D_{t-\vartheta} \tag{5.2}$$

The relationship between investment orders D and investment outlays I is more complicated. Since each order requires a period of time ϑ to be filled, and assuming that the construction of the capital goods proceeds at an even pace (that is, $1/\vartheta$ of each order is executed per unit of time), it follows that the production of capital goods I is equal to:

$$I(t) = \frac{1}{\vartheta} \int_{t-\vartheta}^{t} D(\tau)d\tau \tag{5.3}$$

with τ being the integration variable. This equation means that the output of capital goods at time t is equal to an average – expressed in continuous terms – of the orders placed in the interval $(t-\vartheta, t)$.

Finally, if we call K the capital stock, its first derivative with respect to time ($K'(t)$) is its net increment, so that:

$$K'(t) = L(t) - U \tag{5.4}$$

where U indicates physical depreciation. Kalecki assumes that in the period under consideration U is a constant.

The system can be closed by adding the equilibrium condition of the goods market. In equilibrium, aggregate expenses are equal to aggregate income:

$$C_k + C_w + I = P + wN$$

when workers' consumption is equal to the real wage bill, we obtain Kalecki's profit equation showing gross profits are equal to capitalists' expenditures.

$$P = C_k + I$$

As Kalecki remarked:

> Thus capitalists, as a whole, determine their own profits by the extent of their investment and personal consumption. In a way they are masters of their fate; but how they master it is determined by objective factors, so that fluctuations of profits appear after all to be unavoidable. (Kalecki 1933 [1990]: 79–80)

By replacing P by $C_k + I$ in the investment function (equation (5.1)), Kalecki thus obtains a model of four equations and for unknowns. Equations (5.1), (5.2), (5.3) and (5.4) allow determining the four endogenous variables (D, I, L, K), the exogenous variables being B, ϑ and U.

As we pointed out, investment decisions cause lagged relations in two directions: If investment is rising this entails an increase in both profits and in capital; higher investment will raise demand and profits, and stimulate more investment decisions; but the rising stock of capital will tend to reduce the profit rate and negatively affect investment decisions. It is the interplay of these two opposite forces that creates the cyclical movement. Sooner or later the growth rate of one will overtake the other, and a turning point will be reached. In such a way the system will self-generate four phases of cyclical movements: boom will give rise to recession, recession to depression, depression to recovery, and recovery to boom. The expansion of the productive apparatus hampers the upward cumulative movement, bringing it to an end and to the eventual slump. Expansion is converted into contraction, which assumes a cumulative character by a process inverse to that of cumulative expansionary movement. Investments exert a retarding effect when positive or an accelerating effect when negative. This means that, in a trendless economy negative investments extricate the economy from the slump, just as the accretion of capital stock is responsible for the turning point in the boom. The growth of national wealth contains the seeds of retardation of the growth rate of economic activity. During a considerable part of the cycle, the additional wealth proves to be merely potential in character, as the accumulated capital is substantially underutilized. It becomes productive only in the successive upsurge. Disinvestment, or decapitalization of national wealth, spurs prosperity, breeds forces that put an end to the shrinkage of capital, and stimulates the upswing; but, again, the expansion of capital contains the seeds of depression.

Reducing his system to a linear mixed difference and differential equation, Kalecki expressed formally this business-cycle explanation by suggesting a solution based on the specification of parametres. As it is now well-known, a linear mixed difference and differential equation can give rise to any of the three following types of oscillatory behaviour, depending on the value of the parameters chosen in the equation of the system (the coefficient of the first order term):

a. For a negative coefficient, the amplitude of fluctuation may grow ceaselessly, thus being unstable.
b. For positive coefficient, it may be stable, with ever-decreasing amplitude.
c. If equal to zero, its behaviour may lie exactly in between the other two so that it neither grows nor decreases in strength.

As Goodwin remarked:

> Kalecki very sensibly chose the value zero thus avoiding the dilemma, since his aim, in the Marxian tradition, was to explain how and why capitalism was, by its very nature, bound to oscillate. His solution

> combined theoretical necessity with practical convenience since it determined the one parameter for which he had no evidence. (Goodwin 1989: 249)

Indeed, Kalecki's purpose was to construct a system whose solution would have been endogenous, deterministic cycles of constant amplitude.[4] Therefore, according to him, the demonstration of the intrinsic instability of economy was at stake.[5] This feature of Kalecki's approach becomes all the more evident when compared to Frisch's solution. Contrary to Kalecki, Frisch accepts the idea that economy has a natural tendency to reach its equilibrium state; in other words, that the system is intrinsically stable. From this point of view, if the cycles observed are undamped, this is due to erratic shocks. Referring to Kalecki's presentation in Leyden, Frisch wrote:

> The imposition of the condition that the solution shall be undamped is in my opinion not well founded. It is more correct, I think, to be prepared to accept any damping which the empirically determined constants entail, and then explain the maintenance of the swings by erratic shocks. (Frisch 1935, in Kalecki 1990: 447)

Thus, when Frisch criticized Kalecki's solution, it was in reality Kalecki's approach to the dynamics of capitalist economies that he criticized. This did not escape Kalecki and in successive versions of his theory he abandoned his original approach of an undamped system, and relied on shocks as one of the factors determining the cycles. In other words, after 1935 he changed the course of his research and decided to revise the mechanism at work in his model, analysing especially the factors which made the economy converge to a temporary equilibrium.

Kalecki tried to improve his analysis, especially by dealing more precisely with expectations. From 1936 onwards Keynes exerted a great influence on him; but if Keynes seems to have persuaded Kalecki to treat the expectations issue more thoroughly, this does not mean that he adopted entirely Keynes's outlook. Indeed, Kalecki's *Essays* written in 1939 are clearly an attempt to "generalize" Keynes's theory. We now discuss Kalecki's new version of his business-cycle theory as developed in this book.

Kalecki's 1939 *Essays*

There are two crucial innovations in Kalecki's 1939 *Essays in the Theory of Economic Fluctuations*. In the first place, Kalecki introduces a non-linear function into a dynamical system. In the second place, Kalecki puts forward one of his most important contributions to the analysis of investment decisions, namely the "principle of increasing risk".[6] Indeed, in the previous version of his theory, profits influenced investment only by signaling how profitable new investment could be. In his 1939 model profits play the additional role of providing the requisite finance to fund investment and to have access to the capital market. The second innovation has been recognized as a fundamental one by many commentators of Kalecki's work (Mott, 2004).[7] However, it has seldom been acknowledged that with the first one Kalecki opened up new vistas in the field of endogenous business-cycle theory. Indeed, thanks to this innovation, Kalecki's 1939 model avoids the main problem of dynamic linear models, whereby a small change in the value of the parameters may radically change the nature of the solution; especially by changing cycles of constant amplitude into a solution giving rise to explosive or damped cycles. It is certainly amazing that authors interested in endogenous dynamics usually neglect Kalecki's 1939 model, since it contains the basic ideas of this type of approach and lays the ground for the frequently cited Kaldor model (Kaldor 1940).

In a nutshell, according to Kalecki one could not assume that long-term expectations – expectations of entrepreneurs as investors – during all the adjustment process will remain unchanged. As this process is likely to take a long time, he thought that long-term expectations are likely to vary during the process of convergence of the economy to unemployment equilibrium. Let us see how Kalecki formulated his outlook:

> Let us assume that the rate of investment has really, say, risen so much that the new level of investment... and the *initial* state of expectations give a marginal efficiency equal to the rate of interest. The increase of investment, however, will cause not only the prices of investment goods to rise, but also a rise of prices (or, more precisely, the upward shift of marginal revenue curves) and employment in all branches of trade. Thus because "the facts of the existing situation enter, in a sense disproportionately, into the formation of our long-term expectations", the state of expectations will improve and the marginal efficiency of assets appears again higher than the rate of interest. Consequently equilibrium is not reached and investment continues to rise. (Kalecki 1936–37 [1990]: 538; author's emphasis)

It is useful here to refer to Marshall's concept of demand and supply price of capital for understanding Kalecki's critique. As the reader will probably recall, the supply price of a capital asset is that price which would just induce a manufacturer to produce an additional unit of such assets. The marginal efficiency of capital is then that discount rate which equates the present value of the prospective returns on capital with the current supply price of a unit of capital. The demand price of an asset is simply its present value where the expected net returns are discounted by the current rate of interest. Keynes argued that for a given state of long-term expectations, "the prospective yield [of any given type of capital] will fall as the supply of that type of capital is increased" (1964: 136).

Let us now consider the impact of a decrease in the rate of interest. With unchanged long-term expectations, if the rate of interest decreases, investors will be stimulated to buy a real asset instead of a financial asset. The demand for capital goods will thus increase. If, during this adjustment process long-term expectations increase, the demand will shift upward and equilibrium will not be reached. As Kalecki wrote to Keynes in a letter dated in 1937, in an attempt to convince him:

> [...] the increase of prices of investment goods which equates the marginal efficiency based on the *initial* [author's emphasis] state of expectations to the rate of interest, does not create an "equilibrium"; for at the same time expectations improve to some extent and thus investment increases further. (Kalecki 1990: 524)

All in fact depends on the elasticity of expected profits to current profit. If the elasticity is less than one, a rise in current profit will increase less than proportionally expected profits. The originality of Kalecki's approach is to assume that the elasticity of expectation does not remain unchanged during the business cycle but is instead likely to vary. Let us see how he suggests describing expectations of entrepreneurs over the cycle:

> When things are improving entrepreneurs become more optimistic about their future, and the rate of investment decisions increases strongly; but after a certain point doubts begin to arise as to the stability of this development, optimism ceases to keep pace with boom, and the rate of investment decisions tends to increase less rapidly. In the slump a symmetrical development is likely to occur. (Kalecki 1939a [1990]: 310)

This idea allows Kalecki to describe the process of adjustment of the economy with a non-linear function of investment demand. Assuming that the expected profits of each investment are estimated on the basis of current profits being in a fixed relation with the current national income, Kalecki suggested expressing investment decisions of entrepreneurs, D at time t, as a S-shaped function ϕ of the current national income Y: $D = \phi(Y_t)$.

Clearly, the argument implies the investment demand price will also resemble an S-shaped curve. When activity is low, realized profits do not strongly influence entrepreneurs' predictions about their future. Entrepreneurs wait for a significant improvement before taking new investment decisions. Moreover, if entrepreneurs start initially with important excess capacity, a long time can elapse before they modify their expectations. This tends to be reflected in very inelastic expectations and a constant or even decreasing investment demand price. After a certain time, improvement in activity will strongly ameliorate entrepreneurs' predictions about future profits. This glowing optimism will be reflected in very elastic expectations and a strongly increasing investment demand price. But after a certain point, disappointments and doubts begin. Optimism in the sustained strength of prosperity abates. The rate of investment decisions tends to slow down. Waves of economic optimism are followed by waves of pessimism so that the situation is now reflected by inelastic expectations and a constant or even decreasing investment demand price. In the slump, the process is more or less reversed. Thus we see that the weight of current profit in forming businessmen's expectation about future profits tends to vary during the cycle.

Let us now focus on the dynamic process. When there exists a gestation period of investment, "the investments at a given moment fail to be a variable dependent on other factors acting at this moment, and become a datum inherited from the past like capital equipment" (Kalecki 1937 [1990]: 534). It thus follows that the dynamic process leading the economy to the "final" equilibrium can be described as a "chain of short-period equilibrium", for which the level of investment and capital stock result from decisions taken in the past. But,

> To be able to say more about the mechanism of the dynamic process, we must now examine the motives of investment decisions in order to show how the links of our chain are connected. (Kalecki 1937 [1990]: 537)

At this stage we must consider the principle of increasing risk. If the expected profitability of investment, and the capacity to fund the new investments, did not depend on the scale of the investment undertaken, then there would be theoretically no limit to investments demand. But here Kalecki introduces the principle of increasing risk as one of the main determinants of the investment decision. Indeed, if the marginal risk increases with capital, it becomes possible to justify a definite level of investment, associated with each short-period equilibrium. For whatever the sensitivity of long-term expectations to the current situation, investment spending will reach a definite limit by virtue of the principle of increasing risk.

Let us see how Kalecki analysed the decision to invest of a single entrepreneur aiming at investing an amount k. For this investor, the price of investment goods, as well as the stock of capital in the economy, is a datum when he assesses the profitability of his programme. The eventual rise in all these variables are instead the effect of the realization of all programmes – an unpredictable result, since it depends on decisions taken by investors as a whole. Similarly, this investor takes as given the present and expected price of raw materials as well as the present and expected money wages. For the different given set of present and excepted prices, the entrepreneur is thus able to estimate the series of anticipated profit flows (differences between revenues and effective cost) $R_1^e, \ldots, R_n^e$ during the prospective life of the capital k he intends to invest. Given these parameters, the marginal efficiency of this capital invested (ε) is defined as follows:

$$k = \frac{R_1^e}{(1+\varepsilon)} + \ldots + \frac{R_n^e}{(1+\varepsilon)^n}.$$

The prospective profit π is thus equal to the product εk. Now, let us see how the entrepreneur decides on the optimum k, that is, the size of the investment. If he must charge the capital invested at the market rate of interest r and make some allowance for risk, the rate of which Kalecki denotes by σ, its prospective gain is equal to $g = \varepsilon k - (r + \sigma)k$. The entrepreneur will thus obtain the maximum gain at the value of k for which the marginal efficiency of capital is equal to the sum of interest rate r and rate of risk σ, that is to say when $dg/dk = 0$ and thus when $\varepsilon = r + \sigma$.

When the marginal efficiency of capital is decreasing with k, the optimum amount to be invested is finite and determined at the intersection of curves ε and $(r + \sigma)$. Yet, according to Kalecki, the two reasons generally advanced for justifying that decrease, "large scale diseconomies" on the one side and "imperfect competition" or "the limitations of the market" on the other are not relevant. Regarding the first one, Kalecki's idea is founded on the following considerations.

> The first reason seems to be unrealistic. Clearly it has no technological basis. True, every machine has an optimum size, but why not have 10 (or more) machines of this type? There remains the argument of difficulties of management arising out of large-scale enterprise. But this also is doubtful (why not start 10 factories instead of one with 10 independent directors?), and anyway could apply only to industrial giants far above the average size of investment of existing enterprises." (Kalecki 1939a [1990]: 287)

Regarding the second reason, as Kalecki puts it, first of all, the degree of imperfection becomes relevant only for very large-scale firms; moreover, this is not a deterrent to the firm's investments as such, but only to their concentration in a single sector: the limits set by the size of single markets can be overcome by spreading investments over various fields; finally, this factor "leaves unexplained the existence of large and small firms in the same industry".

If imperfect competition in the goods market cannot be claimed as an ex ante limitation factor, this is however not the case regarding the capital market whose functioning is regulated by the principle of increasing risk. Indeed: i) The danger an investor undergoes in case of failure will be greater, the greater investment are in relation to his wealth: "For the greater the investment, the greater is the reduction of the entrepreneur's income from his own capital when the average rate of profit falls short of the rate of interest" (Kalecki 1939a [1990]: 287–288). ii) Access to credit and financial markets is more difficult – or more costly – the greater is indebtedness compared to the investor's own capital. iii) As a result of point ii), the risk of suffering illiquidity rises with expansion of initiatives not backed by an adequate volume of capital belonging to the firm. Indeed, if the entrepreneur wants to obtain credit, banks will charge a higher rate of interest when the capital of firms is illiquid. The true collateral is not the capital invested but the liquid capital owned by firms. As a consequence:

> The enterprises started in a given industry at a given moment are not of equal size because the private capital of the various entrepreneurs is not the same. "Business democracy" is a fallacy: the amount of

the entrepreneur's private capital is a "factor of investment". (Kalecki 1939a [1990]: 289)

Given these conditions, the appraisal of risk is larger the higher the ratio of programmed investments to the value of entrepreneurial capital, so that, to be offset, it requires a growing difference between expected marginal profitability and the interest rate. Conversely, with a given spread between these two variables (and with given entrepreneurial capital), investment decisions will be taken up to the point where the marginal risk balances this gap.

The above considerations provide the elements for identifying the equilibrium level of investment decisions in a given moment, that is to say, the amount of these decisions that exhausts the convenience of investing in the given conditions. Further decisions may take place only as a result of changes in net marginal profitability or in the risk factor: from this point onwards, Kalecki's entire research on investments focuses on the causes of change of these factors, and on their consequences for the business cycle.

If marginal risk increases with capital, it becomes possible to justify the definite level of investment associated with each short-period equilibrium. For whatever the sensitivity of long term expectations to the current situation, investment spending will reach a definite level by virtue of the principle of increasing risk.

Let us now study the dynamics by which the economy converges, for a given capital stock, to a stable equilibrium. Assuming that the relative share of wages in real national income is given and determined by the degree of monopoly, Kalecki shows that real national income is related to investment spending by means of a function:

$$Y_t = f(I_t)$$

Further, under the assumption that there is an average gestation lag of investment equal to ϑ we can rewrite Y_t as a function of D_t.

$$Y_{t+T} = f(D_t)$$

The dynamics of the economy can be described with both ϕ and f in the (D,Y) plane. When the dynamic process – made of a "chain of short period equilibrium" – leads economy to a stable equilibrium, we have a picture as in Figure 5.1.

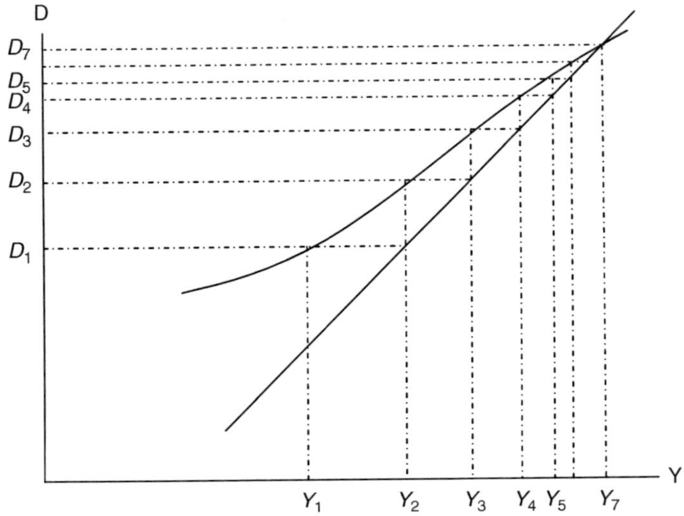

Figure 5.1

Now, we can divide time into periods of length τ. In the first τ period the level of national income is Y_1 and the rate of investment decision is D_1. Since investment decisions determine the national income in the next τ period, the national income will be Y_2 in the second period. But, for this new level of income, the rate of investment decision is above D_1 and equal to D_2. Therefore, national income is growing. However, "after a relatively small number of periods the divergence between Y, D and Y_A, D_A is negligible, i.e. the position of equilibrium is practically reached" (Ibid: 315). Of course, if the point (Y, D) is below the f curve so that investment decisions are lower than those which have determined the present national income "this process is reversed, and the system travels downwards towards A" (Ibid: 315). In a nutshell, if capital stock is constant, a deviation of income from equilibrium, whatever the reasons, initiates an adjustment process towards the stable equilibrium A.

It is worth mentioning at this stage that Kalecki focuses only on this type of situation which, in retrospect, can appear puzzling. Indeed, with a non-linear function, we could have expected Kalecki to have discussed also the case in which ϕ cuts f from below, that is to say a situation in which the economy can attain both stable and unstable equilibrium. As we shall see, it was precisely because Kaldor took into consideration this possibility neglected by Kalecki, that he succeeded in offering a new theory of the business cycle built on the latter's system. We will discuss briefly about Kaldor's approach later on, but before that it is still necessary to consider how Kalecki explains the dynamic process when capital stock is variable.

Up to now, we have implicitly assumed that investment spending doesn't affect the capital stock during the dynamic process so that the economy reached equilibrium by moving up ϕ. However, we will see that by relaxing this assumption, the dynamics of the economy changes. It results from the existence of the investment time-lag previously mentioned, which introduces two time lags into the system. A first one between investment decision and investment spending which increases global demand; and a second one between investment decisions and deliveries of equipment which, by affecting positively the capital stock, and negatively the profit rate, decreases investment decisions and global demand. Then, since the paces of variation of investment decisions and of the capital stock differ, the dynamics becomes cyclical. In order to represent this, Kalecki kept reasoning in the (Y, D) plane. However, he then drew a family of ϕ curves related to different levels of the capital stock, and hence to a given value of investment necessary for the maintenance of the existing capacity (the amount of depreciation being given, higher curves are connected with a lower level of capital stock). For, with a same level of income, investment decisions are greater when the volume of equipment is lower. From this conclusion, it follows that if equipment deliveries are weaker than the maintenance level of equipment, so that the equipment is decreasing, the increase in the investment decision described previously will be strengthened. That is to say that the ϕ curve on which the economy moves up will also move upwards. By contrast, if the volume of equipment deliveries is greater than the volume of depreciated equipment, the dynamic process will be hampered, so that the ϕ curve on which economy moves up will move downwards. Therefore, if at the intersection of curves f and ϕ, investment decisions are greater than the maintenance volume of equipment, the volume of capital will grow and the economy will move up on a downward-shifting ϕ curve instead of being in equilibrium. However, if investment decisions are lower than the maintenance volume of equipment, the reverse will occur. Kalecki thus suggested a representation of the trajectory of the economy, as shown in Figure 5.2.

As we can see, the case considered is a self-stimulated cycle. In order to understand the conditions necessary to obtain this result, we need

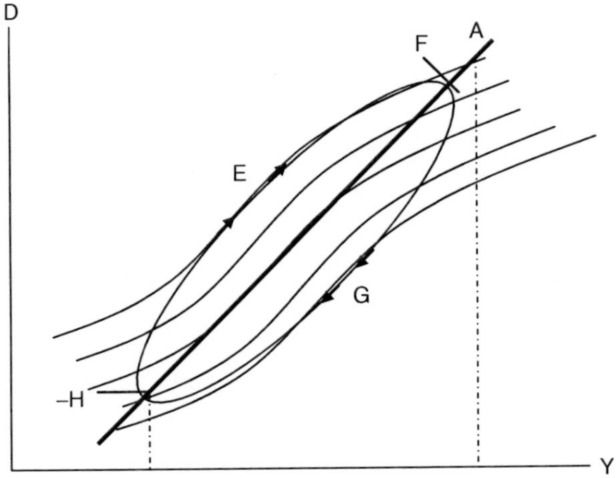

Figure 5.2

to focus on Kalecki's explanation of the cyclical mechanism. Let us first consider the intersection point *E* for which the deliveries of investment goods are just equal to the maintenance level of the equipment. Thus, as the volume of equipment is constant, the ϕ curve is stationary in the considered period, and since *E* is above *f*, national income increases and the point *Y, D* tends to move up this curve. However, in the following period investment activity increases causing the growth of equipment, and the ϕ curve shifts downwards. As a consequence the "self-stimulating process" of the rise in investment decisions and national income is hampered and the economy attains point *F* located on a lower ϕ curve. At this point, where ϕ intersects *f*, national income is neither expanding nor shrinking. However, because of deliveries of investment ordered previously, capital equipment is expanding. Consequently, investment decisions fall causing a decrease in income, which in turn depresses investment decisions. Graphically the ϕ curve shifts downward causing point *Y, D* to move vertically and up until investment activity is equal to the level of maintenance. As a consequence, from this moment, capital equipment shrinks, thus putting a stop to the downward movement. Finally, point *Y, D* reaches *H*. Here, income ceases to fall, but the ϕ curve shifts upwards because of the decrease of equipment, "thus the moving point comes back to point *E* and a new cycle begins" (Ibid: 317).

At first sight, it would appear that Kalecki's cycles are purely accounted for by the underlying economic mechanism. However, this is not the case, and Kalecki himself emphasized it when he wrote:

> Clearly it is an arbitrary and even unlikely assumption that the moving point comes back to its initial position *E* – the trajectory may well be a spiral and not a closed curve. If the fluctuations produced by our mechanism have a tendency to subside, this means that the spiral converges towards point *A*, and in this way the system tends to attain long-run equilibrium. But as shown by the investigations of Prof. Frisch...this is prevented by the existence of "erratic shocks". Since the relationships represented by f and ϕ are in reality not quite stable functions, the actual dynamic process may be imagined as the result of the operation of the mechanism described above and random shocks. Now Professor Frisch has shown that, if the basic mechanism produces slightly damped fluctuations, the existence of shocks establishes a state of relatively regular undamped fluctuations with an average period similar to that of the fluctuations created by the "basic mechanism". (Ibid: 318)

Consequently, as Kalecki recognized, his theory, though non-linear, is only semi-endogenous: its degree of endogeneity depends on the magnitudes of the parameters involved. More precisely, it depends on the importance of the shifts of the investment decision curve ϕ and hence on the sensitivity of investment decisions to capital variations. Indeed, it is only in the case when these shifts are sufficiently strong that a monotonic return to the stationary equilibrium does not occur.

Kalecki, however, rapidly started doubting that Frisch's solution was a suitable one:

> An important point about any trade cycle theory is whether the cycle may be damped down or not. Indeed, the course of the cyclical fluctuations as determined by the fundamental equation may be such that the amplitude diminishes from cycle to cycle so that the system gradually approaches a state of equilibrium. It is true that it has been shown that a combination of a damping mechanism with erratic shocks (due to the fact that the economic relations as represented by the fundamental equation are rather loose) produces cycles with an amplitude which has no tendency to decline. But if damping is strong such cyclical movements would be of extremely irregular character. Thus, because it is difficult to prove why the coefficients of the

> fundamental equation should be such as to exclude strong damping, these theories have a serious loophole. (Kalecki 1943c [1990]: 73)

The purpose of Kalecki'1943 version was precisely to overcome this difficulty.

Kalecki's 1943 version

Kalecki introduced two important innovations to his model in the 1943 version. The first one is that the new model is broader in scope. In the 1943 version Kalecki had an additional objective for his cyclical model, which has to do with the simultaneous and mutual conditioning of economic growth and economic cycles. He now wanted to develop a macro model that would be simple enough to solve analytically, and yet rich enough to have an intimate union of the analysis of trend and cycle. As Steindl put it: "The problem of the trend is, for Kalecki, not separable from that of the cycle. He deals with them together, in their interrelations, and with the same methods: functional equations describing a dynamic process which evolves in time from one period to the next, in contrast to the methods of moving equilibrium or 'growth path' which almost exclusively dominate" (Steindl 1981: 603–04). We will have time to go into greater detail into this aspect when referring to the 1954 version, because in that one the author refers to it more extensively.

The second innovation concerns the nature of the model and its solution. Kalecki obtains his 1943 model by examining a case of his 1939 theory suggested by Kaldor (1940 [1960]). The latter author pointed out that a consistent endogenous business-cycle theory – which is not dependent on the special values of the parameters of the system – must possess at least one non-linear function to make the stationary equilibrium unstable. And from this point of view, the theory "nearest to it, [...] is Mr. Kalecki's theory given in chapter 6 of his *Essays in the Theory of Economic Fluctuations*" (Ibid: 188). For if Kalecki's non-linear investment function is used to obtain this result, the dynamic system becomes robust and business cycles can be explained without having recourse to stochastic shocks. It is precisely by following Kaldor's remark that Kalecki renewed his business-cycle theory by considering the case in which the stationary equilibrium, instead of being stable is unstable. A simple way to see it is to refer to Kalecki's 1939 diagram.[8]

In the plane (Y, D) used previously, let us draw (see Figure 5.3) a family of S - shaped curves ϕ_{e1} ... representing the rate of investment decisions at time t, given the quantity of equipment available, where e_1 represents

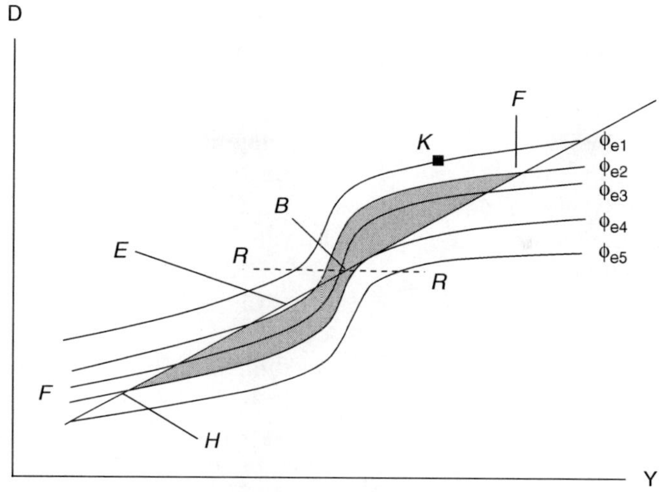

Figure 5.3

a smaller quantity of equipment then e_2, and so on. However, in contrast to the case envisaged in Kalecki (1939 [1990]), let us assume that for a given quantity of equipment (e_3 in the chart) a ϕ curve cuts f from below, which corresponds to an unstable equilibrium. That is to say a point from which, if disturbed, the system will diverge. As regards the cyclical mechanism, this change is vital for it allows us to consider the case where the stationary equilibrium, in which saving equals investment and net investment is zero, is an unstable one. Hence there can be a configuration in which if the economy is not initially at this point, it can never attain it, whatever the parameter values may be. That is to say, situations for which cyclical fluctuations are entirely explained by the underlying economic mechanism. The trajectory of the economy can now be represented by the point *FGHE*.

Supposing that, in the initial position, the system is at *K*, under the latter assumption, the system will move up the same ϕ curves and reach the point *A*. Here, owing to the gradual accumulation of equipment (the economy is above *RR* which represents the locus of points on the ϕ_e curve where the level of investment decisions corresponds to replacement so that net investment is zero) the economy will move up the f curve until it reaches *G*. At this point, since equilibrium is unstable, a downward moving cumulative process is set up which lands the system at *H*. Then, as *H* is below *RR*, capital equipment shrinks so that the economy moves up the *f* curve until it reaches *E*. But, as with point *G*, the latter is unstable. Consequently, an upward cumulative movement follows which lands the system at *F* and a new cycle appears. In conclusion, whatever the initial position – unless the economy is initially at *B* (the stationary equilibrium) – the development of the economy will inevitably be cyclical. Indeed, if at the beginning the system is placed in proximity of *B*, a moving cumulative process is set up which to the right of *B* is downward and to the left is upward, which will give rise to an endogenous cycle.

As in the 1939 *Essays*, the non-linearity of the investment function is mainly explained by evolution of the expectations of the entrepreneurs supposed to be subject to waves of pessimism and optimism. In 1943, this factor becomes the main cause of instability while factors such as the profit rate are pushed into the background. Indeed, whatever the upward or downward shifts of the ϕ curves caused by the evolution of the capital stock, the economy cannot stabilize at the point of stationary equilibrium and will be bound to fluctuate indefinitely. For this reasons, we see "subjective" factors dominating "objectives" factors. In fact, in this version expectations are of primary importance: it is because entrepreneurs are successively optimist and pessimist that the economic situation successively ameliorates and deteriorates. Here lies without doubt the originality of Kalecki's approach. It is precisely this point that T. Scitovsky emphasized in his review of Kalecki's 1943 *Studies*, concluding on the superiority of Kalecki's approach to that of Kaldor.

> Mr Kaldor... has shown that the amplitude of the business cycle is stabilised by the fact that the influence of incomes on investment and of investment on incomes (the multiplier effect) vary with the phases of the cycle – being weakest at the top of the boom and the bottom of the depression. Dr Kalecki's argument in the volume under review is very similar, except that he neglects the variations in the multiplier and pins his main argument on the entrepreneur being cycle-conscious, and hence more cautious in his investment decisions after a prolonged boom than at the beginning of it. (Scitovsky 1946 in Kalecki [1990]: 548)

It is also this feature that Kalecki noticed when comparing his approach to Kaldor. Dealing with the way Kaldor introduces both non-linear investment and saving functions, he noted:

> He obtained [Kaldor] his results by examining a special case of my theory in the *Essays* which I have failed to consider. His theory

> is therefore based on the assumption of a particular shape of the functional relation between income and the rate of investment decisions [functions ϕ and f in Kalecki's model]; and it is difficult to advance any satisfactory a priori reasons for this shape being necessarily such as he assumes. In my present theory the cycle is prevented from being damped down by variations in a (the coefficient of the influence of profits upon the rate of investment decisions), and the pattern of these changes in variations seems to me much better founded than the shape of Mr. Kaldor's curve. (Kalecki 1943c [1991]: 175)

Although Kalecki maintains that the presence of a non-linearity frees his model from the difficulties related to the persistence of the cycle, he only gives a qualitative discussion of how his coefficient fluctuates in the course of the cycle, without supplying an analytical proof. The lack of precise formal specifications in such an equation seem to have prevented commentators (both his contemporary and more recent ones) from recognizing the novelty and importance of Kalecki's non-linear model; and most of them have preferred Kaldor's 1940 version, even though Kaldor does not either provide a mathematical proof of the cyclical nature of his model. Anyway, Kalecki soon abandoned this path. In the following, and last, discussion of this issue, Kalecki returned to a linear model but slightly amended Frisch's approach.

Kalecki's 1954 version

Kalecki's 1954 theory of the trade cycle has some similarities, but also some differences, with his 1943 version. We deal with the most important of them in due course.

Let us first consider the one very relevant difference. In the latter version, the particular non-linear configuration used in 1943 to explain why cycles are undamped is abandoned, and Kalecki comes back to a linear system. This change of methodology may appear at first sight puzzling, because his analysis of Kaldor's model most likely showed him that a non-linear specification might lead to a mathematically more robust endogenous explanation of the cycle. However, we can make an educated guess about the reasons motivating his preference. Surely, this was not caused by a lack of a proper mathematical apparatus, because he was well-versed on the theory of dynamical systems.

We would suggest that his choice was first and foremost influenced by his observation of facts. Here is the relevant quote:

> Some authors (for instance, Kaldor and myself) have assumed that after investment in fixed capital has reached a certain level in the boom it grows more slowly in response to determinants than in the early stage of the boom and that an analogous phenomenon occurs in the slump. Our scatter diagrams do not seem to bear out this hypothesis. (Kalecki 1954a [1991]: 297)[9]

An additional reason why Kalecki decided to return to a linear model is that he became convinced that erratic shocks of a plausible nature could indeed maintain the cyclical movement of the economy. But before we deal with this issue it is best to give an outline of the specification of the 1954 model.

In the latter model (as in the previous one of 1943), investment decisions are related to two broad categories of factors: first, the change in financial resources available to the firms which occurs as firms make gross savings; and second, their profitability prospects represented by the change in profits on the one hand and the change in capital stock on the other.

Profitability prospects of firms are based on projection of recent experience, in that they are taken into consideration by postulating that the amount of fixed capital decisions per unit of time are an increasing function of the change in profits ($\Delta P_t / \Delta t$) – considered as a reflection of the increase in sales – and a decreasing function of the change in the capital stock ($\Delta K_t / \Delta t$) – considered a reflection of the increase of competition between firms and thus more claims for the available volume of sales. The argument here is simply that, all other things being equal, an increase in profit or in the capital stock during the course of a given period makes certain new investment prospects, more or less attractive and permits either extensions or contractions of the boundaries of investment plans in the course of the period.

Once investment decisions are determined on the basis of these factors, they are followed by investments with a fixed time-lag. The equation for investment in fixed capital can be written as follows:

$$D_t = aS_t + b\frac{\Delta P_t}{\Delta t} - c\frac{\Delta K_t}{\Delta t}$$

Where S_t is the total saving, and $\Delta P_t / \Delta t$ and $\Delta K_t / \Delta t$ the change per unit of time in profits and in the stock of fixed capital, respectively. Apart from the equations describing the investment process, the equations defining profits remained fundamentally the same as in the previous version. After some transformation, Kalecki arrives at a linear dynamic equation of net investment in terms of finite differences:

$$I_{t+\theta} = mI_t + n\frac{\Delta I_t}{\Delta t}$$

where m, n and Θ are constant and positive.

This equation conveys the view that investment decisions are driven by the past level and rate of change of profits and therefore (via the multiplier) by the past level and rate of change of investment. Depending on the parameters' values, cycles will be damped, constant or explosive. Following Frisch's approach, Kalecki admitted that the system is asymptotically stable but kept alive by shocks. Being well aware of the difficulties of this approach, he however added:

> The experiments made seem to suggest that, if the damping is not weak, the resulting cycle is very irregular and its amplitude is of the order of magnitude of the shocks. Since there is no reasonable basis for the assumption that the interrelation between investment, profits, and output should necessarily be such as to produce a weak damping, the value of the theory becomes questionable. (Kalecki 1954a [1991]: 309)

To deal with this problem, Kalecki suggests that the erratic shocks to which an economy is exposed are subject not to a uniform distribution, but to a normal frequency distribution.[10] And under this more realistic assumption he shows that business cycles remain alive even if when the underlying deterministic process tends to dampen down.

With this line of approach, he carried out experiments with his cyclical model. In these experiments, he took some plausible values for the variables of his model obtained from data from the US. Then, he simulated two situations of cyclical development, one with a mild and the other with a heavy damping. He concluded:

> Curve D, which corresponds to much heavier damping, shows a pattern very similar to that of curve C [i.e. with mild damping, JL and MA]. Both have a fairly clear-cut average period amounting for curve C to about 8 years, and for curve D to about 7.5 years...The amplitude of curve D is only moderately smaller than that of curve C.

> ...the phenomenon itself is virtually certain: the cycle generated by shocks with a normal frequency distribution shows a considerable stability with respect to changes in the basic equation which involve substantial increases in damping. Thus, even with relatively heavy damping such shocks generate fairly regular cycles.
>
> This result is of considerable importance. It shows that a semi-regular cycle may be in existence even though the "business cycle equation" involves substantial damping. (Kalecki 1954a [1991]: 321)[11]

Let us now deal with Kalecki's attempt to encompass, in his model, both the trend and the business cycle; a subject recurring in all the versions from 1943 onwards. Mathematically speaking, depending on the value of the parameters, the dynamic system encapsulating his economic theory yields either cyclical solutions without trend, or a trend solution without cycles. How, then, to reconcile this economic theory with the empirical observation that capitalist economies do show a trend *cum* business-cycle long-run behaviour?

In relation to this point, Kalecki was convinced that on the basis of his theory, and for realistic values of the parameters, he could find a plausible explanation of the cycle, for which there is hardly a satisfactory substitute. Therefore, he was led to the conclusion that the source of long-term growth must be found in factors somewhat external to the mechanism generating the cycle; namely, forces superimposed to the basic mechanism and which could not be explained by current economic events. This source he saw in innovations.[12] He considered this a semi-exogenous factor, because innovations cannot, in his view, be made dependent on the current economic situation or on purely economic factors having taken place in the recent past.

Already in his earlier *Studies in Economic Dynamics* (1943), Kalecki had distinguished between positive and negative effects of invention and innovation on profit expectations. Formally, this effect is represented by a function of time $F(t)$ in the complete equation of trend and cycle. The trend is represented by a particular solution of this complete equation, and the pure business cycle by the deviations from this trend. This function $F(.)$ is however not totally exogenous. Kalecki especially considered that an important factor contributing to a positive long-run trend is the link between the profitable investment opportunities opened up by invention and the size of the capital stock. Investment flowing from the application of a given flow of new ideas will "be proportionate to the volume of capital equipment" (Kalecki 1943c [1991]). This represents the "semi-exogenous" aspect of investment associated with innovation as well as the sense in which long-run growth is semi-exogenous. As Steindl 1981 [1991] stressed:

> Thus Kalecki agrees to a large extent with Rosa Luxembourg, who could not see any motive for expansion in a capitalist economy unless it came from outside; but, unlike her, he included in these outside influences not only foreign expansion, war, and armament, but also the stream of innovations. This stream has to continue to provide the demand for expansion. (604)

Kalecki however perceived a theoretical cost associated with the way in which he had incorporated innovations and technical change into his model. This cost was a relative neglect of the connection between the trend and the cycle (endogenous mechanism). For the most part these are separate aspects, at least in the formal parts of the argument. To correct this deficiency was the main aim of the 1968 paper.

Kalecki's 1968 version

Kalecki starts his 1968 paper recognizing a limitation of his previous versions. In his words:

> I myself approached this problem [to the theory of growth, JL and MA]...in a manner which now I do not consider satisfactory: I started by developing a theory of the 'pure business cycle' in a stationary economy, and I later modified the respective equations to get the trend into the picture. By this separation of short and long-run influences I missed certain repercussions of technical progress which affect the dynamic process as a whole. (Kalecki 1968a [1991]: 435)

Kalecki's discussion of the determinants of investment in his new paper centres on the difference between the actual and the "standard" rate of profit *of new investment,* which affects investment decisions.[13] This "standard" rate of profit is the reciprocal of the so-called pay off period, namely that period during which entrepreneurs expect "normally" to recover the capital invested. Denoting this standard rate by π, and the level of new investment which "fetches" under conditions prevailing in the year considered the rate of profit π by $I(\pi)$, Kalecki refers to two determinants of the increment of "real profits" of the new investments.

Ignoring for a moment the impact of technical progress, the first arises when any new investment captures only a small proportion (n) of the increment of profits during the year (ΔP). Kalecki's argument is based on imperfect competition: thanks to their market power, the old equipment tends to retain the markets and profits it had before. We have therefore:

$$I(\pi) = \frac{n\Delta P}{\pi}$$

so that

$$\pi = \frac{n\Delta P}{I(\pi)}$$

The second determinant arises when allowance is made for technical progress. New equipments being more productive than older ones, profits accruing to them comprise an additional gain, while for a given volume of total profits the profits fetched by old equipment falls by the same amount. This last component of profits (denoted as δP) together with $n\Delta P$ make up the total profit flow captured by new plant, consistent with what is referred to as the "standard rate of profit". The standard rate of profit is therefore associated with a particular level of investment according to the relation:

$$I(\pi) = \frac{n\Delta P + \delta P}{\pi}$$

For the capitalists, this profit rate π serves as a benchmark of the correct rate of profitability. The reinvestment of entrepreneurial saving-determined by past profit flows – will thus depend on how this standard investment level compares with the actual investment level. In other words, Kalecki writes for investment decisions:

$$D = E + r\left(I(\pi) - I\right)$$

Where E is total entrepreneurial savings and r is a positive constant. Hence, if the term within parenthesis is positive (negative), investment decisions will amount to more (less) than entrepreneurial savings. Kalecki then assumes entrepreneurial savings are a constant proportion (e^{14}) of total savings S (which are equal to total investment I), and including the impact of innovations ($B(t)$), puts forward his equation for investment decisions as:

$$D_t = eI_t + r\left(\frac{n\Delta P_t + \delta P_t}{\pi} - I_t\right) + \mathrm{B(t)}$$

After several manipulations he arrives at the dynamical equation for investment as:

$$I_{t+\vartheta} = aI_t + b\frac{\Delta I_t}{\Delta t} + F(t)$$

where a and b are positive constant. This equation is not unlike the dynamic equation of Kalecki's earlier 1954 model for investment, derived on a somewhat different basis. As regards the problem of the trend, we see however that here, as in the 1943 and the 1954 versions, Kalecki maintains a semi-exogenous term, which is included to take into consideration factors which do not strictly depend on the equations of the model. He concluded his 1968 paper explaining his option:

> It follows that in our approach the rate of growth at a given time is a phenomenon rooted in past economic, social and technological developments rather than determined fully by the coefficients of our equations as is the case with the business cycle. This is very different from the approach of purely "mechanistic" theories... but seems to me much closer to the realities of the process of development. To my mind, future enquiry into the problems of growth should be directed, not towards doing without such semi-autonomous magnitudes as A(t) and B(t), but rather towards also treating the coefficients used in our equations... as slowly changing variables rooted in the past development of the system. (Kalecki 1968a [1991]: 450)

Final Remarks

We have mentioned several times that Kalecki's central concern was the analysis of how in capitalism business cycles and long-term growth are generated; and that he first presented his theory of effective demand in the context of a model of cyclical growth. Moreover, he kept on working on this issue practically without interruption during all his life.[15] In this sense, the long-run theory of effective demand was in fact, the central core of Kalecki's theoretical concern.

It seems important to conclude our review of Kalecki's dynamic model with two general remarks, which will allow us to clarify his difference with today's dominant theoretical approach.

In the first place, Kalecki developed a model in which there exists a continual movement through a series of short-period equilibria or quasi-equilibria. Moreover, this movement will be cyclical and any position of "final equilibrium" will never be reached, because business fluctuations will permanently take place.

We may or may not agree with Kalecki´s theory of the cycle. But, to our mind, we should not lose sight of the fact that he was the first economist to provide a rigorous analytical framework, alternative to the general equilibrium theory, to study the general properties, and more specifically the stability properties, of a capitalist (or decentralized, to use the parlance of the general equilibrium theory) economy. Within this analytical framework, the issue of unemployment in capitalism can be given a dynamic explanation.

In the second place, in his model, Kalecki assumed that the expansion of demand is not only a necessary condition for growth in the long term, but in addition it is a sufficient condition. More precisely, Kalecki's long-run theory of effective demand was a long-run theory of investment decisions.[16] Now, we must make it clear that Kalecki did not purport to consider all those factors that can affect investment. Rather, his objective was to formulate a general theory of investment decisions under normal conditions; thus excluding situations such as "crisis of confidence".

Anyway, Kalecki implicitly supposes that the level of *effective* economic activity is always below the *potential* level; which is to say that, in every moment of time there exists unutilized productive capacity. Kalecki specifies this when he states that "a laissez faire capitalist economy used to achieve a more or less full utilization of resources only at the top of a boom, and frequently not even then" (Kalecki 1968a [1991]: 438). This is why Steindl (1981 [1991]) concluded, "It may be remarked in conclusion that Kalecki's analysis of the trend is purely in terms of demand. The only parameter in his equation through which an influence of supply could enter is the lag between decision and investment. He implicitly recognized the importance of supply as a constraint on growth (if booms hit the ceiling, the trend would be influenced too), but the stream of demand appears as the primary mover, the sine qua non of growth" (605).

Kalecki's position thus differs drastically with the classical (old and new) view, as well as with the so-called New-Keynesian view, which are hegemonic today in our discipline, and which assume that the capitalist economy has a built-in mechanism securing a return to full employment, or a return to the full utilization of the capacity, whenever a shock displaces it from this equilibrium.[17]

Appendix 5.1

Investment decisions, the business cycle and the trend

What follows is a transcription of Kalecki's lectures delivered in the 1967–1968 academic year at the Central School of Planning and Statistics. Kalecki explained as follows the scope and aim of his lectures:

> These lectures ... are concerned with determinants of investment decisions which together with the relations between investment and profits as well as national income permit to examine the dynamic process of the capitalist system consisting of trend and the business cycle ... I start from a theory of investment decisions patterned on Harrod's approach. By amending gradually this theory I pass to my approach of the EJ 1968 paper. (Kalecki 1991: 608–609)

We begin the study of investment decisions of a private and closed economy stating the basic assumptions. We assume wages are entirely consumed.[18] We also assume that overhead labour is negligible and thus the profits-to-income ratio, here denoted the exploitation rate ε, is approximately the same as the profits plus overhead-to-income ratio.

Profits (P) are spent on fixed capital investment (I) and capitalist consumption (C_k), we thus have:

$$P = I + C_k \tag{A5.1}$$

Capitalist consumption (C_k) may be divided into an autonomous part (A), and a part dependent of profits (λP, where $0<\lambda<1$), which we assume is spent immediately. That is, we assume no time-lags occur in the C_k function. Thus:

$$C_k = A + \lambda P \tag{A5.2}$$

We assume A is constant in the short run, but changes slowly in time (i.e. $A = A(t)$)

By substituting (A5.2) into (A5.1) we get

$$P = I + C_k = \frac{I + A}{1 - \lambda} \tag{A5.3}$$

which means that profits depend on the constant term $(1 - \lambda)^{-1}$, on capital investment and on autonomous consumption of capitalists. It seems evident that the level of profits will be larger if λ approaches unity, and smaller if it tends to zero.

We also know that a part of national income is profits,[19] which can be expressed as

$$P = \varepsilon Y \tag{A5.4}$$

We can reinterpret Y in terms of e (the exploitation rate) and of equation (A5.3) as

$$Y = \frac{P}{\varepsilon} = \frac{I + A}{(1 - \lambda)\varepsilon} \tag{A5.5}$$

Equation (A5.5) says that the determinants of Y are the same as for profits *and* the share of these in national income (the exploitation rate).

The level of investment is previously decided upon, with a certain lag z, which implies that

$$I_t = D_{t-z} \tag{A5.6}$$

We now see that fixed capital investment at period t (I_t) depends on the decision of capitalists of effectively carrying out investment at period t–z (D_{t-z}), as we can see from Figure A5.1.

We start our analysis by making use of Harrod's (1951) theory of economic growth, although here his model has been adapted for the

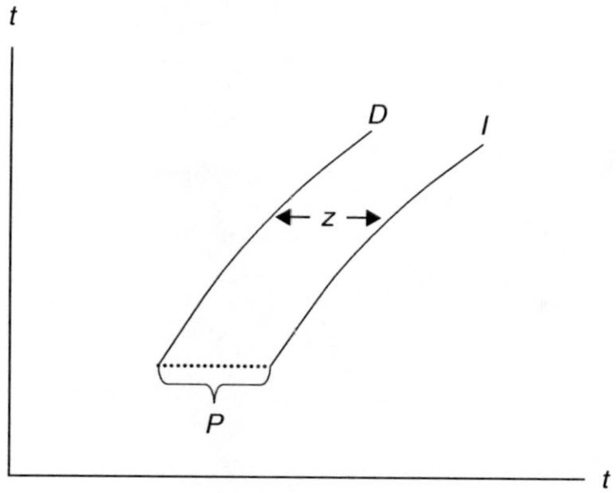

Figure A5.1

analysis of the cycle. We recall Harrod's concept stating that investment would remain constant if previous investments have proved adequate or correct according to some standard. Of course, in actual life investment fluctuates due to the inadequacy and/or incorrectness of decisions. We proceed as follows.

In the first place, in order to know the level of net investments, we must subtract from (gross) investment the level of (real) depreciation investments, U. This is

$$I_N = I - U \tag{A5.7}$$

Let us assume that, from the beginning to the end of one year, income grows by ΔY. Let us further assume that, in the same period investment grew by $\Delta I = I - U$. Now, according to Harrod's approach, to bring about ΔY under normal conditions a volume of capital equivalent to $\Delta Y \cdot m$, where m is the capital – output ratio, would be required. We thus state that if:

$$\Delta Y \cdot m > I - U \tag{A5.8}$$

then the amount of investment effectively done has proven exactly adequate.

Let us now consider different scenarios for the inequality of the right-hand side and the left-hand side of equation (A5.8). If

a) $\Delta Y \cdot m < I - U$ then we say that there was over-investment

b) $\Delta Y \cdot m = I - U$ adequate investments

c) $\Delta Y \cdot m > I - U$ Under-investment

Now, as always according to Harrod's approach, we posit that new investment decisions will be influenced by how capitalists evaluate their previous decisions. More precisely, with their new investment they will tend to correct previous errors. For the cases a) and c) this effect may be written as

$$D = I + \alpha[\Delta Y \cdot m - (I - U)] \qquad \alpha > 0 \qquad \text{(A5.9)}$$

While for case b) we may see that Harrod's approach would imply:

$$D = I \qquad \text{(A5.10)}$$

In anticipation for later consideration, we notice that m depends on output growth as well as on technical capital intensity. When idle capacity exists, only a part of ΔY will imply demand for the new firms, and m will be correspondingly lower. Besides this, we call attention that Harrod's theory does not refer to profitability but to sales. In the third place, we remark that the value of depreciation, U, will depend partly on the rate of technical progress. Finally, we note that a fifth point not considered in Harrod´s framework is the quantity of financial resources the firm accumulates in the period considered. According to the theory of "increasing risk", availability of finance influences investment.

We reorder our previous (9) equation as:

$$D = I + \alpha[(m\Delta Y + U) - I] \qquad (\alpha > 0) \qquad \text{(A5.9)}$$

This means that investment decisions depend on a comparison between the actual, and the "necessary" investment plus depreciation.

We must now consider the problem of reinvestment of profits. Instead of I, we consider the savings of firms (βS). Formally, I will be replaced by βS (with $\beta < 1$). Rentiers' savings will be $(1 - \beta) S$, for S reflects the total amount of savings. Then we would have:

$$D = \beta S + \alpha[(m\Delta Y + U) - I] \qquad \text{(A5.11)}$$
$$D = \beta I + \alpha[(m\Delta Y + U) - I]$$

We now turn to the problems not considered in Harrod´s model, referred to above. These are:

a) Profitability problem
b) Technical progress problem

In order to analyse the first problem, let us assume that there is no technical progress and that U equals zero. The result will be

$$D = \beta I + \alpha(m\Delta Y - I)$$

Now, capitalists have a given conception about the *correct* or *normal* rate of profitability. The increase in profits of the new investments must fulfil such profit rate. Therefore we posit:

$$D = \beta I + \alpha(n\Delta P - I) \tag{A5.12}$$

Technical progress – realized in new establishments – means that the real cost of producing in them is lower than costs in old establishments. In relative terms, new firms' returns will be higher than the old firms' returns. The outcome will be a crowding-out of P from old to new firms. It is then necessary to add something to $n\Delta P$ that indicates such crowding-out, which will be proportional to technical progress.

We will then define $Y–P$ as the real labour costs of old firms. We consider that due to technical progress the real labour cost associated with old equipment rises year after year and, conversely, the real profits yielded by that equipment fall. Now, given the total profits, the loss in profits yielded by old equipment is the gain in profits captured by the new plants. We will add therefore that proportion, namely $\gamma(Y–P)$, where γ must be strictly positive, to $n\Delta P$, to express the increase in profits of the new plants. We thus have:

$$D = \beta I + \alpha\left[n\Delta P + \gamma(Y - P) - I\right] \tag{A5.13}$$

An additional effect of technical progress is that it opens new investment opportunities, and thus stimulates new investment decisions. We express these stimuli by adding and additional argument, denoted by $B(t)$, to our previous equation (A5.13) to get:

$$D = \beta I + \alpha\left[n\Delta P + \gamma(Y - P) - I\right] + B(t) \tag{A5.14}$$

Where B indicates the addition to I that firms are encouraged to make due to technical progress. We assume that B is constant in the short run, but changes slowly in time (namely, $B = B(t)$)

We may now rewrite equation (A5.4) as

$$P = (I + A) \cdot (1 - \lambda)^{-1}$$

Equation (A5.5) may also be rewritten as:

$$Y = P \cdot \varepsilon^{-1} = Y - P = P \cdot \varepsilon^{-1} - P = P\left(\varepsilon^{-1} - 1\right)$$

As we saw before, investment decisions are decided upon with a certain time-lag, therefore

$$D_t = I_{t+z}$$

By substitution in (A5.14) we obtain

$$D = \beta I + \alpha\left[n\left(\frac{\Delta I + \Delta A(t)}{1-\lambda}\right) + \gamma\left(\frac{1}{e} - 1\right)\frac{I + A(t)}{1-\lambda} - I\right] + B(t)$$

$$D = I\left[B(t) + \frac{\alpha\gamma\left(\frac{1}{e} - 1\right)}{1-\lambda} - \alpha\right] + \frac{\alpha n}{1-\lambda}\Delta I + \frac{\alpha n}{1-\lambda}\Delta A(t) + \alpha\gamma\left(\frac{1}{e} - 1\right)\frac{A(t)}{1-\lambda} + B(t)$$

We now have three expressions: the first depends on I, the second on ΔI, and the last one only on the variables that are supposed to be constant in the short run but evolve slowly in time. In order to simplify the analysis we set:

$$a = \beta + \alpha\left[\frac{\gamma\left(\frac{1}{e} - 1\right)}{1-\lambda} - 1\right] \tag{A5.15}$$

We assume that $0 < a < 1$

$$b = \frac{an}{1-\lambda} \tag{A5.16}$$

and

$$F(t) = \frac{an}{1-\lambda}\Delta A(t) + ay\left(\frac{1}{e} - 1\right)\frac{A(t)}{1-\lambda} + B(t) \tag{A5.17}$$

Based on the assumptions that $0 < a < 1$ and that $F(t)$ is a function that changes slowly in time, it can be said that a particular solution would be y_t. If from

$$I_{t+z} = aI_t + b\Delta I_t + F(t) \tag{A5.18}$$

We subtract:

$$y_{t+z} = ay_t + b\Delta y_t + F(t) \quad \text{(A5.19)}$$

We obtain real investments, minus investments given by the long-run movement.

$$i_{t+z} = ai_t + b\Delta i_t \quad \text{(A5.20)}$$

This is independent of *F(t)*, thus the general formula I_t can be decomposed into

$$I_t = y_t + i_t \quad \text{(A5.21)}$$

B(t) are additional decisions that are made because capitalists see that new equipment makes them earn more than the old ones. In this way, businessmen believe they will earn more if they invest more, for they take more advantage of technical progress. Of course in the current period they will not fetch higher profits, because *Y* (*Y* – *P*) is given. However, capitalists will in fact earn higher profits in the next period because additional investments will make *Y* and *P* grow.

$$D = \beta I + \alpha[m\Delta P + \gamma(Y - P) - I] + B \quad \text{(A5.22)}$$

Equation (A5.22) thus may be written as:

$$i_{t+z} = ai_t + b\Delta i_t \quad \text{(A5.23)}$$

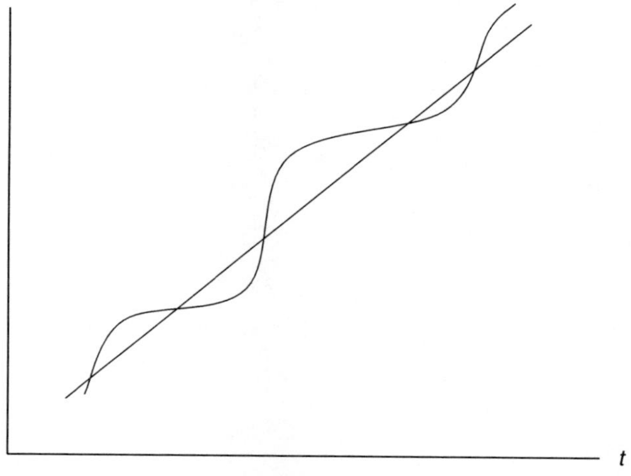

Figure A5.2

The same separation of trend and fluctuations can be made for profits and nominal income:

$$P_t = \frac{I_t + A_t}{1-\lambda} = \frac{\overset{B}{\overbrace{i_t}}}{1-\lambda} + \frac{\overset{A}{\overbrace{y_t + A_t}}}{1-\lambda} \tag{A5.24}$$

and, considering the effect of time in equation (A5.5) as

$$Y_t = \frac{P_t}{\varepsilon} \tag{A5.25}$$

In equation (A5.25), because B depends on i_t and it fluctuates cyclically, B does so too. Part A is thus subject to a trend

$$Y_t = \frac{i_t}{\varepsilon(1-\lambda)} + \frac{y_t + A_t}{\varepsilon(1-\lambda)} \tag{A5.26}$$

Let us now go back to the investment equation $i_{i+z} = ai_t + b\Delta i_t$ and assume that $z = 1$. Therefore

$$i_{t+1} = ai_t + b\Delta i_t \tag{A5.27}$$

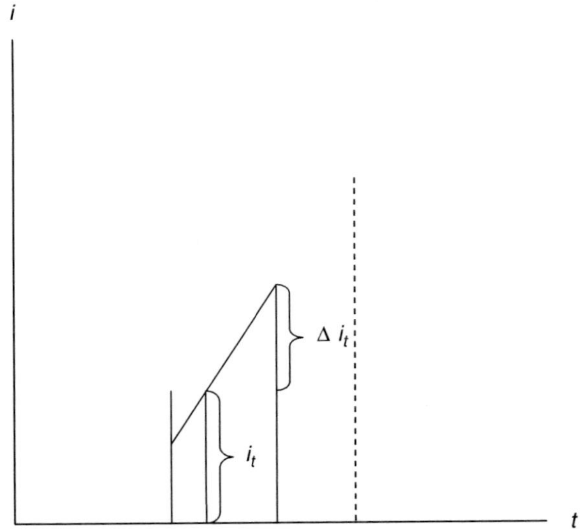

Figure A5.3

With $|b|<1$.[20]

Let us now transform equation (A5.27) into

$$i_{t+1} - i_t = b\Delta i_t + (a-1)i_t \tag{A5.28}$$

or

$$i_{t+1} - i_t = b\Delta i_t - (1-a)i_t \tag{A5.29}$$

but, as we assumed that $0 < a < 1$

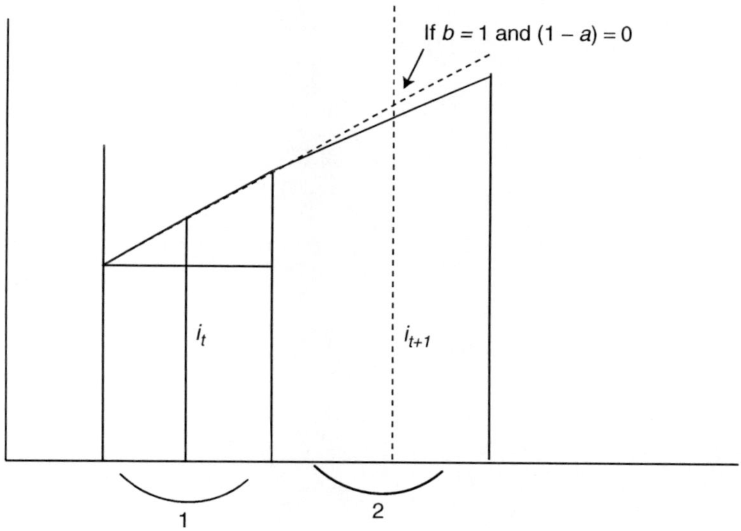

Figure A5.4

If $b = 1$ and $(1 - a) = 0$ then the lengthening of the dotted line determines i_{i+1}. But as, on the one hand, $-(1 - a)$ is negative and greater than zero in absolute value, and $|b| < 1$, we then have that the line breaks, which means that the absolute increase of investment keeps on diminishing.

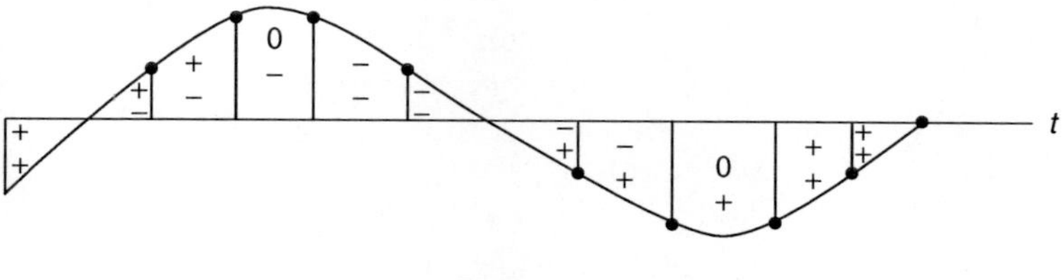

Figure A5.5

Upper part: $\Delta i_t = 0$
Lower part: $(1 - a) < 0$

What happens if $|b| < 1$? In such a case growth will occur quite fast. Up to a certain point the productive reserves will not be sufficient, an enlargement of the time span for delivery of capital goods will result and, because $\Delta_i = 0$ and because $(1 - a)$ acts negatively, this will also produce a fall on the level of economic activity.

Now then, if $|b|$ is sufficiently small, the result will be

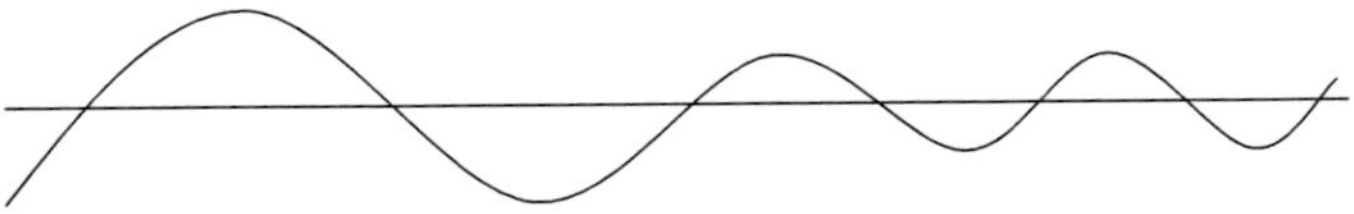

Figure A5.6

On the other hand, if b is sufficiently large

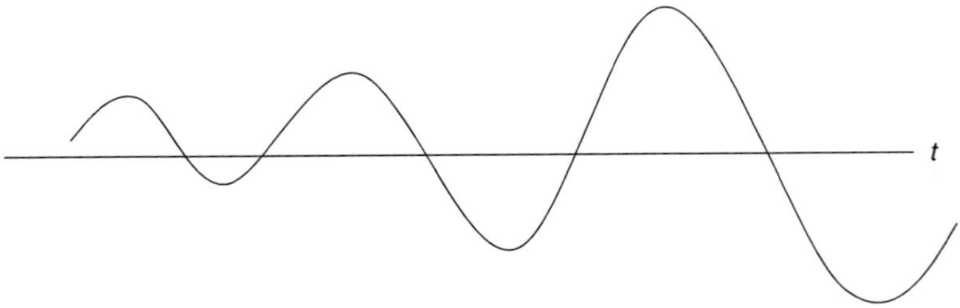

Figure A5.7

There is only one value of b for which the cycle would be regular ($b = 1$).

In the first case, that is when the cycle dampens down, one could imagine that there is a moment in which there is no cycle at all. But it can be demonstrated (through the incorporation of stochastic elements) that this disappearance of the cycle does not occur, and we will have a more or less regular cycle. The case of the explosive (or diverging) cycle is similar to the one in which productive reserves limit the cycle.

What is the economic cause (interpretation) of the positive effect of Δi, and the negative effect of i. The sole fact that i is positive implies an enlargement of the productive apparatus; but the fact that it is constant implies a constancy of profits; it thus follows, in essence, a fall in the rate of profits. In the case where b is sufficiently large so as to eliminate the cycle in general, the lower limit is given by the fact that investments on fixed physical capital cannot be lower than zero.

6
Kalecki's Macroeconomics of Public Finance and of Monetary Policy

After many years of being considered a forbidden weapon by both governments and many economists and as a consequence of the depth of the current world financial crisis, public spending, and even deficit spending, has regained a place of honour in the arsenal of acceptable economic policy instruments. This new situation is hailed by publicists and pundits as a revival of Keynes and Keynesianism.

There is much truth in this opinion. Indeed, the Keynesian revolution changed completely the approach to the economic role of government and taxation. During the period when Keynesianism was influential, taxation was no longer looked on simply as a method of financing government expenditures, but as one of the ways of government intervention for actively influencing, mobilizing and allocating real resources with the aim of ensuring general economic and monetary stability. It was thus recognized that, when resources are underemployed, "functional finance" does not divert real resources from private capital formation to make them available for government good and services, but in a certain sense government deficits perform the compensatory function of making up for a low level of private spending.

However, it is as well to recall that Keynes was not the first economist to put forward the idea of utilizing government expenditure as a tool to fight unemployment; and that he saw the deficit only as an instrument of last resort.[1] It was rather Michal Kalecki who persistently advocated the use of budget deficits. When the latter author firstly put forward his version of the principle of effective demand, he immediately gave a prominent place to government spending as an additional source of demand, with the bonus that he emphasized the role of the budget deficit in determining the aggregate profits. Moreover, he considered that budget deficits might be necessary as a permanent feature of full employment capitalism, and not merely as a last resort instrument used only under circumstances of crises.

Writers who identify themselves with the so-called Post-Keynesian school have always insisted on the beneficial effect of government expenditure, and of government deficit, when idle resources are abundant (see especially Wray 1998, and Arestis and Sawyer 2003 and the bibliography cited therein). In this context, they usually refer to Abba P. Lerner, and to the so-called theory of "functional finance", associated with this author (Lerner 1943).[2] They have also remarked that even a rising public debt need not be a cause of concern, for if output is growing at a sufficiently high rate and the interest rate is low, the burden of the debt will not be a problem. Here they (see for example Wray 2008 and Vatter and Walker 1997) normally quote Domar's (1944) classic paper, which gave a formal proof of this idea. Later, we will show that Kalecki, previously or at about the same time, came to similar conclusions, and in fact went beyond the two previously mentioned authors.

In this chapter, we will consider Kalecki's analysis of the role of government expenditure and its effect on demand. We will analyse public spending, distinguishing between deficit financing and government expenditure financed through taxation. In the final section, we will discuss Kalecki's view of the effects and the limits of monetary policy. In the main text, we conduct the analysis at a purely verbal level; and in the Appendix we formalize the reasoning with respect to public finance.

Public deficits and effective demand

The gist of Kalecki's reasoning can be put as follows. Let us assume an increase in government spending. Unless such an increase carries with it, or induces, *a decrease in private spending* (which Kalecki thought unlikely), aggregate demand will rise, and with it output and employment. Further, Kalecki showed that whether private demand does or does not fall cannot be determined without first specifying how the larger state expenditure is financed.

The most clear-cut case occurs when the government finances its expenditure with money creation, or obtains funds that otherwise would have been hoarded (for example, selling bonds to the public), for in this situation the demand of capitalists and wage earners need not simultaneously fall. To use a contemporaneous expression, public expenditure will not necessarily "crowd-out" private expenditure. Let us expand on this issue.

We know that workers' consumption is not self-governing, but induced by autonomous expenditure and distribution of income. To facilitate the intuitive reasoning underpinning Kalecki's outlook, let us assume income distribution is given, and let us split workers' consumption into two parts; one related to capitalists' expenditure and the other to government expenditure. Now, given the distribution of income, the workers' consumption induced by capitalist expenditure will remain constant if the latter does not change. Accordingly, the increase in government spending (that in this case is equivalent to an increase of the budget deficit) will induce a direct (through its purchases) and indirect (through higher workers' spending) increase in total effective demand, which will give rise to greater output, profits and wages. Of course, idle capacity should exist in those sectors where new demand is forthcoming. We may refer here to Kalecki's formulae for profits and output in a closed economy where the government finances its expenditure via budget deficit:

$$P = I + C_k + B \tag{6.1}$$

$$Y = \frac{I + C_k + B}{e} \tag{6.2}$$

where Y stands for output, B for the budget deficit, I and C_k for private investment and consumption respectively, and e for the share of profits in national income. We recall that Kalecki assumed that capitalist expenditure ($I + C_k$) is predetermined, in that it follows from decisions previously taken, which are difficult to cancel. In short, in Kalecki's view the deficit-financed public expenditure stimulates a higher level of economic activity. Further, just like any increase in demand, when idle capacity exists, the increase in the deficit does not have to induce price increases, but instead will cause output expansion. It's appropriate here to recall Kalecki's words, taken from one of his first theoretical papers:

> Let us assume that the government issues treasury bills and sells them to the banks. The government spends the money, e.g. on construction of railroads ... [therefore] employment in investment goods industries increases and subsequently, as a result of the higher

> purchasing power of the workers, in consumer goods industries as well. The amounts spent by the government flow as profits directly or through spending of the workers into the pockets of capitalists, and return to the banks as their deposits. On the side of bank assets, the government debt accrues in the form of discounted bills; on the side of liabilities, there is an increase in deposits equal to the additional profits. Thus the government becomes indebted, via banks, to the private capitalists by an amount equal to the value of the investment effected." (Kalecki (1935c [1990]): 193)

In a previous paper, Kalecki had called "domestic exports" as a situation whereby "the government borrows from the capitalists at home, spending the proceeds of the loan, e.g. on armaments, payment of unemployment benefits, or public works" (1933a [1990]: 167). He drew the following analogy:

> If a government borrows from capitalists at home, spending the proceeds of the loan, e.g. on armaments, payment of unemployment benefits, or public works, the result is very similar to that of securing a surplus in foreign trade. To the surplus of exports over imports there corresponds here the sale of commodities, used for the purposes mentioned above…. The equivalent of these sales of commodities is the increase in the claims of the capitalists on their government, just as the equivalent of the surplus achieved in foreign trade was the increase of foreign claims or the reduction of foreign debts. (Ibid)[3]

The notion that an increase of the government deficit has no adverse effect but rather stimulates private spending was so completely at odds with the orthodox view of the effect of public finance that it could not fail to confront harsh criticisms. Some of these criticisms were raised during the 1930s and 1940, and they were duly answered by Kalecki (or by Keynes, or by both); while some are of more recent vintage. It is, therefore, useful to examine some of these criticisms to review Kalecki's answers and to speculate on how our author might have replied to more recent orthodox views on the matter.

The first of criticisms raised against the financing of the deficit with banking resources emphasized two related effects: on the one hand, it brings about a rise in interest rates; and on the other, that it reduces the lending capacity of banks. For both reasons, it was argued, an increase in the deficit would cause a fall of private spending; and specifically in private investment and in credit-financed consumption expenditure.

With this, it would also follow that a budget deficit simultaneously reduces profits, negatively affecting the long-run growth rate of the economy in the medium and long term; because higher interest rates and lower profits reduce the stimuli to invest.

However, Kalecki pointed out that the rise in interest rates and credit restrictions are not a necessary consequence of an increase of the deficit. For example, if the Central Bank issues additional money to finance government expenditure, the amount of money available will necessarily increase, avoiding any rise in the interest rate.

However, it could still be argued that when the State borrows money from the commercial banks to finance its deficit, credit lines to individuals would have to fall due to the diminution of the loanable funds of the commercial bank as a result of government borrowing. But again according to Kalecki, this is not correct; or at least overstates the problem: when the State pays to the individuals, that money returns to the banks in the form of deposits. Having thus recovered the deposits, banks will be able to carry out new credits (if demand for such exists). That is to say, for the public expenditure financed with loans from the commercial bank to "crowd-out" private spending, it would have to happen that the individuals that are paid by the State kept all that money in a box, rather than return that money to the banks. But the latter is obviously a rather far-fetched assumption. Kalecki put his argument as follows:

> Will not the rise in the budget deficit force up the rate of interest so much that investment will be reduced by just as much as the budget deficit is increased, thus offsetting the stimulating effect of government expenditure on employment? The answer is that the rate of interest may be maintained at a stable level however large the budget deficit, given a proper banking policy. The rate of interest will tend to rise if the public do not absorb the government securities, by the sale of which the deficit is financed, but prefer to invest their savings in bank deposits. And if the banks, lacking sufficient cash basis (notes and accounts in the central bank), do not expand their deposits and do not buy government securities instead of the public doing so, then the rate of interest must rise sufficiently to induce the public to invest their savings in government securities. If, however, the central bank expands the cash basis of the private banks to enable them to expand their deposits sufficiently while maintaining the prescribed cash ratio, no tendency for a rise in the rate of interest will appear." (Kalecki 1944a [1990]: 360)[4]

A second criticism put the accent on the alleged unsustainability of the public debt. Let us suppose that the government debt continuously rises. Will not this increasing debt burden set a limit to deficit spending? Again, Kalecki had a prompt reply:

> In the first place, interest on an increasing national debt ... cannot be a burden to society as a whole because in essence it constitutes an internal transfer ... Secondly, in an expanding economy this transfer need not necessarily rise out of proportion with the tax revenue at the existing rate of taxes. The standard rate of income tax necessary to finance the increasing amount of interest on the national debt need not rise if the rate of expansion of the national income is sufficiently high. (Kalecki 1944a [1990]: 363)[5]

But Kalecki went even further:

> However, even if we leave this factor aside, it is fairly easy to devise a system of taxation to service the debt which will not involve any disturbances in output and employment.
>
> Imagine, for instance, that the interest on the national debt is financed by an annual capital tax, levied on firms and persons ... The ... aggregate income [of capitalists after payment of capital tax] will remain unaltered ... Further, the profitability of investment is not affected by a capital tax because it is paid in any kind of wealth ... And if investment is financed by borrowing, its profitability is clearly not affected by a capital tax, because borrowing does not mean an increase in wealth of the investing entrepreneur." (Ibid)[6]

Let us detail Kalecki's reasoning. A rise in national debt will have a twofold effect. On the one hand, it will increase the amount of capital tax to be collected. On the other hand, it will increase the interest-yielding assets (inclusive of government securities) in private holdings, which would not have come into existence if the budget had been balanced. Thus, the after-tax current income of some property owners will be lower, and of some will be higher, than if the interest of the national debt had not grown. One may therefore notice that their aggregate income will remain unchanged. Hence there is no reason to see consumption varying. Moreover, the profitability of investment is not likely to alter appreciably. Indeed, the capital levy is paid on any type of wealth in possession. The same capital tax is paid on the principal, irrespective of whether it is in the form of cash, government securities or investment made on real capital goods. If investment is financed by borrowing, its profitability is not affected by the capital tax because it is not imposed, since no increase in the wealth of the investing businessman takes place. For these reasons, Kalecki concluded that a rise in the national debt, if the interest on it is financed by annual capital tax, is in the main "neutral" as far as forces governing private investment and capitalists' consumption are concerned.

In other words, the rise in capital taxation rates does not reduce net profitability of investment (which covers risk) or increases the interest rate. If someone borrows funds to build a factory, neither he increases his own capital by such an action nor does he pay a higher capital tax. And if he finances it by his own funds, he pays the same tax as he would if he abstained from investment. Thus the net profitability of investment is unaffected by capital taxation. Unlike income tax, the capital tax is not a cost of production in the long-run either. Similarly, everybody is prepared to lend at the prevailing interest rate; for the capital tax is not affected by whether he lends or not. Hence the propensity to invest is not dampened by an increase of the rate of capital tax if expected returns are unaffected.

Anyway, as we all know, the arguments put forward by Kalecki and Keynes, as well as Lerner, Domar and many others, apparently do not carry enough weight to convince most members of the economics profession to definitely abandon the orthodox view of public finance. On the contrary, such a view reapers time and time again, under a different guise.[7] It is therefore tempting to give still more thought to the issue under discussion, and speculate a bit on how could Kalecki have responded to some more recent versions of the orthodox view.

Probably the best-known version of the new orthodoxy in public finance is the one put forward by Barro (1974), according to whom agents are fully endowed with rational expectations, and anticipate that a budget deficit has to be paid in the future with higher taxes. Accordingly, as soon as the government announces a deficit, they immediately reduce their expenditure and save to pay future tax payments. In fact, the critique to government spending is even more extreme, in that it assumes that any government expenditure, even one not entailing a deficit, will be fully offset by lower private expenditure. Therefore, larger government expenditure is immediately offset by lower private expenditure.[8]

There are two points in this argument. One is purely theoretical in nature, and the other one is empirical.[9] The theoretical dispute can be easily dismissed with a simple Kaleckian-inspired counter-argument.

Let us suppose that agents are indeed endowed with rational expectations, but that these are of a different kind. Namely, let us assume that they anticipate that a budget deficit will bring about *higher* profits, output and income. It is self-evident that in this case their expenditure, and also the multiplier of government expenditure, would be higher than would otherwise have been.

The proof is almost trivial. Let us recall Kalecki's basic profit and effective demand equations (where we consider now the effect of workers savings S_w). Let us assume that capitalist expenditure and workers's savings depend on the expected budget deficit B^e, such that:

$$P = I(B^e) + C_k(B^e) - S_w(B^e) + B \qquad (6.3)$$

$$Y = \frac{P}{e} = \frac{I(B^e) + C_k(B^e) - S_w(B^e) + B}{e} \qquad (6.4)$$

It is plain that the impact of a higher (expected or actual) deficit on output and employment, and on profits and future investment, will depend on the sign of the partial derivative of capitalist expenditure and workers' savings with respect to B^e. The multiplier of the budget deficit will be higher if capitalists spend more when they expect a higher deficit, and when workers save less when they expect a higher deficit.

As a conclusion, we can restate Kalecki's response to the idea of a government's deficit expenditure that crowds-out private spending. In fact, the opposite happens: when idle capacity exists, and when the monetary policy is adequate, the increase of the deficit causes an increase in the profits and on the levels of economic activity in the short term, which also tends to stimulate a growth of the economy in the medium and long term.

Tax-financed public expenditure, profits and effective demand[10]

We will now study Kalecki's view of the macroeconomic impact of tax-financed public spending. Here the author differentiated two extreme situations. He considered, first, an increase of public spending financed with taxes on wages.[11] In this case, taxes will lower wage-earners earnings, and therefore also private consumption in the considered period. However, state expenditure increases. Therefore, when workers do not save, the increase of public spending is entirely offset by the smaller demand of wage-earners. Total effective demand is unchanged.[12]

However, Kalecki argued that taxes on profits would normally have a positive impact on demand. To follow his reasoning, it may be useful to recast here the author's formalization of his theory of effective demand. Let us start with the enlarged formula for profits in a closed economy, which now reads (under the assumption that workers do not save):

$$P^b = I + C_k + B + H \tag{6.5}$$

Where P^b is (gross) profits *before taxes.*

Effective demand and output are determined as:

$$Y = \frac{I + C_k + B + H}{e} \tag{6.6}$$

To reach a conclusion on the impact of higher taxes on profits, on effective demand and on output, it is necessary to analyse how this affects the total expenditure of the capitalists, and then how the tax would affect the distribution of income.

As we already know, if investment or capitalist consumption, or the budget deficit go up, then total profits before taxes will rise. Furthermore, this being the novel point, if taxes on profits rise, the remaining items composing the right-hand side of equation (6.5) will not change. Besides, given the relative share of profits in national income, according to equation (6.6) total demand and output will rise by so much, that after-tax profits will remain constant.[13]

However, if the rise in government expenditure financed via taxes on profits brought about an increase in the degree of monopoly (and consequently in the relative share of profits in national income), then its impact on effective demand and output would be nil. More precisely, if firms completely transfer the tax into prices, then, with higher prices and given the nominal wage, the real wage drops; even as income distribution changes against wages.[14] We note here that while the demand of workers falls, the government's demand rises, and accordingly the total demand is constant. The capitalist expenditure is constant, and the greater demand ensuing from the rise in the public spending is entirely compensated by the fall in the demand due to a lower workers' purchasing power. This case is then identical to the one of an increase in government spending financed by taxing workers.[15]

Suppose, however, firms do not increase their prices, but absorb this tax. As we already know, capitalists' expenditure will be constant. The increase of the public spending will be added to the total demand, and this will induce an extra spending of workers. Therefore, demand and output will rise by an amount equivalent to the rise of government expenditure plus the induced rise in workers' consumption.[16]

In sum, under conditions of underutilization of productive capacity and supposing that firms absorb the tax, the introduction of this new tax will have an expansionary effect on the level of economic activity. Also on this point, Kalecki fully anticipated the notion, later formalized by Haavelmo (1945), that a balanced government budget may be expansionary. In fact, he also specified the conditions under which this could be the case; namely, the tax should not affect workers' disposable income.[17]

On the contrary, Kalecki identified an additional beneficial effect of taxing profits. Government expenditure financed with corporate profit tax changes income distribution in favour of workers. Indeed, total wages will increase in proportion to the increase in output and, as total profits are constant their share in the total income will diminish. Profits will now represent a smaller share of a greater output.[18]

Kalecki and Keynes on taxing profits and effective demand

We shall now introduce a hypothesis to show some contrasts between Kalecki's and Keynes's views on the consequences of taxes on profits and on effective demand. This issue motivated a lively debate between the founding fathers of the principle of effective demand, and also that underlies the differences in economic policy preferences. An exchange of letters regarding a paper sent by Kalecki to the *Economic Journal* (of which Keynes was the editor) deals directly with this disagreement.[19] It was in this paper, "A theory of commodity, income and capital taxation" (Kalecki 1937 [1990]), where Kalecki originally presented his view regarding the expansionary impact of government expenditure financed with taxes on profits.

We have already mentioned two key assumptions involved in Kalecki's argument. According to the first, the announcement, and even the enactment of the new tax, levied to finance an increase in government expenditure, will not bring about an immediate reduction in capitalists' expenditure because they will wait until the end of the current decision period and see what happens. According to the second assumption, firms will not raise prices when the tax rises.

It seems worthwhile to present the main passages of the exchange of letters already alluded to. Keynes did not object to Kalecki's second assumption, regarding the constancy of prices and profit margins after the tax. But he strongly criticized the first assumption. He wrote to Kalecki: "If capitalists *assume* that their income subject to tax will remain the same, the effect of the tax will surely be to reduce their spending. It is only if they have read your article and are convinced by it that profits will rise by the amount of the tax that they will maintain their spending as before" (Kalecki 1990: 559; emphasis added).

Kalecki replied: "After the introduction of new tax the entrepreneurs even if they expect their incomes to fall *cannot* immediately reduce their investment because it is the result of previous investment decisions which require a certain time to be completed. [...] Their consumption remains also unaltered, if their propensity to consume is not changed... [T]he expectation of future fall of income can influence the present propensity to consume. I think, however, that the capitalists' consumption is rather insensible to *expectations*..." (1990: 560; emphasis in the original).

He added, "I think that this assumption [i.e. about the behaviour of capitalists following immediately the introduction of income tax] is essential not only for the problems of taxation, but for the whole of the General Theory. If, for instance the rise of money wages caused the capitalists to reduce immediately their consumption in expectation of future fall of profits, the result would be rather in accordance with the classical theory."

Keynes's rebuttal went as follows:

> I regard the assumption that investment is fixed as unplausible. Firstly, because it ignores the possibility of fluctuation in stocks. Secondly, because it ignores the possibility of altering the pace at which existing investment decisions are carried out, and thirdly, because at best it can be overcome after a time lag, which may be very short indeed.
>
> I think it unplausible to suppose that capitalists' consumption is insensitive to their expectations, for the latter are affected by the change in the taxes on their incomes...
>
> ...I hope you are not right in thinking that my General Theory depends on an assumption that the immediate reaction of a capitalist is of a particular kind. (Kalecki 1990: 561–562)

In Chapter 2 we presented some empirical evidence that seems to us to give support to Kalecki's hypothesis. We referred to studies that show that private investment responds only with a lag to the current economic environment, rather than to Keynes's view that change, not only in the current situation but also in expectations, would immediately affect investment. We will not, therefore, further discuss the issue. What we would want to call attention to now is a different point, namely the important practical implications of the differing views of the two authors, in the discussion about the finance of government expenditure in Britain during World War II.

Here Keynes and Kalecki had to deal with a full-employment situation, which is quite atypical in capitalism. As the reader will recall, Keynes produced what became his famous pamphlet "How to pay for the war" (Keynes 1940). To curtail private consumption, and free resources for the war, he proposed a scheme of compulsory saving based on post-war credits; that is, compulsory savings to be repaid after the war ended.

Kalecki, however, was very skeptical about the impact of a tax on consumption; and particularly of consumption by the upper classes. He believed:

> The fundamental problem of the war economy is to curtail the purchasing power of the population so as to prevent a violent rise in prices, which is bound to come, since the productive resources are limited ... A solution ... has been proposed by Mr. Keynes. His scheme of compulsory saving raises, however, two important objections:
>
> (i) Compulsory savings will be in many cases offset by reduction in voluntary savings, or even by dissaving ...
>
> (ii) Mr. Keynes's scheme does not attempt to establish a certain maximum for the consumption of the rich before compulsory saving is imposed on the poor. Moreover, it is clearly chiefly the rich who may elude the curtailment of consumption by dissaving" (Kalecki 1940b [1997]: 3).

Accordingly, to avoid an excess demand situation, and the ensuing inflationary pressures, Kalecki advocated rationing.[20] He thought that this was the only alternative to cope with a tendency to excess demand, while safeguarding price stability and ensuring that the poorer strata of the population were not excessively harmed.

The end of this story is probably well-known. Hesitantly at first and later at full speed, the British government had to end up rationing private consumption (and even private investment). But of course this does not mean that they opted for the Kalecki's proposal, because others had also called for rationing, and a series of considerations and events forced the final decision.

Kalecki on monetary policy

We have seen that Kalecki considered that the positive impact of deficit financing on output and employment would be reduced if monetary policy failed to accommodate the additional needs of liquidity from the public. In this sense, monetary policy was an indispensable tool of any expansionary policy. However, Kalecki was skeptical about the efficiency of monetary policy to determine the adequate level of investment. In particular, he doubted that the impulses generated by changes in liquidity may affect significantly the long-term rate and by this way also the investment. To understand this point of view, it is worth recalling Kalecki's general monetary thought and in this context to consider his theory of the interest rate.

Kalecki's early argument regarding the possibility of a business upswing rests on the fact that the credit system will furnish – *ex nihilo* – enough financial means to firms to finance the additional investment decisions. Without enough supply of finance, investment growth would be blocked by a rise in the interest rate. This two-step process was present in Kalecki's writing right from the beginning and is certainly one of the most original aspects of his monetary views. Regarding the determinants of the rate of interest, this conception opens up new vistas. Later on he would be more precise:

> It has been stated above that the rate of interest cannot be determined by the demand for and the supply of capital because investment automatically brings into existence an equal amount of savings. Thus, investment "finances itself" whatever the level of the rate of interest rate ... The rate of interest is, therefore, the result of the interplay of other factors. (Kalecki 1954a [1991]: 262)

Since 1933, Kalecki envisaged that the demand for money could be related to the rate of interest. He considered that liquidity preference was related only to the specific requirements of transactions and financing of investments, rather than to speculative motives. Later, Kalecki related the demand for money to the state of confidence, and the rate of interest. In so doing, he developed an approach based on the distinction of three kinds of financial assets: money (including current accounts), short-term assets ("bills") – time deposits, commercial bills, Treasury bills – and long-term securities ("bonds"). The differences between these instruments refer to liquidity, risk and profitability. Money is the most liquid and safe asset but does not earn income while bonds depending on the degree of their illiquidity are more or less profitable. From this distinction, Kalecki suggested the following portfolio analysis for the determination of the term structure of interest rates. The short-term interest rate results from a portfolio choice between money and bills while the long-term interest rate results from a portfolio choice between bills and bonds. Regarding the determination of the first rate, Kalecki (1954a [1991]: 262–263) notes:

> The higher the short-term rate the greater is the inducement to invest money for short periods rather than to keep it as cash reserve. Or, to put it more precisely: transactions can be managed with a larger or a smaller stock of money; however, a larger stock of money in relation to turnover means on the average a smoother and more convenient handling of transactions. The higher the short-term rate of interest the more expansive is this convenience as compared with the alternative of investing in short-term assets.

With T the volume of transactions, M the supply of money (notes and current account deposits), V the (ex ante) money velocity of circulation, and ρ the short-term rate of interest, and T the value of transactions, we have:

$$V = V(\rho), V' > 0 \tag{6.7}$$

and

$$V(\rho) = \frac{T}{M} \tag{6.8}$$

This equation also defines the demand for money as an inverse function of the rate of interest, for a given amount of transactions. Its characteristics depend on habits and the state of confidence, making it potentially a highly unstable function. The short-term interest rate is therefore determined by the volume of transactions, the money supply policy and liquidity preference.

Kalecki's analysis of the determination of the long-term rate rests on the assumption that the public takes as reference the estimated length of a long-term investment, and on this basis evaluates the relative advantage of investing in short-term or long-term securities. The terms for comparison are, on the one hand, the present rate of interest rate r on long-term bonds and, on the other, the sequence of expected short-term rates ρ spanning the entire period of the investment, that is, those accruing by reinvesting the sum every time until the end of the reference period; from this sequence an average short-period interest rate ρ_e is derived which represents the term comparison with the long-term rate. Other elements to consider are the cost ε of reinvesting in short-term securities every time they come to maturity and the risk of depreciation γ involved in possessing a Consol. In equilibrium, the no-profit condition implies that the difference between the two rates has to be:

$$r - \rho_e = \gamma - \varepsilon$$

The most delicate aspect of the question is the assessment of the risk. In this regard, Kalecki writes:

> If the present price of Consols is p and the holder has a certain, more or less definite, idea based on past experience about the minimum to which this price may fall, p min, it is plausible to assume that u is roughly proportionate to $\frac{p - p_{\min}}{p}$, i.e. to the maximum percentage by which the price of Consols is considered apt to fall. (1954a [1991]: 81)

It follows that

$$\gamma = g\left(1 - \frac{p_{\min}}{p}\right)$$

or, given the inverse relationship between the price and the rate of interest of Consols

$$\gamma = g\left(1 - \frac{r}{r_{\max}}\right)$$

from which the conclusion is inferred that in equilibrium:

$$r = \frac{\rho_e + g - \varepsilon}{1 + \frac{g}{r_{\max}}}$$

Given coefficients g and ε, and given r_{max}, this last equation expresses the long-term rate as a function of the series of expected short-term rates; there is, therefore, a substantially univocal relationship between the two rates, which rests on the short-term one being – as the remuneration for forgoing the convenience of holding cash in its pure form (Kalecki 1954a [1991]: 74) – a fundamentally psychological variable, as in Keynes. The tendency of rates towards equilibrium not only relies on adjustments to the long-term interest rate but also on the fact that the risk for Consol holders increases:

a) with the gap between the percent long-term rate and that viewed as "maximum";
b) with the rise in the weight, within portfolios, of long-term rate compared to the short-term ones and to money.

Finally, from the stability condition we may deduce the long term rate compared to the short term, since

a) changes in the short-term rate only partially affect the estimate of ρ_e;
b) given the parameters of this equation and r_{max} the long-term rate varies to a smaller extent than ρ_e.

There is therefore a long sequence to cover before the impulses generated by changes in liquidity may affect the long-term rate, and their shock is dampened on the way. We thus here understand why Kalecki doubted monetary policy could be a relevant way for achieving a state of full employment. Kalecki was well aware that "this method is not very effective because the long term rate of interest changes rather slowly and (what is more important) because it cannot be reduced below a certain limit" (Kalecki 1944a [1990]: 370). Somewhat later he added:

> The purchase of securities [through open market operations – JL and MA] and the consequent increase of cash balances of the public **as such** would not contribute to the increase of effective demand ..., for any single individual or firm could have sold securities and used the proceeds for consumption or investment without open-market operations. Thus the only channel through which open-market policy could stimulate consumption and investment is the consequent fall in the rate of interest, and in particular in the long-term rate.

The fall in the rate of interest would probably tend to stimulate consumption mainly through inflating capital values of the existing assets. This effect would be significant, most probably, only if the fall in the rate of interest were considerable... Even when effective, this [an open market policy to reduce the rate of interest – JL and MA] seems to me the wrong way, from the social point of view, to increase employment because the method boils down to the stimulation of capitalist consumption.

The reduction of the long-term rate of interest would stimulate investment by increasing its net profitability. Here again a substantial fall in the rate of interest is necessary in order to make the effect significant. (Kalecki 1946 [1990]: 403)

Kalecki's empirical studies

At a very early stage of the development of his work, Kalecki carried out some empirical studies where he found support for the essential aspects of his theory of effective demand and of public finance. Thus, in Kalecki (1932b [1990]) he already anticipated, before Hitler came to power, the expansionary effect that the Nazi economic plan, based on public works and "inflationary" finance, could have in Germany.[21] He also foresaw both the limits arising from the external constraint to German economic expansion, and how the ensuing rise of employment in that country would hardly benefit the working class because of wage control and the rise in the price of necessities. He completed all this with an outstanding and brief paper on Nazi Germany (Kalecki 1935a [1996]). There, he was certainly the first economist to use the principle of effective demand, already in a refined stage of its development, to analyse Hitler's economic policies and their macroeconomic consequences.

After several years, Kalecki came back in different papers to the empirical study of advanced capitalist countries, and particularly the US economy. We shall refer now to two of these papers.

To carry out his analysis, Kalecki devised a special methodology with two purposes in mind. First, to separate those components of income which determine changes in its volume, from those which play a purely passive role. Second, to analyse the impact of government expenditure on effective demand.[22]

Accordingly, he divided the national product in three parts: "(i) private accumulation, (ii) 'net revenue of the government from persons', and (iii) personal consumption of goods and services" (Kalecki

1956 [1997]: 281). Gross (or Social) accumulation is made up of investment in fixed capital, increase in inventories and the export surplus. However, private accumulation is a larger concept because in it also "the budget deficit should be taken into consideration, because it means an increase in the government indebtedness to capitalists. Finally, we also include in private accumulation revenue from the corporate profit tax as accumulation ceded to the government" (Ibid: 281–282). On the other hand, "Item (ii) represents the budget revenue exclusive of taxes on corporate profits but only to the extent to which they are spend on business products. Thus this is a surplus of personal income tax, contributions to social insurance plans, and indirect taxes over and above the expenditure on the remuneration of the armed forces ... and of government employees, on social insurance benefits, and on the interest of the public debt" (Ibid: 281–282).

We can easily see that a rise in any of the items included in Gross (or Social) accumulation, or in government expenditure financed via budget deficit, raises by an equal amount profits and has a large multiplier effect on effective demand. On the other hand, when the government finances its expenditure taxing corporate profits, effective demand is boosted but profits do not rise (so that the multiplier is smaller than in the previous case). Finally, when government expenditure is financed with "net government revenue from persons," it crowds out private expenditure. Therefore, effective demand and output remain unchanged.

In the first of the papers that we will discuss here, Kalecki compared the pre-war and the post-war situation in the US. He pointed out that between 1937 and 1955, the productive potential had doubled and questioned as to how was it possible that the productive facilities were in fact utilized? He stated, "the discrepancy between the development of productive forces and the market for their products constitutes one of the main contradictions inherent in the capitalist system ... [a contradiction that] in the period considered tended to grow more acute ... [because] ... big business's relative share of accumulation of the national product increased significantly" (Kalecki 1956 [1997]: 280).

In his study he found that the most important changes in the structure of final demand in the US between 1937 and 1955 had been, first, the change of sign of the trade balance (from a –0.5% of GDP to +1.3%). Second, the rise in taxes on corporate profits (from 1.9% to 5.8%). Third, the fall of private consumption (from 78.7% to 72.5%). Fourth, the rise of what he called "Net government revenue from persons"; namely, the net balance between personal taxes and transfers (from 4.9% to 6.3%). He thus concluded:

> The increase in the relative share of private accumulation in the national product...did not cause any underemployment of productive resources for the following reasons: the additional private accumulation was absorbed by armaments and by the export surplus, whose increase was associated with "foreign economic assistance" or with the construction of bases abroad which provided the wherewithal for importing American goods. (Kalecki 1956 [1997]: 284)

The second paper was devoted to analyzing the shape and peculiarities of the business cycle in the US between 1956 and 1961. He concluded: "The course of the business cycle in the USA in 1956–61 confirms the view that the capitalist economy still shows a tendency to go into recession, but that a high level of government expenditure during crisis, payouts of unemployment benefits, and such measures as easier credit for housing construction soften the course of the recession and accelerate the upswing" (Kalecki 1962a [1991]: 398).

Thus, in his study Kalecki found that expansionary fiscal policy in the US was not based on budget deficit, but on expenditure financed with taxes on profits. Therefore, he saw substantiation for his hypothesis that a balanced budget can be expansionary when taxes are levied on corporate profits. He also confirmed his critical stance on capitalism, because in spite of the rise in employment private consumption rose at a rather modest pace.

We conclude this section by noting that it is unfortunate that Kalecki had almost no following regarding his empirical studies of capitalist economies, and that his methodology has not had the impact it deserved.

Appendix 6.1

A simple model

Let us start off specifying the demand and output equation in a closed economy, with a non-negligible government:

$$Y = I + C_k + C_w + G \qquad \text{(A6.1)}$$

where G is government's expenditure on consumption and investment (I refers exclusively to private investment).

Let us now study the consequences of government expenditure in the easiest case, that of deficit financing. Kalecki formalized the analysis of the effects of a deficit using his schemes of reproduction. In addition to the original three vertically integrated departments, we add a fourth sector which produces only the goods that the government demands. We also suppose that all the government's expenditure takes the form of deficit (B).

Department	I	II	III	B	
Wages	W_1	W_2	W_3	W_b	W
Profits	P_1	P_2	P_3	P_b	P
Income	I	C_k	C_w	B	Y

If we assume that there are no unwanted changes in stocks, profits of the department that produces wage goods will be:

$$P_3 = C_w - W_3 \quad \text{(A6.2)}$$

This surplus, by its material characteristics, is equal to the demand of wage-earners of the other three departments: That is:

$$P_3 = W_1 + W_2 + W_b \quad \text{(A6.3)}$$

If we add $P_1 + P_2 + P_b$ to both sides of this equation, we get:

$$P = I + C_k + B \quad \text{(A6.4)}$$

Therefore, capitalists get greater profits from greater deficit spending. The financing of this greater government spending allows us to say that capitalists receive more profits without paying greater taxes.

Moreover, we can specify output as follows

$$Y = \frac{I + C_k + B}{e} \quad \text{(A6.5)}$$

From the previous equations and remembering that capitalist consumption can be divided into two parts ($C_k = A + \lambda P$) the following is verified:

$$P = \frac{I + A + B}{1 - \lambda} \qquad \text{(A6.6)}$$

and also:

$$Y = \frac{I + A + B}{e(1 - \lambda)} \qquad \text{(A6.7)}$$

This means that when there is an increase in the budget deficit, profits are increased in the following magnitude:

$$\Delta P = \Delta B \,/\, (1 - \lambda)$$

Since $\lambda > 0$, the increase in profits is greater than the increase in the deficit ($\Delta P > \Delta B$), because capitalist consumption increases too ($\Delta P = \Delta B + \Delta C_k$).

However, if the coefficient of income distribution (e) is constant, then the increase in the deficit will cause an increase in income greater than the increase of profits ($\Delta Y > \Delta P$), because it will also increase wage consumption ($\Delta Y = \Delta P + \Delta W$). This is expressed as follows:

$$\Delta Y = \Delta B \,/\, (1 - \lambda)\, e$$

This way the government deficit will increase profits and national income.

We will now formalize Kalecki's analysis of government expenditure financed by taxing profits. Let us assume that a new tax on profits is introduced which does not bring about a rise in prices. Total profits before taxes (P^b) can be expressed as follows:

$$P^b = I + Ck + B + H \qquad \text{(A6.8)}$$

and:

$$P^b = P + H \qquad \text{(A6.9)}$$

In which P^b is profits before taxes, P is profits after taxes, and H is the amount of the tax on profits.

The coefficient of income distribution (e) will now have the following expression:

$$e = \frac{P^b}{Y} \tag{A6.10}$$

Let us suppose now a rise in H, which does not entail a rise in prices. We must first of all note that since neither prices nor the unit *prime* cost have changed, the degree of monopoly is unchanged. But then, also the ratio of profits (before taxes) over income is kept constant.

Considering that:

$$Y = I + C_k + C_w + G$$

Let us assume:

$$Y = P + W + H \tag{A6.11}$$

Let us further suppose:

$$Cw = W; H = G \tag{A6.12}$$

We then get:

$$P = I + C_k \tag{A6.13}$$

It is clear that, since P is entirely dependent on $I + Ck$, our assumption that $I + Ck$ does not immediately change after the tax, entails that profits after taxes do not change either.

Moreover, let us suppose that capitalists' expenditure depends on net after tax profits, then:

$$C_k = A + \lambda P \tag{A6.14}$$

Therefore we can deduce:

$$P = \frac{A + I}{1 - \lambda} \tag{A6.15}$$

Consequently, we obtain:

$$Y = \frac{\left[\frac{A+I}{1-\lambda}\right]+H}{e} \qquad \text{(A6.14)}$$

That is, if the government collects a tax levied on profits, which it spends in the same period, the capitalist expenditure will remain constant. If such expenditure is not altered, total profits (after tax) will not change either. Why? Because, as a consequence of government expenditure, the output and sales increases are of such magnitude that there will be an *increase of total profits before taxes* such that *profits after taxes remain constant.*

Furthermore, the rise in output – which has been caused by the greater public expenditure – will cause an increase of workers' consumption that will be proportional to the increase in the level of economic activity. As profits after taxes are not altered and the total realized output increases, the ratio of the after-tax profits to total income will decline. That is why the greater total expenditure that is financed with a profit tax, not transferred to prices, will expand production, increase the level of employment and bring about a shift from profits to wages.

7
Kalecki's Open Economy Macroeconomics

In previous chapters our discussion has been confined to Kalecki's analysis of a closed economy. The aim of this chapter is to show how he included the effects of foreign trade in his approach to effective demand. Maybe not everybody, not even Kalecki's most unconditional admirers, would entirely subscribe to Joan Robinson's assertion: "Keynes's **General Theory** was worked out in terms of a closed system. ... Here also Kalecki's work claims priority" (Robinson, Preface to Kalecki (1969)). But we claim that Kalecki had a very original and novel approach to analyse open economy macroeconomics. Of course, some of the points he raised are now of common knowledge. However, we submit that in any case this part of his theory is still worth studying because, as is usually the case with this author, one can always find something which is unique and appealing in his reasoning.

Foreign trade, profits and effective demand

We have seen that, according to Kalecki, in contemporary capitalism actual output may be lower than potential output due to insufficient demand. To study how and to what extent foreign trade can affect demand we may consider a short time-period, and take up the case of a country where the productive capacity is not fully utilized, and which opens up to foreign trade and makes some exports but imports nothing. In this way, it accumulates gold or monetary reserves, or receives as payment its own previously issued liabilities. If we assume as given the autonomous components of domestic expenditure as well as the wage share, it follows that the total demand for domestic output will be higher when exports rise. The country will absorb purchasing power from abroad and, also, will increase its own domestic purchasing power. Demand is raised, in the first instance, by an amount equivalent to exports; but there is a second rise associated with the increase in workers' consumption.[1]

In short, from the point of view of effective demand when exports go up, output, the degree of utilization of productive capacities, profits and wages, all rise. It is easily seen that foreign trade will be favourable for a country whenever its trade balance is in surplus.[2] The financial counterpart to this situation is "capital exports". In other words, countries get into debt with the country that has a trade surplus; or the debt, which the surplus country holds with other countries, is reduced.[3]

It may be appropriate here to make a short digression, briefly referring to how Kalecki envisioned foreign aid, because he discussed this issue with the help of this part of his theory. He considered the situation of a donor country which "does not fully use its productive capacity, because of lack of effective demand" (Kalecki and Sachs (1966 [1993]): 63). In such a case,

> the export surplus... has a "multiplier" effect so that the aggregate domestic expenditure after deduction of the export surplus thus generated is higher than the income which would be generated without the export surplus. We may say, therefore, that by giving economic aid to other countries a developed country with free productive capacity assists its own economy in obtaining a higher level of economic activity. Foreign aid, far from being a burden on it, can perform a very useful role in achieving full employment. (Kalecki and Sachs (1966 [1993]: 63)

We come back now to our previous discussion. While capitalists' profits in a closed (and private) economy depend only on their investment and consumption decisions, in an open economy, profits depend also on their ability to gain net foreign markets. Kalecki immediately made the following remark on the political economy of the export surplus:

> It follows directly that the export surplus enables profits to increase above that level which would be determined by capitalist investment and consumption. It is from this point of view that the fight for foreign markets may be viewed. The capitalists of a country which manages to capture foreign markets from other countries are able to increase their profits at the expense of the capitalists of other countries. Similarly, a colonial metropolis may achieve an export surplus through investment in its dependencies. (Kalecki 1954a [1991]: 245)[4]

As mentioned, an export surplus implies that the creditor country does not spend the total received value of its exports in the form of imports. Some proportion of the domestically produced goods is traded, not for goods, but for gold, for foreign exchange, or debt instruments of other countries. In other words, the rest of the countries get into debt with the country which gained the net foreign markets. It is in this sense that Kalecki speaks of *capital exports*.

Now let us analyse this problem from the point of view of the foreign exchange situation. An economic upswing caused by an increase in exports implies that the country receives the international means of payment to pay for the greater imports directly and indirectly required by the increase in exports.

Let us compare this with the effects of an increase in investment. Both an increase of exports and an increase of investment expand effective demand and profits.[5] However, they are not identical in other aspects. In the case of an economic upswing via an increase of investment (or any other kind of increase of internal demand), the upswing does not bring about a gain in gold or in international reserves. In other words, the increase of investment (and in domestic demand in general) does not augment foreign exchange but, on the contrary, it uses additional amounts of foreign exchange to purchase the new imports required by the new investments.

Kalecki (1933b [1990]: 173) commented on this point that:

> the tension in the balance of payments which accompanied "domestic exports"[6] from the start, in the case of an upswing stimulated by securing a surplus in foreign trade arises only at the point when investment has reached a level several times greater than this surplus, i.e. at an advanced stage of the boom. Moreover, it is probable that prior to this a considerable improvement in the economic situation which does not involve balance of payment difficulties will lead to an inflow of foreign capital ... It is worth mentioning that the "natural" upswing based on the automatic increase in investment activity does not enjoy these advantages, and if there is not inflow of foreign capital, it will be confronted with the same balance of payments difficulties as the upswing based on domestic exports.

Wages and profits in the open economy

When we discussed the relationship between changes in wages and changes in output and employment in a closed economy, we saw that, in Kalecki's theory, a wage increase does not affect the amount of profits, since these depend entirely on the capitalist expenditure which may be assumed to be given in the current period. This being the case, the cost increase ensuing from the wage rise is exactly matched by the increase of sales due to the higher spending level of the workers.

In an open economy the final result is different. A part of both the wage consumption and of the intermediate material is bought outside the domestic economy. When wages increase[7] domestic sales swell, in the first place, by as much as wage consumption on domestic goods rise (we suppose that the wage-earners do not save). To this we should add the increase of domestic input sales. However, costs increase by an amount equivalent to the total increase of wages, plus the increase in the imported wage consumption, plus the increase in the cost of total inputs, both home-made and imported.

From the previous argument we can deduce that, in the open economy, when wages increase, the increase of sales is less than the increase of costs, and thus the total gross profit will be reduced. It is also easy to appreciate that the reduction of profits will be greater when the ratio of imports of the economy is greater; in particular, such reduction will be greater when the ratio of consumer imports to wage consumption is greater.

Let us now discuss the relationship between wages, output and employment in the open economy. This is a crucial point because, as mentioned time and time again, classical and neoclassical macroeconomics claim that (downward) flexibility of nominal (and real) wages can ensure full employment. Now, let us assume that a fall in money wages and the consequent real currency depreciation are indeed capable of bringing about an expansion of both employment and output. Then it would follow that capitalist economies are endowed with a very powerful built-in full employment mechanism. In fact, unemployment would sooner or later bring about a reduction in nominal wages, to be followed by a decline of domestic prices. Given the nominal exchange rate, the decline in prices would improve competitiveness. The latter would expand the trade balance and stimulate effective demand, thus mitigating unemployment. The process would only stop when the economy achieves full employment because only then nominal wages would cease to fall.

It is no wonder, then, that *practical* orthodox economists nowadays put much more emphasis on the repercussion of flexible wages upon international competitiveness. Of course, *academic* orthodox economists still pay lip service to either the so-called Keynes effect or the

Pigou effect or both, as the mechanisms that would allegedly ensure full employment. But the real point that mainstream policymakers have in mind when recommending, for example, downward wage flexibility is that the country will gain foreign markets which will bring about the absorption of unemployment.

As the reader will remember, in his *General Theory* Keynes devoted only few sentences to discuss the effects of wage reductions on unemployment in an open economy; and he did not state a clear-cut conclusion. But "the other" founding father of the theory of effective demand did consider this issue in detail, and came to a very straightforward conclusion. We will begin our exposition with a detailed presentation, in Kalecki's own words, of his outlook. He wrote:

> A reduction in wages and the consequent fall in prices will obviously improve the competitive position of the goods produced by a given country in the world market, and thus will contribute to an expansion in the volume of exports. This would affect production and employment favourably. However, the reduction of wages ... exerts an opposite influence as well, so that the final outcome is by no means certain.
>
> Indeed, the reduction of wages in a given country has obviously no influence on the price of imported raw materials. Therefore the prices of goods manufactured from them decline ***pro tanto*** more slowly. As a result, real wages decline (in addition to the decrease caused by the "rigidity" of prices)...Consequently the purchasing power of the workers is correspondingly lower, and has an adverse effect on the industries producing wage goods.
>
> The final outcome of the reduction of wages depends on the extent to which the reduction of wages and prices will increase the volume of exports." (1939c [1991]: 37; emphasis in the original)

As mentioned, Kalecki remarked upon the similarity between a wage fall and a depreciation of the currency, adding that "[t]he two cases differ only in that in the former the wages decline and the prices of imported raw materials remain unchanged, while in the latter the wages remain unaltered (in terms of domestic currency), and the prices of imported raw materials increase in inverse proportion to the currency depreciation" (Kalecki 1939c [1991]: 38).

Based on his analysis, he concludes: "even in such a case [in an open system] the reduction of wages does not necessarily lead to an increase in employment, and the prospects of raising the aggregate real income of the working class are even dimmer. In particular, under the system of high and rising tariffs it is very likely that a reduction of wages will have an adverse effect on employment also in an open economy " (Kalecki 1939c [1991]: 38).

Kalecki's analysis is concise, but we can elaborate on it and rigorously examine the effects of a wage fall in an open economy with the help of his theory.[8]

Let us first of all recall that aggregate demand depends on total profits, divided by the relative share of profits in the national income. Total profits are equal to the autonomous component of expenditure; namely, capitalist expenditure on consumption and on investment, plus the trade surplus (we assume away government expenditure). It follows that, when the Marshall–Lerner condition is fulfilled, the wage fall will bring about an improvement in the trade balance, and so also in total profits and in the autonomous components of expenditure.

As previously mentioned, Kalecki was rather skeptical about the elasticity of exports with respect to improved competitiveness, especially when trade barriers are high. However, let us assume that the trade balance does improve and that profits rise. Does that mean that output and employment are also going to rise? Not necessarily, because we still need to see what happens with the relative share of profits in the national income. In Kalecki's theory, this share rises when the degree of monopoly increases, or when the ratio of aggregate cost of materials to the wage bill rises. Now, there are several reasons why the relative share of profits in output may rise when nominal wages drop.[9]

In the first place, the wage drop entails a rise in the ratio of the materials bill to the wage bill, because the price of imported inputs has not fallen. This is one reason why the profit share may rise when wages fall. But there is more.

In the second place, under imperfect competition it is possible that firms raise their mark-up on unit prime costs; that is, Kalecki's "degree of monopoly" may rise. The reason is as follows. It is true that unit prime costs fall thanks to the wage fall, which might stimulate a price fall. However, the domestic price of the competitive imports does not fall, and this may prevent domestic producers to pass on to consumers their cost reduction in its entirety. If they do reduce prices, they are likely to do so in a smaller proportion than the cost fall, because the price of competitive imports does not fall. This is why Kalecki' degree of monopoly may rise when wages fall.

Now, when the relative share of profits in income increases, income gets re-distributed against workers, who have a higher propensity to consume than capitalists; consequently, aggregate demand is bound to fall. In other words, the shift from wages to profits would impart a deflationary bias to output, and may offset, or more than offset, any improvement in the trade balance on effective demand, or would magnify its reduction if it had actually fallen.

On the basis of Kalecki's approach, we therefore come to the conclusion that in an open economy, output may also contract as a result of a fall in wages, because this fall tends to reduce the share of wages in value added. Moreover, *this fall may take place even when the Marshall–Lerner condition is fulfilled.*

Finally, given the equivalence between a wage fall and currency depreciation, we can infer from Kalecki's reasoning another important result. Namely, the effect of currency depreciation on output and employment may also be negative; a conclusion that is contrary to the one envisioned by conventional economic analysis. Indeed, the latter assumes that a flexible exchange rate can guarantee both trade balance equilibrium and full employment. But in Kalecki's view there is no guarantee whatsoever that a more competitive real exchange rate will, by itself, ensure full employment.

Critics of Kalecki's conclusions may raise two objections. One, that his analysis might have been valid in the international circumstances of his times, when barriers to trade were high, but not in the present international setup. The other, that even if a wage fall may contract aggregate demand, it will be a short-run result. In the medium- and long-run, the situation will be reversed. Let us ponder over these two objections.

Indeed, Kalecki confined his conclusion to a "system of high and rising tariffs." (Ibid: 38). Nowadays, when trade has been greatly liberalized, we can expect that a change in a country's relative wages, and prices, vis-à-vis other countries, may have a greater effect on the trade balance. In other words, if we assume a wage fall, we may expect that – disproving Kalecki's skepticism from his previously quoted paragraph – the trade balance, and so also profits, will rise.

However, we must consider two other effects of greater openness on trade, which affect the relative share of profits in output. First, the importance of the international market, and of competitive imports, for domestic producers is greater than in the past. Second, imports today have a greater weight in material costs and in total direct costs.

To discuss the consequences of bringing in the first factor, let us assume that together with wages, the unit prime cost also falls. If the domestic price of competitive imports does not fall (and it will not fall unless competitive imports are "priced to the market"), then domestic prices may fall in a smaller proportion than unit costs. Also, since prices abroad have not fallen, prices of exports may fall proportionately less than costs. In other words, both firms catering to the domestic market and to the export market may raise their degree of monopoly when wages fall, because the pressure of international competition becomes weaker.

The second factor, the greater weight of imports in material costs and total direct costs, also plays a relevant role. To examine this issue, let us again assume wages fall. Then, other things equal, this would entail a rise in the ratio of the materials bill to the wage bill. Moreover, the more rigid the prices of material inputs, the rise will be all the greater. We may expect that when the share of imported material inputs is larger, their prices will also be stickier.

In sum, in economies more open to trade than in Kalecki's time, there are also strong factors that may prevent any compensatory rise in aggregate demand when wages, and consumption per worker, fall.[10]

We discuss now the long-run inference about the association between a wage fall and output and employment. Let us assume that a wage fall in an open economy does cause a decline in output and employment. Is it really true that this will be only a short-lived situation? Not necessarily; the contraction of output and employment may be drawn out. This is a likely occurrence because the reduction in the degree of utilization of capacity will probably have a detrimental effect on investment decisions in the present and future. In other words, the short-run negative impact of a wage fall may extend into the long-run.

We may recall here the recent discussion that has taken place amongst Post-Keynesian economists on the so-called wage-led and profit-led regimes.[11] This discussion has made it clear that whether a wage fall will stimulate investment, and long-run growth, or not depends on the weight of the different determinants of the investment function. Indeed, the wage fall raises profits in an open economy, but may reduce the degree of utilization of productive capacity, which are two arguments that we may assume that should be included amongst the determinants of investment.

Let us consider a situation where the "Marshall–Lerner" condition is fulfilled, such that a wage fall brings about an improvement in the trade balance and in profits, but causes a decline in aggregate demand. Let us moreover assume a simple investment function, where investment depends positively on profits and on capacity utilization. Then, if the elasticity of investment with respect to profits is higher than its elasticity with respect to utilization, a wage fall will have a short-run negative effect on output and employment, but that effect will reverse after a certain time-lapse, because investment will start growing at a faster rate (a "profit-led" regime). But, of course, if the elasticity of utilization is greater, then the short-run negative effect on output of the wage fall will extend to the long run.

Taxes, profits and employment in the open economy

We will consider now the effects of an expansionary fiscal policy stance on the trade balance, making use of Kalecki's theory. As should be obvious, just like any increase in demand, a rise in public spending will cause an increase in output, and therefore also in imports. This has a twofold implication. On the one hand, the rise in imports will reduce the expansive effect of this expenditure on output (the "multiplier") and on profits, "leaking" part of the increase of demand towards the rest of the world. The outward "leakage" will be greater, the higher the coefficient of imports to output.

In the extreme case when the internal productive capacity is totally or almost totally utilized, then the increase in demand will cause a rise in internal prices; also the coefficient of imports will rise. As a result, the increase of demand will almost totally or totally "leak" towards the rest of the world. Output and employment, as well as profits, will not rise or they will rise very little.

Anyway, the increase in the public expenditure will cause a worsening of the trade balance of the country that – given the magnitude of the increase – will be greater accordingly to the magnitude of the expansive effect of the expenditure and the size of the import coefficient. This normally will affect the balance of payments of the country even more because the worsening of the trade balance can stimulate capital flight, in view of the fear of a future currency devaluation or exchange controls.

We can also infer that in economies having structural difficulties to keep the balance of payments in check, the capacity of the State to manage demand through its expenditure is considerably limited by external considerations.

Finally, it is also easy to see that in an open economy, Kalecki's statement that taxing profits will not reduce profits after taxes is no longer valid. We can easily understand this point when we recall that profits after tax in an open economy include the trade surplus. If indeed taxes on profits do not immediately diminish capitalist expenditure, then they will bring about an expansion of demand; but the latter will provoke a rise in imports and a reduction in the trade surplus. Accordingly profits will be reduced.

Does it follow then that in an open economy taxing profits will have a negative effect on private investment, thus jeopardizing the long-run growth of output and employment? Not necessarily; and we may use here again a type of reasoning advanced previously. Indeed, if the elasticity of investment with respect to capacity utilization is high, and is larger that the elasticity of investment with respect to profits, then investment need not fall at all, because capacity utilization will rise. For in this case the fall in profits will be more than offset by the rise in capacity utilization. Therefore, long-run growth may even be stimulated.

Proposals for a New International Economic system

Kalecki was well aware of the vital role of the foreign sector and of the availability of international liquidity for the evolution of any economy, and conscious of the importance of coordinated action by different nations for expansionary measures to achieve complete success. Thus, in a very early paper (published under the pseudonym, Henryk Braun, in a socialist magazine) he put forward the idea that, "we should mention yet another possibility [to overcome the world crisis of the 1930s], namely... individual states, or group of states, starting up major public-investment schemes, such as construction of canals or roads, and financing them with government loans floated on the financial market, or with special government credits drawn on their banks of issue" (Kalecki 1932d [1990]: 53). He remarked, however, "if it were to be carried out on a large scale, it would have to be co-ordinated by an international agreement of the individual capitalist governments, which, given today's quarrelling imperialism, is almost out of the question" (Ibid: 53).[12]

For a time, Kalecki did not elaborate further on the topic. However, during the 1940s, surely stimulated by the debate initiated by Keynes on the organization of the post-war system of international trade and finance, he published two short papers where he reflected on the macroeconomic links between nations, both from the point of view of world effective demand and with a proposal to amend Keynes's original scheme. We will discuss these two papers later on, but now it will be appropriate to present in some details Keynes's proposal, and to the extent possible, in his own words.[13] This will set the stage to clearly understand the debate as well as Kalecki's contribution.

The aim of Keynes's proposal was to encourage expansion rather than contraction, in the sense of a promotion of the international division of labour, and also of facilitating an increase of effective demand in any country wishing to carry out full-employment policies. He envisioned the situation as follows:

> The problem of maintaining equilibrium in the balance of payments between countries has never been solved, since the methods of barter gave way to the use of money and bills of exchange...
>
> To suppose that there exists some smoothly functioning automatic mechanism of adjustment which preserves equilibrium if only we trust to methods of ***laissez-faire*** is a doctrinaire delusion which disregards the lessons of historical experience without having behind it the support of sound theory. (Keynes 1971–1982, Vol. 25: 21–22)

He then stated the following requirements for a well-functioning new world order:

> (a) We need an instrument of international currency having general acceptability between nations...
> (b) We need an orderly and agreed method of determining the relative exchange values of national currency units...
> (c) We need a quantum of international currency, which...is governed by the actual current requirements of world commerce, and is also capable of deliberate expansion and contraction to offset deflationary and inflationary tendencies in effective world demand.
> (d) We need a system possessed of an internal stabilising mechanism, by which pressure is exerted on any country whose balance of payments with the rest of the world is departing from equilibrium in either direction, so as to prevent movements which must create for its neighbours an equal but opposite want of balance.
> (e) We need an agreed plan for starting off every country after the war with a stock of reserves appropriate to its importance in world commerce...
> (f) We need a method by which the surplus credit balances arising from international trade, which the recipient does not wish to employ for the time being, can be set to work...without detriment to the liquidity of these balances and to their holder's faculty to employ them himself when he desires to do so.

(g) We need a central institution, of a purely technical and non-political character...

(h) More generally, we need a means of reassurance to a troubled world, by which any country whose own affairs are conducted with due prudence is relieved of anxiety, for causes which are not of its own making, concerning its ability to meet its international liabilities. (Keynes 1971–1982, Vol. 25: 168–169)

Keynes then went on to the following proposal:

> The proposal is to establish a Currency Union...designated an International Currency Union, based on international bank money, called...bancor, fixed (but not inalterably) in terms of gold and accepted as the equivalent of gold by...all...the members of the Union for the purpose of settling international balances. The central banks of all member states...would keep accounts with the International Clearing Union through which they would be entitled to settle their exchange balances with one another at their par value as defined in terms of bancor...Measures would be necessary...to prevent the piling up of credit and debit balances without a limit....
>
> The idea underlying such a Union is simple, namely, to generalise the essential principle of banking as it is exhibited within any closed system. This principle is the necessary equality of credits and debits. If no credits can be removed outside the clearing system, but only transferred within it, the Union can never be in any difficulty as regards the honouring of cheques drawn upon it. It can make what advances it wishes to any of its members with the assurance that the proceeds can only be transferred to the clearing account of another member. (Keynes 1971–1982, Vol. 25: 170–171)

Finally, Keynes made more precise his proposal by suggesting that each member of the Union be given a quota according to its importance in the world trade,[14] by defining permissible upper bounds to the debit and credit balances of each member of the Union, and by establishing fines that would be charged to both credit and debit balances when the country exceeded its permissible quota in either direction.

Let us now come to Kalecki's reflections on the issue. His first paper, written with E. S. Schumacher, was a direct response to Keynes' and White's plans; basically suggesting amendments to the former.[15] His second paper dealt in more general terms with the requirements to make multilateralism workable; that is, the requirements to ensure that any country wishing to carry out full employment measures did not find obstacles to meet its international liabilities. These obstacles could easily arise if countries with a balance of payments surplus, simply sterilized their surplus, thus depriving the other countries of the requisite international liquidity. We will first consider the second paper, given its more general approach.

In this paper, Kalecki recognized that "world multilateralism can secure a better utilization of world resources than bilateralism or regional blocks (although in the latter case the difference may not be so great). Nor does multilateralism raise the political issues that may be in the formation of regional blocks. It is therefore superior to other systems provided that it is workable; that is, provided that it is operated under conditions of such a kind that no difficulties in balancing imports of goods and services with exports arise for full-employment countries" (Kalecki 1946 [1990]): 409–410).

Kalecki then argued that, on one hand, multilateralism would be unworkable if employment in major industrial countries is subject to strong fluctuations. On the other hand, he was skeptical that the trade balance problems of the full-employment countries could be solved by introducing trade restrictions or currency depreciation. Trade restrictions would mean "the failure of multilateralism to secure the international division of labour" (Ibid: 412). Currency depreciation may not solve the situation for the reasons given earlier in this chapter.

Kalecki finally inquired about the necessary conditions for a viable multilateral system. He showed that if all countries maintained full employment on the basis of a sufficient level of internal demand, then no country will experience difficulties in balancing its foreign trade. However, if some major countries do not achieve full employment but have a great demand for imports, other countries may still reach full employment without difficulties in balancing their foreign trade. The reason is simply that when a country has a balanced trade, it is not subtracting international liquidity to the other countries. On the contrary, high import demand from major not fully employed countries can provide the rest of the world with the requisite international liquidity to carry out their full employment policy.

Kalecki then argued that other possibilities exist to make multilateralism compatible with the pursuit of full employment. He mentioned two cases. The first one would occur when "each country must maintain full employment based on domestic expenditure and on foreign net expenditure financed by long-term loans. Thus, each country must maintain such a domestic expenditure that this expenditure plus export surplus financed by foreign lending (or minus export deficit financed by foreign borrowing) is adequate to assure full employment. Indeed, if a country has an export surplus which is not financed by foreign long-term lending, and if, in accordance with our assumption, it will not cut its domestic expenditure, the effective demand will exceed the full employment mark and an inflationary situation will arise. To deal with it, the country will have to increase its imports or to reduce its exports, or both. In this way, the surplus which is not financed by foreign long-term lending will be eliminated" (Kalecki 1946 [1990]: 414).[16]

Another possibility would be the following: "If some countries are not fully employed, this does not mean that the full-employment countries will necessarily experience difficulties in balancing the proceeds and outlays of foreign exchange. The imports of not fully-employed countries plus their foreign lending may provide the full-employment countries with foreign exchange adequate to cover their imports from the former countries" (Ibid).

Kalecki warned, however, that if these conditions were not met "a breakdown of multilateralism and its replacement by another system of international trade is unavoidable" (Ibid: 416).

In the first paper, co-authored with Schumacher, the authors agreed with the aim and with much of the specific proposals contained in Keynes plan. However, they went beyond that proposal. First of all, they stated:

> There is no merit in a general policy aiming at ***current account equilibrium*** for all countries, because different countries are at different stages of economic development, and a regular flow of investment from the more highly developed to the more backward regions of the world may redound to the benefit of all ... .
>
> Is there, then, any merit in a general policy aiming at what we have called "**unbalanced equilibrium**", i.e. at a balance in the current account and the long-term capital account taken together? There is, indeed, a strong case for it. ... if "disequilibrium" destroys the international liquidity of the deficit country ...
>
> If, therefore, the supreme aim of a new international system and a new international policy is to be expansion rather than contraction ... it may be worth while to consider whether the dangers of disequilibrium, which consist of the resulting illiquidity of the deficit countries, could not be overcome by other means [than by inducing

> the surplus countries to ration their exports and by inducing the deficit countries to ration their imports]. (Kalecki and Schumacher 1943 [1997]: 226–227; emphasis in the original)

The authors therefore imagined a very ingenious mechanism, with three main features. First, "countries can have any surplus they may like, but will not, by hoarding their surpluses, endanger or ruin the international liquidity of others" (Kalecki and Schumacher 1943 [1997]): 227). Second, they distinguished three typologies of countries, according to their level of development and to their international economic position (see below). Third, they suggested attaching an International Investment Board to the Clearing Board. We think it is important to describe their proposal in detail.

Kalecki and Schumacher's idea aimed at the following: "(i) to make it possible for any country desiring to have an export surplus to hoard unlimited amounts of gold or bancor ... (ii) to safeguard countries needing an import surplus for purposes of reconstruction, readjustment, and industrialization ["A" countries] against any long-term deterioration in their international liquidity; and (iii) to provide an instrument for ***international*** policy by means of which help can be given to countries which cannot be included under (ii) ["B" countries; namely countries whose deficit in the current balance of payments is due to reasons other than those arising in the course of industrialization, reconstruction, or readjustment] to maintain a long-term balance in their current account" (1943 [1997]: 228).

To carry out this international strategy, they proposed the attachment of an "International Investment Board to the International Clearing [Union] which decides the amount of long-term loans which might be granted to deficit countries" (Ibid: 229), distinguishing between (i) and (ii) countries. Moreover, to ease the international situation of "B" countries the "Board should have the power to direct borrowers receiving development loans to use them fully or partly to increase their imports from specified 'B' countries" (Ibid: 230).

Nevertheless, the authors concluded their reflection with this warning: "If investment decisions have to be taken by an international authority, there arises, of course, a political problem of first magnitude ... investment decisions, and decisions directing a borrower to make his purchases in one particular country, involve a high degree of political responsibility" (Ibid: 231).

Unfortunately, the Kalecki–Schumacher proposal did not receive the attention and the discussion it deserved. In fact, as we know, even

Keynes's proposal was largely abandoned in favour of the plan elaborated by Harry Dexter White, the US chief international economist, at the US Treasury in 1942–44.[17]

Appendix 7.1

We begin with the equilibrium output equation (demand side) in an open economy with no government, which reads:

$$Y = I + C_k + C_w + E \tag{A7.1}$$

$$E = X - M$$

I is (private) investment, C_k is capitalist consumption, C_w is workers' consumption and E is the trade balance. X and M are exports and imports respectively, in domestic currency at constant prices. Thus, if the domestic components of expenditure are given, such as is the case in any short period, effective demand, and therefore, income and output, will be greater when exports exceed imports.

Let us now look at the role of the export or import surpluses with the aid of the schemes of reproduction. In the original simplified model we included three vertically integrated departments, to which we now add a fourth one, which produces the total export surplus E.

We can express this as:

Departments	I I	II C_k	III C_w	IV $E = (X–M)$	Total
Wages	W_1	W_2	W_3	W_e	W
Profits	P_1	P_2	P_3	P_e	P
Income	I	C_k	C_w	E	Y

Let us take into consideration Department III, which corresponds to the production of wage goods. An amount equal to its profits (P_3), equal to $C_w – W_3$, is sold to the workers of the remaining departments, such that:

$$P_3 = W_1 + W_2 + W_e \tag{A7.2}$$

Adding $P_1 = P_2 + P_{e,}$ to both sides of the equation, we get

$$P = I + C_k + E \qquad \text{(A7.3)}$$

Our last equation indicates that the total gross profits obtained over the period equals the capital expenditure and the export surplus.

Let us now examine the effect of the export surplus "multiplier". On one hand, an increase in exports allows effective demand to increase as well, and therefore, profits will increase too. On the other hand, if income distribution is assumed constant, a rise in income will involve a proportional rise in total wages.

The explanation for this export surplus "multiplier" effect is quite simple and comes from the schemes of reproduction recently discussed. Such surplus involves a greater level of domestic output, hence, higher levels of employment, wages and wage consumption. Contrariwise, when purchasing goods from abroad which were previously home-made, the output and employment levels of Departments I and II will be smaller and – given the income distribution – so will be the level of output in Department III. But profits will also be reduced.

Let us now recall equation (A7.3), as well as equations from previous chapters.[18]

$$P = I + C_k + E \qquad \text{(A7.3)}$$

$$C_k = A + \lambda P$$

$$Y = \frac{P}{e}$$

$$Y = \frac{I + C_k + X - M}{e} \qquad \text{(A7.4)}$$

Rearranging and substituting we get:

$$P = \frac{I + A + E}{1 - \lambda} \qquad \text{(A7.5)}$$

$$Y = \frac{I + A + E}{e(1 - \lambda)} \qquad \text{(A7.6)}$$

It can be easily seen that an increase in the export surplus leads to an increase in profits equal to:

$$\Delta P = \frac{\Delta E}{(1-\lambda)} \tag{A7.7}$$

and an increase in effective demand and income equal to:

$$\Delta Y = \frac{\Delta E}{e(1-\lambda)} \tag{A7.8}$$

The previous expression shows that the increase in the total income is greater than the profit increase, due to the increase in wages that accompanied the income increase ($\Delta Y = \Delta P + \Delta W$). However, the profit increase is greater than the export surplus increase because the former leads (even though with a lag) to a greater level of capitalist consumption, which will also lead to greater profits ($\Delta P = \Delta E + \Delta C_k$).

Let us discuss in detail the extent of the expansionary role of the external sector. An increase of exports, for example, causes an increase of profits and of national income. But the increase of exports itself demands greater imports.

Let γ be the ratio of total imports to total output. To simplify, let us suppose that the ratio is the same for all of the productive sectors. Let us now recall equation (A7.6):

$$Y = \frac{I + A + E}{e(1-\lambda)}$$

In an economy where all the productive departments are vertically integrated, we can write this equation as follows:

$$Y = \frac{I(1-\gamma) + C_k(1-\gamma) + X(1-\gamma) - C_w\gamma}{e} \tag{A7.9}$$

We assume now a given level of capitalist consumption in the short term. In other words, we assume away any growth in capitalist consumption that may be induced by higher profits. Then we can obtain the change of income that is caused by a change in exports (ΔY_e).

$$\Delta Y = \frac{AX(1-\gamma) - \Delta C_w \cdot \gamma}{e} \tag{A7.10}$$

That is to say, only a part of the rise of exports expands effective demand and output; the other part of this rise "pays" for the additional imports that the change in exports induces.

From another angle, when an increase in exports happens, just a part of it contributes to the increase in profits. The other part is used for "paying" the ensuing imports. Namely:

$$\Delta X = \Delta E + \Delta M$$

$$\Delta E = \Delta X - \Delta M$$

The expansive effect of the increase of exports (its "multiplier") on profits and on output will be – given the coefficient e – all the greater, the smaller is the ratio of imports (γ) of the economy. In other words, the lower is γ, the smaller the outward leakage of domestic demand will be.

We can now specify the relationship between the change in exports and the change in imports (Kalecki 1933b [1990]). Supposing the ratio of imports γ is constant we obtain:

$$\gamma \Delta Y = \Delta M \tag{A7.11}$$

If we abstract from the change of capitalist consumption that is induced by the change of profits, we get:

$$\Delta Y = \frac{\Delta E}{e} \tag{A7.12}$$

Substituting we get:

$$\frac{\Delta E}{e} = \frac{\Delta M}{\gamma} \tag{A7.13}$$

From here we get:

$$\frac{\Delta E}{\Delta M} = \frac{e}{\gamma} \tag{A7.14}$$

Consequently, we can say that the relation between the increase of the surplus (ΔE) and the increase of imports that it brings about (ΔM) is equal to the ratio between the share of profits in income and the import coefficient. In other words, if a country increases its exports, the relation between the improvement of its trade balance and the increase of imports that it induces, is same as the ratio of the profits to national income to the ratio of imports. Again, given a certain value for e, the ratio between the increase in the export surplus and the increase of imports will be all the greater, the smaller the import ratio γ.

We now discuss the consequences upon profits of a wage rise. When wages increase, national sales increase by as much as the increase of wage consumption on domestic goods (ΔC_{wn}), plus the increase of domestic intermediate goods sales (ΔBI_N). Instead, costs increase in an amount equivalent to the total increase of wages (supposing that the wage-earners do not save, such amount is equal to the increase in the national wage consumption ΔC_{wn}, plus the increase in the imported wage consumption ΔC_{wm}), plus the increase in the cost of total intermediate goods (national intermediate goods ΔBI_n, plus imported intermediate goods ΔBI_m).

$$\Delta \text{Sales} = C_{wn} + \Delta BI_n$$

$$\Delta \text{Costs} = \Delta C_{wn} + \Delta C_{wm} + \Delta BI_n + \Delta BI_m$$

From the previous argument it is deduced that when wages increase, the increase of sales is less than the increase of costs, and thus the total gross profit will be reduced.

To discuss with the help of a formal model the consequences of a wage fall on output and employment in Kalecki's model, we consider the following equations. Let us recall that P stands for profits, I for private investment, C_k for capitalist consumption, X for exports, and M for imports. ω is the relative share of wages in the value added (or output), so that (under simplifying assumptions) $1-\omega$ is the share of profits in output (i.e., what we have denoted by the letter e). k is the "degree of monopoly", or the ratio of aggregate proceeds to aggregate prime costs, (which is also equal to the ratio of average prices to average prime costs). j is the ratio of aggregate cost of materials to the wage bill. Subsequently, p is the price charged by a firm, u is the unit prime cost, p' is the weighted average price of the industry, and m and n are parameters. We thus have:

$$P = I + C_k + (X - M) \quad \text{(A7.15)}$$

$$\omega = \frac{1}{1 + (k-1)(j+1)}, k > 1 \quad \text{(A7.16)}$$

Assuming:

$$e \equiv 1 - \omega \quad \text{(A7.16')}$$

We have:

$$Y = \frac{P}{1-\omega} = \frac{P}{e} = \frac{I + C_k + (X - M)}{e} \quad \text{(A7.17)}^{19}$$

$$p = mu + np' \quad \text{(A7.16)}$$

$$k = \frac{p}{u} = m + n\left(\frac{p'}{p}\right) \quad \text{(A7.16a)}$$

Equation (A7.13) is the well-known Kalecki's equation for total profits in an open economy (where we abstract from workers' savings and from the budget deficit for the sake of simplification).[20] Equation (A7.14) shows that (for a given composition of output) the relative share of wages in the value added is determined by the degree of monopoly and by the ratio of the materials bill to the wage bill. Equation (A7.14´) comes from the notion that, under simplifying conditions, national income is equal to profits plus wages. Equation (A7.15), which encapsulates Kalecki's theory of effective demand, makes total output depend on total profits and the share of profits in output. Finally, equations (A7.16) and (A7.16a) depict the pricing policy of firms. Following Kalecki we assume that firms fix prices taking into consideration their prime cost and the weighted average price of all firms.

To discuss the effects of a fall in nominal wages on profits and on output we concentrate on equation (A7.17). If prices go down, and the nominal exchange rate is constant, that leads to improved competitiveness. In the short run, when capitalists' expenditure is given, the effect of improved competitiveness on profits, and hence on the numerator of equation (A7.15), will depend on the elasticity of export and imports with respect to the real exchange rate. When the Marshall–Lerner is fulfilled, the numerator of (A7.15) will rise after a wage fall.

We discuss now the impact of a wage fall on income distribution ($e \equiv 1 - \omega$). It can be easily seen that the relative share of wages in output is very likely to fall when nominal wages fall. In the first place, the ratio of the materials bill to the wage bill (j) will rise. Moreover, under imperfect competition the degree of monopoly (k) may also rise.

In terms of equation (A7.17), in his analysis, Kalecki argued that the numerator may fall if the Marshall–Lerner condition is not fulfilled, causing (X–M) and P to decline. But most importantly, the denominator will surely rise because ω is likely to fall.[21]

8
Michal Kalecki: A Pioneer of Development Economics

Introduction

Kalecki made important contributions to development economics, which rank him among the founding fathers of this area of economics. The objective of this chapter is to give an account of his contributions, mostly by letting the author speak for himself. We will start the presentation of his ideas summarizing one of the last papers he wrote on the subject (Kalecki (1966b [1993]), where he presented in his usual concise style his overall outlook.

First, he indicates that, "The crucial problem of the underdeveloped economy is different from that of the developed countries (...) as contrasted with developed economies [in the former the capital equipment] is not capable of absorbing all available labour, as a result of which the standard of living is very low" (Kalecki (1966b [1993]: 16).

He then argues: "The crucial problem facing the underdeveloped countries is thus to increase investment considerably (...) There are, however, three important obstacles to stepping up investment. First, it is possible that private investment will not be forthcoming at an adequate rate. Second, there may be no physical resources to produce more investment goods. Third, even if the two difficulties are overcome, there is still the problem of adequate supply of necessities to cover the demand resulting from the increase in employment" (Ibid: 16).

The author then recognizes that these obstacles can be surmounted with appropriate measures. He refers to "the intervention of the government in the sphere of investment with the aim of securing its planned volume and structure, the overcoming of the institutional barriers to rapid development of agriculture, and adequate taxation of the rich and the well-to-do" (Kalecki 1966b [1993]: 19). But he concludes his reflection with this rather gloomy diagnosis: "[These] three problems...clearly present a formidable political problem...The overcoming of all the obstacles to economic development enumerated above amounts to more than the upheaval created in the eighteenth century by the French Revolution. Thus it is not surprising that these reforms are not peacefully carried out. Vigorous but balanced development (...) is hardly encountered in practice. In fact we find two types of development (perhaps with some intermediate cases): either the development is non-inflationary, but extremely slow, or it is relatively rapid and is accompanied by violent inflationary pressures" (Ibid).

We will now discuss in detail Kalecki's theoretical economic analysis of underdeveloped economies. Later we will see how he envisioned an economic strategy to stimulate economic recovery and foster high and balanced long-run growth.

Kalecki's macroeconomics of underdeveloped economies

Kalecki's first written contribution to the study of underdeveloped countries came in his review of Manoilescu (1931).[1] The reader may recall that the Rumanian economist and politician Manoilescu was a vehement supporter of protectionism and industrialization in underdeveloped countries, and a critic of the orthodox theory of international trade based on comparative advantage and the labour theory of labour. His defence of protectionism was severely condemned by conventional economists, but Kalecki supported Manoilescu's outlook claiming that "it is the author [i.e., Manoilescu] who [is] right in [his] solution of the problem of protection in agricultural countries" (Kalecki 1938c [1993]: 181).

Kalecki argued that "it is (...) realistic to assume that in an agricultural country there is some unemployment, manifest or disguised, and thus the supply of new saving is by no means fixed: it is equal to the investment undertaken (...). If some new industry is protected, opportunity for investment increases, and the supply of capital rises *pro tanto*" (Ibid). In other words, Kalecki believed that new industries would be convenient from the point of view of the country because additional investment would bring about its own savings supply due to unemployment. In a later paper he would be more explicit mentioning that, "In underdeveloped countries, the additional labour force will frequently come from rural districts. In many instances, agricultural production will not fall, as a result of 'surplus labour' in agriculture" (Kalecki 1954b [1993]: 28).

However, Kalecki concluded his review of Manoilescu with a more general critique. "The author's tendency to represent protection as the solution of the problem of industrialization of agricultural countries is definitely misleading...To represent free trade as the *only* obstacle to economic progress of backward countries is to divert attention to such urgent social problems as land reform and others" (Kalecki 1938c [1993]: 182; emphasis in the original).[2]

Kalecki continued his reflections on the economics of underdeveloped countries during his work in the Economic Department of the UN Secretariat. Part of his opinions most likely appeared in official documents of that organization.[3] However, he articulated his more personal views as a response to invitations as a consultant, or as an invited lecturer to developing countries.

Probably the best point of departure for a detailed and analytical exposition of his ideas is his paper on "The problem of financing economic development", the result of a lecture he gave in 1953 at the Centro de Estudios Monetarios Latinoamericanos, Mexico City (Kalecki 1954b [1993]). In this paper, his objective is to study the problem of financing economic development; but his analysis is also an inquiry into the factors that limit capital accumulation and long-run growth in underdeveloped economies. We will select paragraphs of this paper which convey his analytical approach; and afterwards we will make some general remarks on Kalecki's ideas.

First, the author specifies the institutional and structural assumptions of the economy he is going to study. He distinguished three main social classes: "capitalists, workers and small proprietors. The last group includes poorer peasants, artisans, small shopkeepers, etc..." (Kalecki 1954b [1993]: 23). He also "...subdivide[s] the economy into two sectors producing investment and consumption goods, respectively [Departments I and II, respectively]. In each sector [he] include[s] the production of the respective commodities from the lowest stage" (Ibid). Department II is further split into agricultural and non-agricultural consumption goods.

Kalecki then criticizes the view whereby it is "the lack of adequate markets [that is] the main obstacle to development rather than inflation. The problem was usually formulated as follows. In view of the small internal demand, there will be no outlet for the products of the newly built factories. Thus industrialization will prove impossible unless it is oriented towards external markets. The answer to this problem is (...) if investment is sufficiently high, it pushes the demand for consumption goods up to the point where the surplus of these goods in Department II meets the higher demand of workers and capitalists in Department I. In this way it is the high level of investment itself that generates demand for consumption goods" (Kalecki 1954b [1993]: 29). Kalecki's view is based on the principle of effective demand, and it is stated in much more precise terms than in the case of other founding fathers of development economics, such as Rosenstein-Rodan (1943) and Nurkse (1953).

Kalecki also notes that "Investment may be limited…by the unwillingness of entrepreneurs to expand their capital expenditures. In such a situation, public investment acquires a crucial importance for the process of rapid economic development" (Kalecki 1954b [1993]: 27). He then goes on to identify inflationary pressures as the main obstacle arising in underdeveloped countries when investment accelerates. Indeed, "in some sectors of Department II the supply of consumption goods may be elastic and in some it is rigid. An important instance of this situation in underdeveloped countries is the case where the supply of industrial consumption goods is elastic because considerable reserves of productive capacity exist or because it may not require a very large investment to increase that capacity. On the other hand, the supply of food may be fairly rigid. This will depend on the fact that under the conditions prevailing in underdeveloped countries food production expands in response to demand less than in developed countries" (Ibid: 28). Later he expanded on this view arguing: "The point is that in an underdeveloped economy agricultural production is beset with a variety of limitations, which would prevent it from growing at a high rate even if all material resources were available. These powerful obstacles to the development of agriculture are the feudal or semi-feudal relations in land tenure as well as the domination of the poor peasants by merchants and moneylenders. Thus a radical acceleration of the development of agriculture is impossible if substantial institutional changes are not introduced" (Kalecki 1966b [1993]: 18).[4]

Kalecki then states: "It may be shown that in some instances the rigidity of the supply of food may lead to the underutilization of non-food consumption goods. This will not be the case if the peasants profit from the increases in food prices, because they will buy more industrial goods out of their higher incomes. However, if the benefits of higher food prices accrue to landlords, merchants, or moneylenders, then the reduction in real wages due to the increase in food prices will not have, as a counterpart, an increased demand for mass consumption goods on the part of the countryside; for the increased profits will not be spent at all, or will be spent on luxuries". (Kalecki 1954b [1993]: 29).

Kalecki then compares the effects of two alternative shocks to his model: an increase in agricultural production, and a rise in labour productivity. "While an adequate food supply is of basic importance in preventing inflation...the increases in industrial productivity work in the same direction. There is, however, an important difference. An increase in the supply of food tends to raise real wages at a given level of non-agricultural employment. On the other hand, an increase in productivity tends to increase real wages through a reduction of the level of employment corresponding to a given level of non-agricultural production." (Ibid: 30). Moreover, "if there is a rise in the degree of monopoly which causes a shift to profits...the rise in prices in relation to wages will reduce effective demand and prevent the full utilization of productive facilities...The final result will be a shift in the distribution of income from wages and agricultural incomes to industrial profits" (Ibid: 32).

Kalecki's analysis is clear, and we need not expand on it.[5] On the basis of his statements, we can single out Kalecki's distinctive approach to development economics. To start with, it may be useful to contrast his analysis with the one put forward by A.W. Lewis's (1954) classic paper.

The reader may recall that Lewis proposed a model of a dual economy in which a modern (industrial) sector coexists with a backward (agricultural) sector. Industrial marginal labour productivity is decreasing but higher than productivity in agriculture. Real industrial wages depend on, and are set at a higher level than, the subsistence wage of agricultural workers. At that level industrial firms can employ as many people as they want, and they will hire workers up to the point where their real wage equals industrial productivity. Lower real wages entail higher industrial profits and all profits are automatically reinvested. Thus, the higher the difference between average industrial productivity and average real industrial wages, the higher the rate of industrial growth and the faster the agricultural labour surplus will be absorbed.

Now, Kalecki did not assume that all profits will be reinvested; neither did he postulate that a higher profit share will necessarily enhance the growth rate of investment and output and bring about a faster absorption of the labour surplus. There are many reasons for this. One is that even if they fetch high profits, firms may be reluctant to invest. Another one is related to the effect of higher profit shares on aggregate demand, total profits and output; a point neglected by Lewis. The latter assumes that higher *profit shares* will go along with higher *absolute profits*, higher profit rate, and higher rate of accumulation. In fact, he goes as far as to argue that a fall in the standard of living of the rural poor will have a positive effect on industrial profits, because it will lower urban wages. This will augment profits and thus will tend to enhance the rate of economic growth and the absorption of the labour surplus.

Kalecki's view is entirely different. A higher profit share – brought about either by the fall of urban wages or by the rise of the degree of monopoly – will not necessarily translate into higher absolute profits. The latter will not rise when wages fall *unless capitalist consumption or investment simultaneously rises*. Moreover, a rise of the standard of living of poor peasants will have a beneficial influence on effective demand and employment on two counts. On the one hand it will expand the agricultural market for industrial consumer goods. Besides that, it will stimulate a rise in real wages which will expand demand for consumer goods in the urban areas.

By the same token, it is only when higher agricultural prices benefit poor peasants that aggregate demand and output will be raised. If the higher profit share in the countryside ensuing from higher agricultural prices is fetched only by landlords, merchants and moneylenders, this will not bring about higher consumption and investment. This is one of the economic reasons why Kalecki strongly advocated for agrarian reform.

In the paragraphs previously presented, Kalecki raised several additional points, which were not taken up, or were considered in a different way by the pioneers of development economics. We will now refer to three issues: i) the presence, and economic importance, of idle capacity in underdeveloped countries, ii) the effects of higher labour productivity on economic growth and iii) the problem of inflation.

When Kalecki formulated the principle of effective demand, by implication he made a thorough rejection of the efficiency criterion hidden in an outlook that sees massive unemployment of people and machines as a natural result; and explains this situation as a consequence of the lack of economic value of the unemployed resources.[6] On the contrary, he considered that idle resources are the consequence of a systemic failure. We find the same idea in his analysis of underdeveloped economies; and he was one of the very few pioneers of development economics to stress that although capital equipment is scarce in backward economies, a part of it may nevertheless remain idle.[7] Furthermore, when labour unemployment goes together with idle capacity utilization, he emphasized the possibility of tapping these resources to accelerate economic growth without, or at a low, cost. Thus, from the point of view of the interest of the economy as a whole he considered that is better to put idle resources into use rather than to keep them unemployed.

However, Kalecki did not think that, in conditions of unemployment, higher productivity itself was a panacea. When a rise in labour productivity is accompanied by a simultaneous and proportional rise in wages, the degree of monopoly does not change. If capitalist consumption and investment do not rise, then aggregate demand and output will remain constant; which will entail lower employment because productivity is higher. Moreover, if the lower unit labour costs ensuing from higher labour productivity are not passed-on to consumers through proportionate price reductions, or if they are not accompanied by proportionate higher wages, the degree of monopoly will rise. Then, for a given level of capitalist consumption and investment, effective demand and output will fall; and the reduction of employment will be greater.[8]

Finally, Kalecki can be also credited for proposing a novel theory of inflation in developing economies, whereby inflation arises because food production is supply-inelastic to prices. Note that inelasticity of supply is not only a short-run, but also a long-run phenomenon. It results from the institutional set-up of this sector, and the limited role of higher prices and higher relative productivity on supply. Moreover, inflation appears before industry reaches a stage of full utilization of capacity, and it does not contribute to raising utilization; it may even reduce effective demand and utilization. Note, Kalecki's ideas on the subject were taken up by Latin American economists, who formulated a structuralist theory of inflation in the 1950s and 1960s (Noyola 1956, Sunkel 1960).

The intermediate economic regime[9]

Kalecki's contribution to the theory of underdevelopment was not limited to economic matters. In the framework of underdeveloped economies, he identified a type of state emerging from political emancipation in which power is taken over by middle-class representatives. The key characteristic of this type of state is that it is constituted as an "intermediate regime"; in between the developed capitalist economies and socialist centrally planned economies.[10] These regimes emerged after World War II as a consequence of struggle against colonialism and other imperialist forms of domination, during a period when both in developed capitalist countries and in the socialist ones state intervention and economic planning became widespread.

Under those international circumstances, of the emergence of new independent nations and of anti-imperialist governments, and of strong state intervention, Kalecki posited that governments led by representatives of the lower middle-class, would have to fulfil some conditions for their permanence. "To keep in power they must: i) Achieve not only political but also economic emancipation, i.e. gain a measure of independence from foreign capital. ii) Carry out land reform. iii) Assure continuous economic growth; this last point is closely connected with the other two" (Kalecki 1964b [1993]: 6–7).

This type of analysis, linking, on the one hand, the social constituency of political power and the corresponding regime with, on the other hand, the path of economic development, is a prominent feature of Kalecki's thought. Like some Latin American economists, he posited that the economic paths countries opt for, and their distinctive characteristics – in terms of the investment and income distribution profiles – are not over-determined by the economic structures. Rather, they depend on correlations among groups, sectors and social classes in power, the insertion of the governments in the international field, and the regimes the elites attempt to establish.

The pattern or type of development the economies pursue depends, to a great extent, on how social and political processes are intertwined with those strictly economical. Kalecki pointed out that intermediate regimes could prosper in their efforts to achieve development through state intervention by the existence of circumstances such as the following. The lower middle-class will not be subject to the will and interests of large corporations, while *top* segments of the same class are weak and incapable of taking up the role of the "dynamic entrepreneurs". At the same time, competition among socialist and developed capitalist countries for influencing the intermediate regimes gave birth to possibilities of foreign credits with lesser degrees of domestic economic political conditioning (Kalecki 1964b [1993]: 8). These circumstances widened the possibility of a capitalism based on public enterprises and organizations, on investment-led policies, on creation and utilization of productive capacity, as well as on re-distribution of income.

The examples of characteristic intermediate regimes were India and Egypt, to which Kalecki added Bolivia. This last one was anomalous because of the high participation of mine-workers in the government born from the 1952 revolution (Kalecki and Kula, in Kalecki 1970 [1993]: 169–173). The changes in the domestic correlation of the social forces in power, along with their international alliances – some of them not aligned to any bloc; others aligned to one of the big blocs – drove the intermediate regimes through different paths of economic policy.

To conclude, there are at least two important lessons we may draw for developing countries, in terms of the design of a progressive socio-economic strategy.

On one hand, for governments that represent the interests of "dynamic entrepreneurs", middle classes', workers' and other important groups of the population, the room for manoeuvre for state intervention is a function of the possibilities of international agreements and alliances concerning the mobility of foreign capital. This is a first lesson when favourable conditions are searched for an investment pattern capable of ensuring sustained economic growth.

On the other hand, governments representing social group coalitions that are formed to support economic policies that favour development and the progressive redistribution of income must recognize the limits emerging from the lack of political competition among international economic blocs. The second Kaleckian lesson can thus be formulated in the following fashion: whenever there are diverse conceptions between the international dominant economic blocs about what must be done to foster growth in underdeveloped countries, the possibilities of carrying out affirmative and effective actions are widened. Korea might be a good example of how the divergent conceptions about economic development in the 1970s between the US and Japan favoured a higher bargaining power for state intervention.

Development strategy

Based on Kalecki's ideas outlined in the preceding section, as well as others taken from what he wrote, we will now study how he envisaged a growth strategy for a developing economy. This is a somewhat speculative exercise, because the author never formulated a specific proposal. Nevertheless, when he discussed the problems of developing economies, and even more so when he acted as an invited consultant, he provided many insights on how he visualized an economic strategy. We will put the stress on an underdeveloped semi-industrialized economy because it will allow us to combine three theoretical lines developed by such author. Indeed, as Sachs puts it, "Kalecki's unique position in contemporary economic thought rests on his seminal contributions to each of the three main areas of political economy: the dynamics of monopoly capitalism, growth under socialism and the theory and practice of development planning in mixed economies" (Sachs 1977: 47). With this exercise we will try to show the validity and currency of Kalecki's theoretical framework for the study of underdeveloped economies.

We shall be led, to a great extent, by the study Kalecki carried out for the Israeli economy (Kalecki 1951 [1993]). In our judgement, such a study is of great importance for two reasons. First, because it is the only work in which the author explicitly considers the case of what we nowadays call a semi-industrialized economy. Second, because here Kalecki formulates a series of strategies and economic policy proposals for a capitalist economy with State intervention. In other words, he is proposing measures that could be undertaken in a mixed economy. In the next chapter we discuss his proposals for an advanced capitalist economy.

In the first place, Kalecki did not consider that only a little government intervention would be enough. He proposed far-reaching radical changes. In his words:

> It is frequently maintained that all problems could be solved at one stroke by abolishing foreign exchange restrictions and domestic controls...The measures recommended below go in exactly the opposite direction. It is advocated that the greatest possible effort should be made to reduce imports and to increase exports and thus to rely as little as possible on import of foreign capital, while maintaining the strictest possible exchange restrictions. These measures for improving the current balance of payments will require a much larger degree of government supervision and interference than has hitherto been the case. (1951 [1993]: 98–99)

General remarks

As a previous step, it is convenient to say that semi-industrialized economies occupy an intermediate place between those of advanced capitalism and those really underdeveloped, which are the ones Kalecki paid most attention to in his theoretical and applied works; and share some of the characteristics of both. We will point out two of their features which resemble more the underdeveloped ones. First, it is not possible to eliminate unemployment in the short- and medium-run, even when the countries fully utilize their capital equipment.

Second, in such economies the income-elasticity of demand for food is high. At the same time, the elasticity of agricultural supply is low in the short-run, and even in the medium-run; due to institutional factors. Accordingly, when per-capita income grows, in many underdeveloped countries, strong inflationary pressures or external deficits, or both, arise. More than four decades have elapsed since Kalecki pointed out this situation; but unfortunately in many underdeveloped, and even semi-industrialized economies, the institutional obstacles to agricultural production are still present.

Nevertheless, semi-industrialized economies resemble also the fully developed ones because, though capital equipment is not so large, usually an important proportion of the productive capacity is not used; especially in the manufacturing sector. Referring to the Israeli economy, Kalecki observed: "It should be stressed, however, with regard to the shortage of equipment that in some branches of industry considerable unused capacity exists. The position in such cases is roughly as follows. The home consumption of the goods manufactured in these not fully used establishments cannot be increased because this would involve higher imports, while exports of these goods have not yet been developed" (Kalecki 1951 [1993]: 98).[11] In this sense, these economies differentiate themselves from those properly underdeveloped in that in the latter, despite the existence of idle capacity, their significance is minor. Idle capacity is an important feature and constitutes a central premise in which a short-run proposal for a semi-industrialized economy could be based, inspired in Kalecki's theory.

Now, Kalecki was of the idea that three conditions must be fulfilled if mixed economies are to achieve a high and sustained output growth rate: i) control on foreign trade and financial operations, ii) control over private investment in order to avoid undesirable projects and readiness of the State to carry out priority projects and iii) price stability, except for corrections from variations in the terms of trade. In particular, since foreign trade can be helpful to overcome most internal bottlenecks, all operations in foreign currency deserve careful handling by the State. Taking these premises as point of departure, we will now outline a growth strategy, distinguishing the short-run and the long-run aspects.

Economic growth in the short-run

It follows from what we said previously that the existence of idle capacity in semi-industrialized economies implies that output could grow significantly in the short-run. A first requirement is obviously the growth of effective demand. In his classic article about economic policies in advanced capitalist economies, Kalecki (1944a [1990]) considered three ways of achieving sufficient growth of (internal) demand so as to ensure full employment of both labour force and capital equipment. Namely:

1. By government spending on public investment (...) or subsidies to mass consumption (...) – provided this spending is financed by borrowing. We shall call this method deficit spending.
2. By stimulating private investment (...).
3. By redistribution of income from higher- to lower-income classes. (Kalecki 1944a [1990]: 357)

Kalecki was not so optimistic about the possibility of founding growth on stimulating private investment. Nonetheless, he was a strong supporter of income redistribution for social-justice reasons, but also due to the favourable impact of such redistribution on demand and employment. In many works he considered the advantages of a wage rise above labour productivity rise (Kalecki 1971 [1991]). But he also observed that in certain less developed countries "(...) white-collar workers and the not very numerous workers of large establishments (...) in underdeveloped countries are in a privileged position as compared with urban and rural paupers (...)" (Kalecki 1964b [1993]: 8).

The previous observation is a first antecedent that suggests that, in the author's view, income redistribution through a generalized rise of wages does not seem to be the best solution.[12] Such rises do not directly benefit the poorest, which in many cases are not employed by formal firms, but rather are peasants with little or no land at all, self-employed workers or employed by informal business; and, in fact, it could even do much harm to them if such rises are transmitted to prices of basic goods. A second antecedent about the best way of redistributing income, is that Kalecki (1944a [1990]) emphasized that public spending can actually have a great redistributive impact, for it can be channelled to the most exposed groups in a more precise way.

As we discussed in Chapter 6, when dealing with how to finance greater public spending, Kalecki (1937 [1990]) supported public deficits, but he also noticed that deficits cause an increase of profits together with demand; and hence do not contribute to improved income distribution. This is a quite serious limitation in semi-industrialized economies, where income can be very highly concentrated.

For such reason Kalecki was, above all, a supporter of stimulating effective demand through public spending financed with taxes levied on high income sectors, because this sort of financing does not increase profits. In a work specifically referred to developing economies, Kalecki pointed out two additional advantages of public spending financed through taxes on profits.

> The reduction of capitalists' consumption will also be beneficial from the point of view of the balance of payments, because it will reduce the demand for imported luxuries (...) In addition to limiting capitalists' consumption, financing public investment by taxation presents still another advantage. It reduces the creation of liquid assets (...). If (...) an inflation spiral has been in existence for some time, the large amount of liquid assets will stimulate speculative hoarding and thus will help to aggravate the primary inflationary process. (Kalecki 1954b [1993]: 41)

In his study of the Israeli economy Kalecki referred to an additional problem related to the accumulation of liquid assets, namely: "The accumulation of unspent liquid funds, combined with the uncertainty of the future official rate of exchange, creates a natural tendency for illegal transfers abroad which depress the Israeli pound in the black market in foreign exchange. Such a black market is the common experience of countries with a strained balance of payments necessitating the maintenance of exchange restrictions" (Kalecki 1951 [1993]: 97).

All in all, we can conclude that, in Kalecki's vision, the reanimation of effective demand should be based on a rise of public spending financed with taxes on profits. Such public spending should prioritize investment, ensuring that "whenever private investment fails, the government steps in so that total investment reaches the desirable level" (Kalecki 1966b [1993]: 16]. Moreover, government expenditure should subsidize the groups with the lowest incomes.

However, a rapid and sustained economic recovery, especially if supported by a high level of employment, generates a great demand for food supplies, meanwhile the internal supply of agricultural goods faces obstacles. He recognized that some measures could "expand agricultural production in the short-term. These measures range from land reform and cheap bank credit to peasants to improvements in the method of cultivation, small-scale irrigation, and cheap fertilizers." (Kalecki 1954b [1993]: 30). If the agricultural output does not rise much, prices may tend to grow and income distribution worsens. If there exists external trade of agricultural goods, the acceleration of growth will go hand-in-hand with a fall of exports of agricultural goods, or with a raise of imports of the same.

More generally, an economic recovery will normally put the trade balance in jeopardy. The response of conventional economics to the problem of the deterioration of the external balance is to counteract such a tendency by improving competitiveness through devaluation of the exchange rate. However, Kalecki recommended different solutions. In his words:

> Considerable excess capacity exists in Israel (...) in such light industries as textiles, apparel, shoes, leather goods, etc. This capacity could be mobilized for exports, provided markets were found for such products abroad (...) However (...) Israel goods of this type are too expensive and require considerable export premiums. It is essential that such premiums be granted, even if they should amount to a relatively high percentage of the value added. Export premiums should nevertheless be kept as low as possible and other inducements should also be used for expanding exports. The allocation of raw materials for production for the home market should be made dependent on the export performance of firms so that they will be encouraged to export at prices lower than those achieved on the home market. (Kalecki 1951 [1993]: 100)

Investment and long-run growth

As we have mentioned time and time again, Kalecki was of the idea that the crucial problem of the underdeveloped economy was to raise its rate of accumulation. We will study now how he envisioned this issue in economies with abundant supply of labour. He argued on this point referring to a socialist economy; but his vision is also valid for mixed economies. His model (Kalecki 1963 [1993]) is a very simple one; let i be the rate of (gross) investment, and k the technical capital–output ratio (i.e., the number of units of capital effectively in use needed to produce a unit of output). Let d be the rate of depreciation, and u the *extra* annual rate of growth of production which a country could get if it uses more and better existing capital equipment (we express i, u and d as ratios to GDP). We denote by r the rate of growth of productive capacity and we specify a long-term growth model as follows:

$$r = \frac{i}{k} + u - d \qquad (8.1)$$

This simple formula shows that, given k, u and d, productive capacity can grow only if the share of investment rises. But Kalecki also emphasized that k, u and d are parameters which a country can modify with economic policy measures. Thus, it can raise *u* by using more (and better) capital equipment. Also, by lengthening the life-span of the capital equipment it can reduce *d*. Finally, it can decrease the capital – output ratio *k* having recourse to more labour-intensive techniques.[13]

From the previous formula, it is clear that in Kalecki's vision, to adequately conduct investment to where it can have better positive effects, or to carry it out with appropriate technologies, could be even more important than making it grow at very high rates. More specifically, he recommended prioritizing fixed capital investments necessary to make a greater and better possible utilization of the inherited, and oldest, capital equipment, to lengthen its useful life.[14] At the same time, when possible, he proposed to choose productive techniques which could decrease the capital – output ratio of new investments (*k*).

Let us consider a growth process based on the increase of the coefficient *u*, or the reduction of the coefficients *k* and/or *d*. In this case, the investment rate will be lower with respect to another strategy that favours the creation of new factories, or that is based on investments on capital-intensive technologies. Therefore, in the short-run, consumption, or its growth rate, will not be reduced, or will be reduced less, in the case of the first strategy.

There are also costs associated with a strategy like the one suggested following Kalecki's ideas. Particularly, if economic growth is largely based on a greater utilization of the oldest equipment, or if it is carried out thanks to less capital-intensive investments, then the level (or the growth rate) of labour productivity will be reduced and thus the demand for manpower will increase.

Therefore, the highest cost to pay in order to achieve growth with a strategy based on a greater utilization of idle capacity comes in the form of lower labour productivity growth rates and thus higher employment requirements. But this is a cost semi-industrialized economies can afford, since in all of them labour unemployment is, in general, widespread. It is only afterwards, once the labour surplus has been absorbed, that a country should shift to a strategy aimed at raising the rate of growth of labour productivity.

It would then seem that an economy which has idle capital and manpower resources, and is able to choose less capital-intensive techniques, could grow at spectacularly high rates. Somehow, this is not the case. There are limits for long-term growth associated with the obstacles they face when they try to accelerate the expansion rates of agriculture, on the one hand, and to the difficulties in ensuring a high growth of exports, on the other hand.

Kalecki emphasized that a high rhythm of economic growth goes hand-to-hand with high growth rates of demand for food. He also insisted on the institutional barriers that hamper production expansion in underdeveloped capitalist economies. He saw a well-designed and implemented agrarian reform as a precondition for high and stable long-term growth. Nonetheless, he also considered that the agricultural sector is clearly "supply-determined". The following remarks by Kalecki refer to a socialist economy, where the institutional barriers have been overcome, but nonetheless structural barriers limit grow:

> An important distinction has to be made between two types of industries (...) We shall call these two categories supply-determined and demand-determined industries. By supply determined industries we mean such activities which have a certain ceiling for the long-run growth rate for technical and organizational reasons, so that even considerable increase in capital outlay will not raise their output at a higher rate...
>
> The technological and organizational factors on which, in turn, the ceilings of the growth rate of the supply-determined industries depend are of a very varied nature. Limited natural resources are the simplest and most obvious example. The time necessary for the adaptation to new technological progress is another example. The most serious difficulties in the way of introducing new techniques are probably encountered in agriculture, where there is always a certain element of spontaneity in the development of production. (1962d [1992]: 225)

It may be argued that the deficit in the internal supply of agricultural goods may be paid out with exports of other tradable goods with high elasticity of supply. In consequence, a rapid economic growth accompanied by a disequilibrium in foreign trade of agricultural goods could be financed with manufactured exports.[15] The problem, however, is that to make foreign sales grow at high and stable rates could be difficult.

Indeed, with well-conceived and well-managed subsidies, a country could make production profitable and competitive. However beyond certain limits the benefits of subsidies become progressively lower. When import requirements grow, and exports have to follow suit, "It may be virtually impossible to place the exports in the foreign markets (...) As a result of the pressure of supply of the products in question, their average prices may fall to such an extent as to make it impossible to achieve the revenue of foreign exchange required for purchasing the necessary imports. Or (...) it may require very high capital outlays in relation to the effects in terms of foreign exchange" (Kalecki 1962d [1992]: 227).

Now, to finish our presentation, we must recognize that from certain point of view, the strategy founded on Kalecki's view, which favours investment devoted to making possible a fuller use of the oldest equipment even as they extend their lifetime, and embodying labour-intensive techniques, may bring a deceleration of technological progress. However, with respect to this, the author's argument raised on this point in his study of the Israeli economy is still valid,

> especially [when] (...) there is no scarcity of labour (...) modernization (...) which would aim at saving labour, does not make much sense from the point of view of the interest of the economy as a whole. It may be argued that modernization is necessary in order to reduce costs and thus increase the ability to compete abroad, which would increase exports. Nevertheless, from the point of view of saving foreign currency, which is the scarcest factor in the Israeli economy, it is much more reasonable to pay export premiums, however unnatural such a subsidization of obsolete methods of production might appear. (Kalecki 1951 [1993]: 103)

Final Remarks

We have shown that Kalecki made important contributions to development economics, both from the point of view of understanding their particular and most relevant features and their way of functioning, and from the perspective of planning their development. We do not claim that he covered the whole field, but he laid the grounds for further theoretical developments in this area of economics.

In contradistinction to other pioneers of development economics, Kalecki did not stress the international forces that hamper development, but put the accent rather on the internal institutions and social and political determinants. In particular, the feudal and semi-feudal conditions in agriculture, the reduced market ensuing from income concentration and widespread monopolization of the economy, and the lack of willingness of entrepreneurs to carry out the necessary investments. Accordingly, his economic policy recommendations emphasized also the internal aspects involved.

We have discussed in some detail the economic policy measures he advocated and the long-run investment strategy that we can infer from his writings. As most socialist economists of his time, Kalecki was quite sceptical about the possibilities of emerging from underdevelopment under capitalism. Nevertheless, with hindsight we can see that in fact some underdeveloped countries, most notably from East Asia, have managed to overcome economic backwardness. But we could also claim that their success was made possible because most of these economies undertook radical agrarian reforms before they could embark on a fast development path, because they all carried out measures very similar to those recommended by Kalecki, and because in all of them the State played a leading role.

This last point is not a minor one. Ultimately, all the measures, and the whole strategy advocated by the author involved a strong intervention of the State into the economy. This is not surprising, because he was an important contributor to one of the most ingenious and rigorous macroeconomic strategy proposals put forward immediately after World War II to overcome unemployment in capitalism. Thus we will end our work quoting the final statement from that study. It refers to a developed economy, but the idea is also valid, and in our view *a fortiori*, for an underdeveloped one.

> It is obvious that full employment will require a greater degree of Government control in economic affairs than has been the rule in the past. And it is this extension of the power of the State which causes apprehension. But the alternative to the controls which full employment brings is not some ideal state of full employment without controls, but unemployment and trade fluctuations. The more sophisticated, and economically the more fortunate, may argue that unemployment is the price of freedom from control, and as such can be tolerated. But it is a false argument. In the first place, sectional controls were prevalent in unemployment... Secondly, the argument ignores the question of hidden controls. In this sense unemployment is the most powerful of all economic controls. (The Oxford University Institute of Statistics 1947: 204–205)

9
Kalecki: The Socialist Economist

Kalecki was a convinced socialist during his whole lifetime. He was part of that fascinating group of Central and Eastern European intellectuals that suffered directly from the ravages ensuing from the great crisis of the 1930s, who were greatly influenced by Marx's ideas. We must keep in mind, though, that during the formative years of that group, Marxism was a very vital intellectual current. Outside of the Soviet Union and the communist parties – of which Kalecki was never a member[1] – there was not an "official" Marxist school of thought, with enough power to impose its own theoretical vision above the rest.

The objective of this chapter is twofold. On the one hand, we want to discuss how Kalecki's theory fits in with Marx's, and with Marxian economic thinking. In this context, we will discuss why, in spite of his background, Kalecki's approach did not leave an imprint on Marxian economic ideas, and why his theories were, and still are, received with suspicion by many Marxist economists. On the other hand, we want to analyse Kalecki's proposals to reform capitalism. Kalecki wrote only a few pieces on this issue, and his opinions on reform proposals put forward by other authors are also rather scant. From what he wrote, it will be seen that he had very definite ideas and a very radical outlook. In fact, from today's perspective his ideas may look too radical. However, we must recall that during those times such a radical outlook was common to great number of social thinkers, and that many "left Keynesians" put forward ideas not too distant from those in which Kalecki believed.

Kalecki and Marxian economics

Let us first of all link Kalecki's and Marx's theories; not with the purpose of giving him a "Marxist" credential, but rather to show how in some general principles formulated by Marx, one finds in embryo the theory of effective demand, as well as some points later developed by Kalecki (and by modern heterodox economists). It is our contention that had Marxists followed the path opened by Kalecki (and by other similar "iconoclasts"), they would have been able to develop a much more interesting economic theory.

Realization and effective demand

We begin with a comparison between Kalecki's theory of effective demand with the so-called problem of realization of Marxist economic thought taking first a purely national accounts perspective. Consider a private, closed economy in conditions of "expanded reproduction".[2] Following Kalecki, we will suppose that all the sectors of this economy are vertically integrated; and we will also assume that workers are paid at the end of the production period.

Using Marx's categories, we can state the problem as follows. At the beginning of any productive period, the capitalists possess a certain endowment of means of production and hire a labour force. At the end of a productive period, part of the means of production has been used up. In their place, the capitalists now have commodities, which must be sold. The entirety of these commodities is equivalent to the global (gross) output; which, in terms of value, can be separated into constant capital, variable capital and surplus value (or, simplifying, net profits).

The realization of these commodities takes place in the course of the process of circulation. Its starting point is the money which the capitalists throw into the market, a part of which they use to replace the machinery and equipment worn out during this period. This expenditure (and demand) serves to realize that part of the constant capital included in the global product corresponding to depreciation. Another part of this money is used to pay the labour force hired. The workers spend all of their wages to buy the necessities of life which they themselves have produced during the period of production. Through this expenditure (and demand) the variable capital is realized. In the third place, the capitalists spend money for their personal consumption and to expand their endowment of the means of production. Through the latter two types of expenditures, as much for their personal consumption as for their (net) accumulation, the capitalists realize the surplus value (or net profit) contained in the global product. Therefore, the surplus value is realized through the consumption of capitalists and their accumulation or net investment.[3]

As we can see, there is almost a one-to-one correspondence between Kalecki's and Marx's conceptions of how output and profits are realized. And in fact, Kalecki used Marx's schemes of reproduction to illustrate his theory whereby profits equal capitalist consumption plus their investment (Kalecki 1939a [1990]: 252–255, and 1968b [1991]). However, the Marxian foundations of Kalecki's approach go beyond purely accounting principles.

Indeed, even though Marx did not formulate a theory of effective demand, he established certain fundamental, very general principles which could serve as a basis for such a formulation. These principles are embedded in what Sweezy (1942) called the qualitative aspect of the theory of value, and which were taken up in Kalecki's theoretical construct. Synthetically, the idea is the following. In capitalism, which is a developed mode of commodity production, the products of labour appear as "commodities", that is, as goods which are produced for others. Thus, the search for a profit, which is contained in the prince of production of the commodities but which can only be obtained from its sale, will be the incentive to production.

The topic of effective demand is directly related to Marx's proposition of capitalism as a fully developed mode of commodity production. The labour contained in the sum of commodities produced – the total product – only reveals itself as socially necessary if commodities are realized; that is, sold at their prices of production. But this is far from certain.

Moreover, both authors identify investment demand (or accumulation, in Marx's parlance), as the moving force of the capitalist economy. As we saw in previous chapters, Kalecki argued that in a capitalist economy nothing guarantees that output is produced at a level compatible with the full employment of the productive forces. Marx was well aware of this possibility.[4] As Kalecki (1968b [1991]: 465) put it, "Marx was deeply conscious of the impact of effective demand upon the dynamics of the capitalist system follows clearly from this passage of the third volume of Capital 'The conditions of direct exploitation and those of the realization of surplus value are not the same. They are separated not only by time and space, but also logically. The first ones are merely limited by the productive capacity of society, the second ones by the proportion of the various branches of production and by the consumer power of the society'. However, he did not systematically scrutinize the process described by his reproductions schemes from the point of view of the contradiction inherent in capitalism as a result of the problem of effective demand".

Marx's insistence on the difficulty of realizing the surplus value contained in the sum total of commodities led at least one of his followers, Rosa Luxemburg, to strongly deny that expanded reproduction could take place in capitalism. Her denial followed from her notion that capitalists had no reason to accumulate, because they knew beforehand that the surplus value could not be realized. Therefore, realization of profits could only take place through foreign trade, through exchange with non-capitalist sectors of any given country, or thanks to government purchases of goods and services (e.g., in armaments).

Kalecki was a great admirer of Luxemburg's work. He recognized that in her quest for the motives of expanded reproduction, she emphasized the essential role of capital accumulation, which led naturally towards a theory of investment decisions. He also thought highly of her intuition on the role of foreign markets and government expenditure in the realization of profits. But he rejected her overall conclusion about the impossibility of expanded reproduction in capitalism. He also proved that it is not total exports, or total government expenditure, which contribute to raise profits, but only a trade surplus, and a budget deficit. He concluded: "Rosa Luxemburg ... stressed the point that, if capitalists are saving, their profits will be 'realized' only if a corresponding amount is spent by them on investment ... the necessity of covering the 'savings gap' by home investment or exports was outlined by her perhaps more clearly than anywhere else before the publication of Mr. Keynes's General Theory" (Kalecki 1939a [1990]: 255).

Theories of value and of distribution

We will contrast now Kalecki's and Marx's theories of distribution. As an antecedent, let us first recall that, according to Marx's "law of value",[5] prices are only a transfigured form of values, which are determined by the total amount of labour, socially necessary to produce a commodity. Prices in particular sectors will deviate upwards (downwards) from values, whenever the "organic composition of capital"[6] in the sector is above (below) the average. However, in the aggregate, the surplus value, as well as variable capital and constant capital, will have the same magnitude if they are expressed in values or in prices. Also it would follow that capitalist profit is quantitatively equivalent to the unpaid work. Capitalists can exploit workers because they can pay them a wage which though equivalent of the "value" of their labour power, is below the "value" of what they produce.

Further, in Marx's approach, income distribution is determined, ultimately, by the struggle and the strength of capitalists and workers.

The rate of surplus value, equivalent, *grosso modo*, to the relation between net profits and the wage bill, is determined by the productivity and the real wage per worker. The first is considered as a given for purposes of analysis; the second, however, converges towards the value of labour power, which depends on "historical and moral" factors and which can change over the medium or long term.

However, in Marx's analysis, changes in the real wage and in the rate of surplus value appear to be determined exclusively in the labour market. Let us state this in another way: in Marx's theory of distribution, prices seem to play a passive role, in the sense that, he works with the (implicit) assumption that businesses are "price-takers", and that they cannot influence the latter.

It is well-known, particularly after Sraffa's (1960) work, that logical reasons do not exist to state that prices are derived from "values"; nor that profit is (quantitatively) equivalent to unpaid labour[7]; nor, lastly, that the movements of the profit rate are determined univocally by the movements of the rate of surplus value. In this sense, the Marxian "Law of value" has serious problems. Nevertheless, Marx's point can be stated in somewhat different terms. We could say that at the core of Marx's concept is the notion that in the capitalist mode of production, economic, political and social conditions are such that, the capitalist can pay the productive workers with wages which, when expressed at prices of production, are less than the net product (at its price of production) which they themselves (the workers) have produced. Or what adds up to the same thing, the capitalists obtain a profit because they can charge a price which is over and above their production costs (including wage costs).

Kalecki did never (to our knowledge) refer to the "Law of value", and he did not use it to explain the existence of a surplus accruing to capitalists. We may assume – though he never said it explicitly – that he agreed with Marx and classical economics that profits are indeed a surplus.[8] Moreover, he did not start from values to arrive at production prices, but conceived prices as determined by firms which mark-up unit prime costs. One of the arguments determining the mark up could actually be the "organic composition of capital" (a term he did not use), because those sectors with higher-than-average ratio of overheads over wages will tend to have also higher-than-average mark up. But other factors, and particularly the degree of imperfection of the sector's market, will also contribute to shape the level of the mark up.

Kalecki, however, retained the general focus of Marx and in particular the idea that the distribution of income is determined ultimately by the class struggle (see especially Kalecki 1971 [1991]). But he took into consideration the new reality of imperfect competition, as an element which is not marginal, but rather predominant, in contemporary capitalism. He also used in his approach the theories on imperfect competition which had appeared in academic thought. In his conception, businesses are now "pricemakers", in that that they can fix their prices in accord with their monopolistic control over their markets. Thus, the distribution of income is determined as much in the labour market as in the market for commodities.

How far on this particular point does Kalecki depart from Marx? We are of the opinion – not too much. In fact, we can quote here another of Marx's sentences which point in the same direction in which Kalecki developed the theory:

> The monopoly price of certain commodities would merely transfer a portion of the profit of the other producers of commodities to the commodities with a monopoly price. A local disturbance in the distribution of the surplus-value among the various spheres of production would take place indirectly, but they would leave the boundaries of the surplus-value itself unaltered. If a commodity with a monopoly price should enter into the necessary consumption of the labourer, it would increase the wages and thereby reduce the surplus-value, if the labourer would receive the value of his labour-power, the same as before. But such a commodity might also depress wages below the value of labour-power, of course only to the extent that wages would be higher than the physical minimum of subsistence. In this case the monopoly price would be paid by a deduction from the real wages...and from the profit of the other capitalists. (Marx 1993, Vol. III, Part VII, Chapter L)[9]

It is unfortunate that this intuition of Marx whereby monopoly prices may affect the distribution of income was not developed by his followers.

Profits and wages

We can now consider the connection between wages, profits and effective demand. Here, as we will see, there is a fundamental difference between Kalecki and Marx.

Of course, Marx was aware of the double role of wages in capitalism. He recognized that wages are simultaneously an element of demand and an element of costs. Now, his judgement of the effects of a change in wages on profits is very clear: in whatever circumstance, a rise (lowering) in wages provokes a fall (increase) in profits. Both variables move in an inverse direction. As we saw in the previous chapter, Kalecki's conclusion is different, since he acknowledged that a fall (rise) in wages will not bring about a rise (fall) in profits; but will rather expand demand and output such that capitalists will get a higher share of a lower output, whereby their total profits will remain constant. We may, of course, say that Kalecki's conclusion is valid only in the case of a closed economy. In the more realistic example of an open economy, an increase in wages will indeed, reduce profits, because the increase in sales of domestic businesses (equivalent to the increase in the consumption of workers) will be lower that the increment in costs (equivalent to increase in wages plus the increase in imports). Thus, we might argue that Marx was closer to the truth in regards to the negative effect of a wage rise on profits. But we should recognize that Marx was also reasoning within a closed-economy context.

Anyway, it can be seen that unlike Marx, when he studied the relation between wages and profits, Kalecki does not suppose that the total product is given. On the contrary, it changes with changes in effective demand; and the latter changes with real wages (and the real consumption of the workers). We may conclude that, on this point, the contradiction of interests between capitalists and workers is less strong in Kalecki than it was in Marx.

The destiny of capitalism

Kalecki was convinced that capitalism was essentially a contradictory social system. In his masterful piece "Political aspects of full employment", he put forward the general and political conclusion he derived from his theory, stating: "although most economists are now agreed that full employment may be achieved by government spending, this was by no means the case even in the recent past. Among the opposers of this doctrine there were (and still are) prominent so-called economic experts closely connected with banking and industry. This suggests that there is a political background in the opposition to the full employment doctrine, even though the arguments advanced are economic" (Kalecki 1943a [1990]: 349).[10]

In this paper, Kalecki argued that in contemporary capitalism a "political cycle" tends to appear, induced by "stop and go" policies of State expenditure. In a nutshell, his view was that a lasting boom would bring about political changes – fear of a greater State intervention, weakening of "worker discipline" – and economic changes – especially inflationary tendencies – which induce the capitalist class and its allies to struggle to reduce government expenditure, even though this would provoke a fall, not only of output, but also of private profits.

However, when there exists too low a level of employment, as a result of pressures from the masses or even without these pressures, capitalist governments are stimulated to intervene in order to revive the economic cycle and to reduce unemployment.[11] He therefore inferred: "The regime of the political business cycle would be an artificial restoration of the position as it existed in nineteenth-century capitalism. Full employment would be reached only at the top of the boom, but slumps would be relatively mild and short-lived" (Kalecki 1943a [1990]: 355).[12]

He then asked the following question: "Should a progressive be satisfied with a regime of political business cycles ... ? I think he should oppose to it on two grounds: (i) that it does not assure lasting full employment; (ii) that government intervention is tied to public investment and does not embrace subsidizing consumption. What the masses now ask for is not the mitigation of slumps but their total abolition. Nor should the resulting fuller utilization of resources be applied to unwanted public investment merely in order to provide work" (Ibid: 355). And he then concluded:

> "Full employment capitalism" will, of course, have to develop new social and political institutions which will reflect the increased power of the working class. If capitalism can adjust itself to full employment, a fundamental reform will have been incorporated in it. If not, it will show itself an outmoded system which must be scrapped. (Ibid: 356)

Kalecki, however, remained for a long time very skeptical about the possibility that capitalism could in fact reform itself. In his published works he did not expand much on the hypotheses proposed in his "Political Aspects". From most of what he wrote until his death, one gets the idea that he did not believe that a fundamental change had taken place (see especially Kalecki 1968c)[13]; even though most observers from that period, and contemporaneous writers, are agreed that during the three-odd decades after World War II something like full employment capitalism had in fact been in existence.

However, in one of his last (and posthumous) papers, Kalecki finally came to accept that a "crucial reform" had indeed taken place. In his words: "Let us imagine that the strong pressure of the masses leads to such a radical reform of the system, in spite of the opposition of the ruling class, that, without abolishing existing relations of production, a new valve is opened for the development of forces of production. There will then be a paradoxical situation: a 'crucial reform' imposed on the ruling class may stabilize the system, temporarily at least. As we argue below, we have to do with such a situation in contemporary capitalism" (Kalecki and Kowalik 1971 [1991]: 467).

The two authors then argued: "One can say that during the Second World War the economies of the European capitalist countries largely took the form of centrally controlled capitalism.... Following the end of the war and a short period of reconversion, however, central control of the capitalist economy weakened considerably.... The share of government expenditure in the total demand for goods and services increased considerably in comparison with the inter-war period. Besides this, in some European capitalist countries influenced the economy through nationalized industry...The Second World War accelerated the 'crucial reform' process. Government intervention in the expansion of markets became an institution, making it possible to limit unemployment to a few percent, and hence in practice to accept something similar to the 'right to work' slogan advanced by the revolution of 1948 (Kalecki and Kowalik 1971 [1991]: 472).

Thus, the authors concluded that the "crucial reform" has brought about a considerable improvement in the standard of living and on employment in contemporary capitalism, which are now considerably better than in the "laissez faire" period. But also owing to this "crucial reform", the class struggle has been attenuated, with which capitalism has achieved a greater global political stability.[14]

Conclusions

We mentioned at the beginning of this chapter that a large majority of Marxian economists were suspicious of Kalecki's economics, in spite of its closeness to Marx's overall vision of capitalism, and especially their common critical stand towards capitalism and their rejection of Say's Law. It may be useful to conclude this chapter by pointing out some reasons for this mistrust.

A first reason probably had to do with Kalecki's refusal to use Marx's law of value.[15] He always reasoned on the basis of prices; and in certain Marxian circles this is an unacceptable deviation from basic Marxian principles.

The other reasons are more significant. As also discussed, unlike Marx, Kalecki did not think that wage increases would reduce profits. Rather, higher wages would normally be passed on in prices. Alternatively, if firms could not raise prices as much as unit costs rose, then higher wages would increase sales by as much as wages rose, so that profits would not fall. For some Marxists, this might be seen perhaps as a watering down of one of the inner contradictions of capitalism, and as a support for taming the class struggle.[16] Of course, Kalecki did see class struggle, and struggle for higher wages, as very important for workers' advancement; but not so much because this would reduce profits, but rather because class struggle would bring about a shift from profits to wages, which would favour employment and enhance the bargaining power of workers.

The third reason for the coldness of Marxists vis-à-vis Kalecki is a bit more subtle. In Kalecki's different models of capitalist long-run evolution, nowhere the "law of the falling rate of profit" is given the central place accorded to it by Marx and his followers.[17] Apparently, Kalecki did not believe on the actuality of this "law", or in any case did not consider it important for the future of capitalism. In fact, in the words of one of his closest collaborators and followers, "Kalecki ... as well as most socialists, took it for granted that capitalism was threatened by a crisis of existence.... But found the reason, given by Marx, as to why such a crisis should develop, unconvincing" (Steindl 1990).

The last reason for Marxists' qualms about Kalecki's theory is closely related to the previous one. In Kalecki's theory demand management, especially through fiscal policy, might lead to something close to the demise of business fluctuations. Moreover, growing government expenditure would generate an expansive tendency; thus ensuring high growth rates in the long run. In the first place, aggregate demand would be permanently above what would have been the case if the expenditure had not existed, and in fact growth of output would be only limited by the growth of productive capacities. In the second place, unless the expenditure would be entirely financed with business profits, the levels and rate of profits, as well as the utilization of productive capacities, would also be above their "spontaneous" level, which would stimulate private investment and growth of productive capacities.

Therefore, according to Kalecki's theory, the management of demand by the government could ensure, from a technical point of view, high rates of growth of output and of employment in advanced capitalism, with only very mild cyclical fluctuations or none at all.

Beyond this technicality, this outlook points to a collision of Kalecki's vision with that of Marx and orthodox Marxism. The latter surely could not accept the idea that government intervention, and specifically intervention through government expenditure or a budget deficit, could affect the level of profits and growth. Indeed, a basic tenet of historical materialism, together with the notion that in the long run capitalism is doomed to collapse, or at least to stagnate, is the idea that the "superstructure" cannot have a *lasting* influence on the economic "structure". It is only the latter that gives rise to the inner laws of movement capitalism.

Now, if state expenditure can in fact influence the volume of profits and national income then, on a certain vision, those inner laws could somehow be changed, or even violated. For example, the law of the rate of profit to fall could be counteracted by deficit spending. More in general, the general crisis of capitalism, which might have been delayed somewhat but would sooner or later come into view, could be avoided through government intervention.

Kalecki the radical reformer

The general outlook

In his celebrated "Three ways to full employment", Kalecki (1944a [1990]) developed his most detailed reflection on how a radically reformed capitalist society should carry out a full-employment policy. He started with the consideration that the major problem of economies stuck in a situation of underemployment equilibrium is to overcome the problem of the deficiency of effective demand by finding markets for the output that could or would be produced at full utilization of resources. Kalecki's arguments then concentrates on the relative merits of i) deficit spending, ii) stimulating private investment, and iii) redistributing income from higher to lower income groups; and remarks that these three means are not equally satisfactory. Especially, he asserts that ii), as compared with both i) and iii) when they are supported by appropriate monetary policy, does not provide adequate means for a permanent maintenance of full employment. To fully grasp Kalecki's outlook, it is worth distinguishing, on the one hand the question of the *level*, and on the other the question of the *content* of output and employment. While the three ways may be equal as regards the first question, they however may give rise to totally different outcomes as regards the second question.

Focussing first on the question of the *level* of effective demand in the context of the Great Crisis the world was going through in the 1930s, Kalecki moved later to the second one as full employment was reached in the course of World War II. During the first period, Kalecki was mainly interested in demonstrating the beneficial pump-priming effects of even useless projects, and to fight the classical view regarding investment and saving. In particular he aimed at establishing the relevance of deficit spending as a means to escape from the crisis. Obviously, the second question was to determine where the funds could be spent most effectively and in the best social interest. And from this point of view, Kalecki stated that the various ways of increasing effective demand are not equal if account is taken of their economic, social, and political content, because they may lead to better or worse allocation of resources, income distribution, structure of the economy and society; and produce different side effects. The point was thus to determine the conditions by which full employment is to be achieved even as the corresponding policies contribute to a fundamental overhaul of the system as regards especially the distribution of income and economic power amongst different social groups. (see especially Feiwell (1975))

Kalecki was thus well aware that the process of establishing full employment could be used as a way to change radically the capitalist system both by allowing what he considered a more just distribution of national income and improving the standard of living of the masses. Its treatment of the second question was thus clearly coloured by preferences, and even prejudices as to the future socio-economic structure of the country. One must choose the adequate structure of both private and public consumption and its distribution and of investment and its composition (capital formation in the profit-oriented private sector, infrastructure, welfare-oriented investment not offering sufficient private gain, investment in human capital, etc.). Kalecki's analysis was also marked by a predilection for government direct intervention rather than stimuli to private enterprise, whose results could prove rather uncertain; for resource allocation through comprehensive planning, rather than through the use of the market, etc.

The author was conscious of the political and ideological difficulties that could accompany the implementation of his full-employment programme. He dealt with these difficulties separately. First, on theoretical grounds, he exposed the issues of full employment. Then he concentrated on the practical problems of opposition and resistance. One should, however, take into account that even when dealing theoretically with the different ways to reach full employment, he took care to recall the political and institutional constraints that could arise. Even though he may have decided sometimes opting for a rather less polemical style to convince his readers of the relevance of its recommendations, the political problem raised by full-employment policy remained always present.

Debating alternative proposals

During the War period, government intervention was widespread and full employment was actually achieved. It is no wonder then that government authorities as well as the public at large were convinced that full employment could be reached with adequate measures and policies. This explains why in 1944 three important works were published in England, all dealing with full-employment policies. One was *The Economics of Full Employment*, several times mentioned in this volume, published by the Oxford Institute of Economics and Statistics, containing several papers including one by Kalecki. Almost simultaneously Sir William Beveridge published the report "Full Employment in a Free Society" (1944). And finally, there appeared the *White Paper on Employment Policy*.

Kalecki expressed support for the overall outlook contained in the *White Paper*. In particular, he recognized as positive the fact that "For the first time an official document acknowledges the responsibility of the government for preventing large fluctuations in output and employment. This represents a great advance upon the creed that slumps are natural and even salutary which has hitherto prevailed" (Kalecki 1944 [1997]: 238). However, this support did not prevent him from putting forward his criticisms.

Briefly, in the *White Paper*, the suggestion was that stabilization of effective demand could be achieved by: i) maintaining the balance of payments in equilibrium; ii) trying to stabilize investment by both stimulating private investment and planning public investment; and iii) if the above efforts were not fully successful, by mitigating the changes in private consumption by resorting to taxation policies as well as to policies aiming at varying contribution to social insurance.

Kalecki subjected the three methods to criticism: i) the deterioration of the balance of foreign trade is not necessarily incompatible with the maintenance of full employment. Permanent disequilibrium between exports and imports can be mitigated either by a rise in public expenditures or by a rise in private consumption. ii) Because it may be difficult to manipulate the long-term rate of interest, changing the short rate of interest – reducing it in a recession and increasing it when economic activity recovers – is not likely to be the most effective method of counteracting fluctuations in private investment. iii) The *White paper* also suggested, in the case these methods would not be entirely sufficient to appeal to measures to control fluctuations of consumption. One measure was to implement a scheme whereby contributions to social insurance would fall as employment fall, and would increase as employment was increasing. Allowing firms to cut down costs, one may thus expect an increase in purchasing power. The scheme could be reinforced by a corresponding system of taxation. Kalecki doubts that this intervention would be sufficient let alone, to stabilize national expenditure as a whole.

Kalecki's primary objection to the *White Paper* was that, even if these parts of the proposal proved successful, a state of full employment would not necessarily be reached. According to him, the *White Paper* remain silent on the two main pillars of any consistent full employment program. For one, the *White Paper*, by maintaining the principle of balanced budget, excluded deficit spending as a permanent measure. For another, the *White Paper* did not evoke any forms of income redistribution.

The programme presented by Beveridge was far more along the lines of Kalecki's ideas although Beveridge did not centre on income distribution. As Feiwell remarked, "The program presented by Beveridge in his Plan stirred up great controversies. Its radical features creates considerable disquietude in many quarters; The government found itself not only divided, but also in great difficulties, because on the one hand, in order to win the support of the more radical members of trade unions, a vision of a brighter and more egalitarian post-war environment was needed, and, on the other, there was tremendous opposition to using the war period as an engine of social change." (Feiwell 1975: 182).

Kalecki put forward several objections to the Beveridge Plan, which are rather similar of his criticisms to the *White Paper*. An additional objection referred to the requirement it placed on worker recipients of the social security benefits. Kalecki's view gives us a clear idea of his general attitude on social issues, and is also of interest today, given the current debate on how to reform the social security system. Let us reproduce his criticism almost in full:

> The Beveridge Plan abolishes the means test. It introduces, on the other hand, compulsory attendance at a work or training centre after six months of unemployment. While facilities for retraining may be welcomed, the rigid rule of compulsory attendance at a work or training centre seems to constitute a step backwards as compared with the present system. If handled ruthlessly it may amount to penalizing people who happen to be unemployed longer than six months by compelling them to do uncongenial work to earn their dole.
>
> The reason for favouring such an arrangement may be the erroneous belief that the unemployment benefit suggested in the Beveridge Plan is rather high and that the existing level of wages would not always provide a sufficient incentive to work. With a few exceptions, the present normal earnings ... in both industry and agriculture exceed the relevant benefits under the Beveridge Plan by 25 per cent. This may be regarded as a substantial incentive. (Kalecki 1944d [1997]: 225)

In the remainder of this chapter, our aim is to present Kalecki's vision of the different ways of managing capitalist economies subject to important fluctuations in unemployment. Three points will be treated which will make clear that Kalecki's approach appears to be that of a radical reformer of the more fundamental features of capitalist economies: the effect of government spending, the problem of stimulating private investment and the shortcomings of monetary policies.

Government spending

Kalecki claimed that the stabilization of effective demand and the maintenance of full employment should rely on the following principles: "i) the Government spends so much on public investment and subsidizing consumption of the poorer sections of the population and this secures full employment in combination with that private investment which is necessary to increase the productive capacity of equipment proportionately to the rise in the full 'employment national income' ii) Public investment is carried on at the rate actually required for satisfying the needs of the community, while all government spending above this level is devoted to subsiding mass consumption" [(Kalecki 1945 [1990] :383, quoted by Feiwell (1975): 182). It is worth stressing here that these measures may come with a rising national debt.

The basic rule ought to be that both public and private investments should be carried near the point where they cease to be useful, and not beyond that point.[18] If the effective demand created by public investment is insufficient to ensure full employment, the gap should be closed by increasing consumption, rather than by piling up wasteful public or private capital goods. The problem is similar to that of maintaining full employment by stimulating private investment. Public investment cannot be carried out beyond the point when it becomes useless. When public investment becomes useless, the excess of Government expenditure necessary to maintain full employment over this reasonable level of public investment must be devoted to consumption.

Kalecki's argument is that government measures aiming at increasing public investment or stimulating mass consumption can always prove successful for achieving and maintaining full employment. The problem was hence to eliminate or minimize crowding out effect. To satisfy this requirement, the government should undertake investment which would not be undertaken by private enterprise itself. Otherwise, compensatory adverse effects of public spending on private spending could reduce the expected profitability of private investment and its volume. But such effects will be weak if the government undertake project socially beneficial that businessmen find unprofitable. Kalecki maintained that reduction of profit taxes in a slump, as a device for eliminating as far as possible swings in private investment is promising, but he thought that a more reliable approach to offset the swings would be an appropriate and well-planned timing of public investment. But, as Feiwell noted "the method is not devoid of limitations, owing to i) the urgency of certain types of public investment projects in a given period which makes it very difficult to subordinate their time structure to the needs of stabilization policy; and ii) administrative and political difficulties in view of the insufficient power of direction of the central government over local administrations which are the main agents of public investments." (Feiwell 1975: 183–84).

Alternatively, the government may stimulate effective demand by subsidizing mass consumption either by tax cuts or appropriate transfer payments. Both the burden of direct and indirect taxes may be reduced. These measures can be financed by borrowing. Provided that the central bank kept constant the short-run rate of interest, no crowding out effect is likely to reduce the level of effective demand. Moreover, the maintenance of full employment is likely to come with strong distributional effects. Kalecki was concerned with tax policies in view of these effects; He stressed, especially, that some policies, even if they would reveal able to increase employment, seem to him not desirable, when these policies boil down to the stimulation of capitalists' consumption.

Stimulating private investment

Kalecki was of the idea that a policy which attempts to achieve full employment exclusively or primarily by stimulating private investment can neither be regarded as satisfactory nor is it likely to be successful. In his view, the effects of the stimulation of private investment depend first of all on the difficult-to-predict and changeable moods and reactions of entrepreneurs. It is quite possible that, when businessmen are in a pessimistic mood, they may fail to respond to even considerable stimuli. This clearly happens, for instance, when there is lack of confidence in political leadership or there is insecurity owing to a worsening international situation.

Let us assume however that the government maintains employment at its full-employment level. The question arises, is it possible to stimulate increases of private investment at a constant growth rate?

According to Kalecki, we may expect that policies aimed at establishing full employment may contribute, by reducing the variation and the volatility of profits which are the most important determinants of investment decisions, to stabilize the growth rate of private capital formation. In consequence, it is likely that a macroeconomic policy may succeed in dampening fluctuations in investments and thus stabilizing in part this highly variable and capricious component of national income, reducing risks and appreciably moderating fluctuations.

It is however doubtful that a state of full employment could eliminate totally fluctuations in private investment, for at least two reasons. First of all, it is important to note that under full employment, output and profits exhibit long-term changes due to alterations in the size of the labour force and rise in productivity, which are difficult to predict. Second, since a part of investment is exogenous, stabilizing the growth rate of income will not necessarily stabilize the rate of investment. This is especially the case when we consider investment resulting from technical progress, which is by nature discontinuous and mainly unpredictable. Neutralizing such fluctuations may be difficult since to be successful, public authorities must be able, despite the important lag between their decisions and the implementation of their decisions and different administrative and public difficulties, to determine the good timing.

As mentioned, this type of policy may nevertheless contribute to reducing significantly the variations in private decisions as compared with what they might be under the regime of a laissez-faire economy. Moreover, such a policy, if implemented for a sufficiently long time, may be taken with very small compensatory variations in public investment.

Kalecki dealt also with a second question: what should be the "equilibrium" level of private investment in a regime of full employment? To deal with this second issue, Kalecki starts with the following general consideration. From the employment standpoint, investment has a dual effect: i) capital formation acts on the supply side by increasing future capacity to produce output.[19] ii) Investment expenditures, being a source of effective demand, expand demand for current output through an income effect. Securing a policy for full employment needs to deal with both the supply and the demand effects. Kalecki treats both problems, noting first that dealing with the supply effect of investment involves the intricate concept of productive capacity.

For the purposes at hand we may define the degree of utilization of productive capacity as the ratio of actual output to the maximum capacity. The rate of utilization must be neither too small nor excessive. In the first case there will be idle capacity (waste of resources), and in the second the reserves of equipment will be insufficient to ensure elasticity for adjustment.

Let us consider a situation in which effective demand is adequate to ensure full-employment of labour and a "desirable" rate of capacity utilization. How then to maintain this rate of utilization in the case in which both the labour force and labour productivity (owing to technical progress) are growing? Naturally, to preserve the rate of plant utilization, capacity must grow proportionately to the expansion of the labour force and productivity. Here is a clue to what the level of private investment should be. Private investment must be at that level that ensures the expansion of the capacity of equipment proportionately to the increase in working population and productivity of labour, that is, proportionately to full-employment output. In other words, private investment should be pushed up to a level adequate to expand productive capacity proportionately to the long-run rise in full-employment output, but no more; and it would be absurd to push it beyond that level for reasons of insufficiency of effective demand.[20] Thus, if savings were too high in relation to private investment, the gap should not be filled by the stimulation of private investment. For if investment is above the level at which productive capacity increases *pari passu* with the expansion of full employment that results from growth of population and productivity, it creates overcapacity and this tends to depress long-term investment. These measures to stimulate private investment above a certain level will eventually prove self-defeating.

Moreover, even if investment is sufficiently stimulated to expand, there is no reason that the level of effective demand will allow to achieve full employment. Following Kalecki, one can distinguish two levels of investment: i) the level of gross private investment which creates effective demand sufficient to maintain full employment output, call I_F; and ii) the level which is just sufficient to expand the stock of capital proportionately to the rate of change in the work force and productivity, denoted by I_C. If technical progress entails no change in capital in relation to productive capacity, the expansion of I_C will be sufficient to obtain full-employment output. However, if technical progress entails a rise in capital in relation to productive capacity, full employment will not be sustained: productive capacity will now be insufficient to employ the whole labour force. In that case, As Feiwell notes: "the long-run unemployment that arises is not caused by insufficiency of effective demand, but by a lack of productive capacity; If this state of affairs is to be avoided, a stimulus to profit-seeking investors is required, not to create affective demand sufficient for maintaining full employment, but to prevent the deficiency of productive capacity which would otherwise hinder the system. [...] But if the prevailing technical progress should be of such a variety as to entail an expansion of productive capacity at slower pace than that of the accumulation of capital, even though government intervention can solve the problem of effective demand, it would be 'still necessary to grant cumulative subsides to private enterprise in order to induce it to expand its productive capacity to keep pace with the increase in population and productivity of labour (Kalecki 1945 [1990]: 385).'" (Feiwell 1975: 191).

On the other hand, if the level of private investment is pushed up to the point at which it ensures effective demand sufficient to obtain full employment and if this level is in excess of that necessary to expand productive capacity proportionately to full-employment output ($I_F < I_C$), there will be a continuous rise in surplus capacity and some investment will prove to be abortive. The decline in the rate of utilization of capacity will be reflected in a falling rate of profit, which will, in turn, adversely affect investment decisions. If deficiency of private investment is not here compensated by government deficits, macroeconomic policy must be aimed at averting the decline in the rate of private investment in order to prevent setting in motion the forces of contraction where a fall in investment gives rise to a magnified fall in national income (through the working of the multiplier). Thus the government would have to revert to more of the simulative medicine to spur private investment. After a certain time the need for further stimuli will reappear to offset the influence of the falling rate of profit. Kalecki demonstrated that, under the assumed conditions, to maintain full employment by stimulating private investment alone, it might be necessary to apply the stimuli active measures not only once, but to stimulate in a cumulative way; that is, the rate of interest must fall continuously, and quite rapidly or the profit tax must be continuously reduced or subsides to stimulate investment must constantly rise, that is, a policy of cumulative stimulation in favour of business would be required.

Whatever the case, if private enterprise were unable to meet the task of creating the required rate of new capacity, Kalecki conceived that the logical solution to the problem is for the function of private enterprise in this respect to be taken over partly by the government, by means of state-owned enterprises. This would also be particularly advantageous in those activities which are unprofitable to private interest. For example, in slum clearance the authorities could gradually ban certain obsolete buildings, thus raising the level of necessary investment to preserve housing capacity. Then, instead of stimulating private construction, state housing could be built (Kalecki 1945 [1990]: 385).

Kalecki believed in the efficacy of subsidies for modernizing equipment in the form of granting cheap credits for modernization projects, submitted to government agencies for approval. He also thought that the creation of modern state-owned enterprises might force private firms to modernize; but whether such firms would be more "efficient" and whether they are likely to exert the effect Kalecki anticipated is a controversial question. Nonetheless he emphatically declared that "such activities should not be governed merely by the wish to achieve full employment through investment in the 'private sector'. It is only to the extent that the acceleration of technical change has a social priority over public investment (in the strict sense) and subsides to consumption that such schemes should be put into operation." (Kalecki 1944a [1990]: 371).

Once the state steps in to substitute for private investment activities, forces for cumulative expansion of the government sector will set in. This will magnify the political opposition against what Kalecki considered to be the most rational way of achieving full employment. The very notion of deficit spending and particularly the direction of such spending is clearly not solely a technical economic problem.

As we have mentioned, redistribution of income was another of the ways envisioned by Kalecki to achieve full employment. We already discussed this issue at length in a previous chapter, and need only make a brief reference to it here. Kalecki suggested that the relative advantages of basing a full-employment policy on taxation of profits, or an income tax method, rather than on a budget deficit policy, lies in the fact that it not only secures full employment, but at the same time it renders the distribution of income (after taxation) more egalitarian. But precisely for this reason, "full employment through taxation", is likely to encounter a much stronger opposition than a "Budget deficit policy". Kalecki maintained that, because of this resistance, policy makers cannot simply choose between using the tax weapon as against budget deficit. Rather, they should use the former as realistically as possible, and fill the remaining gap by the latter.

If macroeconomic policy is used as a deliberate weapon for redistribution of incomes, aggregate consumption spending will tend to increase because the lower income groups have a higher propensity to consume (as there are "poor" and "rich" of different income and wealth gradation, the shift to the poorer within each of the broad categories tends to increase the overall propensity to consume). Thus redistribution of income is capable of generating effective demand and achieving full employment; however, the effect of such measures on private investment must be taken into account. Often the increase of taxes on profits, or of the modified income tax that Kalecki proposed, will be insufficient by themselves to maintain the profit incentive, and additional measures would be required to neutralize or offset depressing effects on private investment. With reference to redistribution of income by taxation, for instance, changes in the structure of taxes and transfer payments, such as a progressive rise of tax rates of higher income groups and simultaneous reduction of indirect taxes on necessities or semi-necessities to the same extent, or an increase in transfer payments to the poor, have the effect of increasing the propensity to consume. But the rise in income tax may have depressing effects on investment, imposing therefore specific limits on taxation. Moreover, uncertainty about taxation may depress private investment, as investment is a risky undertaking under most circumstances, and this added factor may have a destabilizing effect.

10
Michal Kalecki's Intellectual Legacy

At the end of our journey, when we want to assess Michal Kalecki's intellectual legacy, we will probably be amazed by the range, the depth, the importance and the originality of his work. Perhaps we should underlie this last point. Nobel Prize winner Robert Solow (1975) remarked, "Michal Kalecki ... seems to have sprung, full-grown, from his own brow; and his important work on macroeconomics is written not in opposition to the orthodoxy of the time, but in utter independence of it".

Even though the qualities of Kalecki's heritage make it difficult to put in few words what his most relevant contributions were, we may take as point of departure for our assessment his formulation of the principle of effective demand. We deliberately use the words "his formulation" because, in spite of his system being similar to Keynes's in many respects, the two of them should not be confused. Kalecki envisaged the issue with a distinctive "class approach", an approach more similar to the classic economists and to Marx than to Marshall. Moreover, having no attachment to the conventional wisdom of his time, he did not make any concession whatsoever to neoclassical economics.

Kalecki starts from the obvious idea that, in a capitalist economy commodities are produced with the purpose of making a profit. His line of approach to the problem of effective demand, therefore, begins with an inquiry of how the potential profits contained in the mass of commodities produced are realized through their sale. In other words, his formulation of the principle of effective demand is intimately associated with his theory of how profits are brought to fruition.

Kalecki first considers a capitalist economy with no foreign trade and no government, made up only of capitalists and workers, in which the latter spend all their wages, and where no unintended growth of inventories takes place. He then reaches the amazing conclusion encapsulated in the sentence popularized to sum up his theory of profits: *when workers spend what they earn capitalists earn what they spend*. The simplicity of the idea, once it has been uttered, should not lead us into conflating the accounting rule with the theoretical deduction. The accounting rule was already there, waiting to be brought into the open. The theoretical deduction demanded more; it demanded an analytical understanding of the causality and of the time sequence involved. Kalecki was the first to state clearly that profits cannot come into existence unless capitalists invest and consume; and in this sense today's capitalist spending antecedes today's profits (while today's profits antecede tomorrow's capitalist spending). Moreover, as the author puts it, "capitalists, as a whole, determine their own profits by the extent of their investment and personal consumption. In a way they are the masters of their fate; but how they master it is determined by objective factors." (1933a [1990]: 79–80).

If Kalecki had written nothing besides his theory of profits, he would still have deserved a relevant place amongst twentieth-century economists. But he gave us much more than that, developing his economic theory of the capitalist economy in many directions.

In the first place, he demonstrated that profits will also be affected by other components of effective demand. In particular, he showed that an export surplus, which absorbs from abroad a greater purchasing power than it cedes to foreign economies, raises sales and thus total profits over and above the level they would have reached in the closed economy. Likewise, the budget deficit, whereby the demand of the government is not offset by a reduction in the purchasing power of the private sector, and which entails a debt of the state vis-à-vis domestic capitalists, enlarges sales and profits. The similarity between these two extra sources of profits led him to label the latter "domestic exports". His finding that both the export surplus and the budget deficit expand profits probably explains his admiration for his compatriot Rosa Luxembourg, the Marxian revolutionary, who had to a certain extent, though imperfectly, anticipated this idea some years before.

In the second place, Kalecki widened his inquiry to consider how not only profits, but also the whole national production is realized. National production cannot exceed the level set by the existing productive capacity; but its real size is determined by effective demand. In developed capitalism demand is usually lower than the potential output, and idle productive capacity allows supply to have some elasticity, even in the short-run. When supply is lower than demand, production tends to increase and the opposite happens when demand is lower than supply; without such changes in demand and output necessarily entailing changes in prices. From the above follows a seemingly paradoxical consequence: *in developed capitalism, demand creates its own supply.*

Kalecki then went on to distinguish the autonomous from the induced components of effective demand. He singled out investment as the central autonomous component of the latter, with the remaining elements of demand being functions of investment. The crucial role of investment in the operation and the dynamics of capitalism, its position as the *primun movens* of capitalism, and the conceptual difference between investment decisions and investment spending, were two points that Kalecki raised at the early stage of the construction of his overall vision. Comprehending what determines investment decisions and investment spending thus became the task he set to himself to further develop his macroeconomic system.

In the first steps of the formulation of his theory of investment decisions, Kalecki gave prominence to the profit rate and to the interest rate as the fundamental determinants of investment; and in a certain sense the real and monetary factors were put on an equal footing. In this context, he assumed endogenous money, whereby banks could, and during the upswing would, accommodate the forthcoming demand for credit ensuing from the needs of investment spending; such that a higher interest rate would not normally be an obstacle to a higher desired level of investment.

However, in the course of the development of his ideas, Kalecki refined his view giving a greater weight to profits than to purely monetary factors, because he realized that investment entails a risk for the entrepreneur, a risk that increases with the size of investment (the "principle of increasing risk"). Therefore he concluded that profits play a dual role in the determination of investment; namely, they (and more particularly the profit rate) provide, on the one hand, an indicator of how lucrative investment has been in the past. But on the other hand higher profits, by providing the internal funds with which to finance investment, reduce the risk associated with any given volume of investment; and higher savings out of profits open up additional sources of finance external to the firm that can be tapped.[1] In this perspective, we can understand why Kalecki accorded a central place in his theory of investment decisions to profits, and to the change in profits and the change in the amount of capital (the latter two together establishing the profit rate). To this he added innovations, which provide an additional stimulus to investment.

Summarizing, we can therefore say that Kalecki put forth an investment theory of demand and a profits theory of investment.[2] Accordingly, he assigned a key role to objective factors and to the past evolution of the economy.

In this respect, he departed considerably from Keynes, who placed a greater emphasis on long-run expectations. And in fact Kalecki criticized Keynes on this issue; writing in his review of the *General Theory* "Keynes does not take sufficient account of the influence of current profitability on investment" (Kalecki 1936 [1990]: 229). Much later he would be more categorical, adding, "Keynes...did not show that capitalists' profits, rather than some nebulous propensity to save, are the mainspring of economic decisions" (Kalecki 1993a: 260). Let us mention here, by the way, that his understanding of the importance on entrepreneurial decisions of objective factors, and of the past economic evolution, probably also explains why he supported the use of statistical and econometric tools; having contributed with original work, both applied and theoretical, also to this chapter of economics. And let us conclude this point reminding readers that the relevance of past profits as a determinant of the volume of investment, as Kalecki assumed, has been borne out by most extant empirical research.

The closure of Kalecki's system to determine total output required linking wages to profits; or, looking at the same issue from a different angle, required linking worker's consumption with capitalists' expenditure. This Kalecki achieved with his *theory of income distribution*, another one of his most original and lasting contributions.

Kalecki's distribution theory picks up Marx's basic idea on class struggle as a decisive element in the configuration of such distribution. But also considers the capacity of firms to affect the determination of prices. We discussed the specific mechanism of Kalecki's theory of distribution in chapter four of this book. Let us recall here simply that, given the structure of production, the relative share of wages in national income depends entirely on the price/unit cost ratio, and on the relative cost of material inputs with respect to wages.

Now, here again we should not conflate the accounting rule with the theoretical principle. Due to the former, the wage share will be entirely determined by the above mentioned factors under whatever circumstances. This, and probably also Kalecki's unwillingness to use the optimization rule, cherished by neoclassical economics, to determine the price/cost – ratio, may explain why an economist of a no less stature than Nicholas Kaldor (1955–56) dismissed Kalecki's theory as being tautological. Kalecki (1968a [1991]: 438) sternly replied: "no problem of *tautology* is involved. If the price is not determined by the equilibrium of supply at full utilization of equipment, on the one hand, and demand, on the other – the prices are fixed by the firms on the basis of the average prime costs and the average price of the product group in question". Indeed, in setting their prices in relation to their costs, businesses also set the distribution of income between profits and wages; and thus between profits and total income.

To sum up, capitalists' expenditure and income distribution determine effective demand and hence the level of economic activity and of employment. Indeed, through their expenditure capitalists determine their profits. Given total profits, and given the relative share of profits to income, total wages and national income are set.

Moreover, when we assume, with our author, that wages are entirely consumed and that capitalist expenditure follows profits with a time-lag, we reach another of Kalecki's *prima facie* paradoxical conclusions: *a rise in wages will not necessarily imply a fall in profits*. Indeed, if wages grow, and prices do not increase (or if they increase in a lower proportion), capitalists will not *immediately* reduce their real expenditure. Thus, as capitalist expenditure does not fall, their profits will not be reduced either. The consequence of the wage increase is a higher demand and production, with which the rise in wages and wage consumption are covered, and an increase in the degree of utilization of productive capacities. Capitalists now fetch a smaller relative share out of a greater output. Moreover, since profits do not fall in the current period, the following period's investment need not fall either.

Thus, without denying the central role of investment in shaping output and employment, Kalecki posited that in theory, with sufficient price and hence profit margin flexibility, the aggregate effect of fluctuations upon investment might be dampened, or even eliminated. In this aspect, his theory anticipated the contemporary New Keynesian claim that with a strong enough price flexibility unemployment might be removed no matter how low investment is. However, Kalecki's viewpoint was different from theirs. In the first place, due to the pervasiveness of market imperfections in modern capitalism, he did not believe that price flexibility would play a stabilizing role. And besides that, he argued that profit margins and the degree of monopoly would have to be flexible *downwards* when labor unemployment arises, whereas real wages would need to *rise* in order for increases in consumption to expand (and sustain) demand; which is the opposite policy conclusion to the one New Keynesian economics postulates.[3]

Finally, in the context of his theory of distribution, Kalecki argued that a wage reduction would, under conditions of imperfect competition, bring about a shift of factor shares from wages to profits. He then drew the following conclusion:

> There are certain "workers' friends" who try to persuade the working class to abandon the fight for wages in its own interest, of course. The usual argument used for this purpose is that the increase of wages causes unemployment, and is thus detrimental to the working class as a whole.
>
> The Keynesian theory[4] undermines the foundation of this argument ... A wage increase ... affects to a certain extent the distribution of income: it tends to reduce the degree of monopoly and thus to raise real wages ...
>
> If viewed from this standpoint, strikes must have the full sympathy of "workers' friends." (1990: 284)

And he concluded:

> It is quite true that the fight for wages is not likely to bring about fundamental changes in the distribution of the national income. Income and capital taxation are much potent weapons to achieve this aim, for these taxes (as opposed to commodity taxes) do not affect prime costs, and thus do not tend to raise prices. But in order to redistribute income in this way, the government must have both the will and the power to carry it out, and this is unlikely in a capitalist economy. (Ibid: 285)

Taking stock of our previous discussion, we can now recap Kalecki's three major criticisms of the neoclassical notion that laissez-faire capitalist economies are endowed with an endogenous full-employment mechanism, triggered by the wage-fall caused by unemployment. In the first place, his endogenous conception of money led him to reject the view whereby lower wages and prices supposedly contribute to raising the real amount of money which would bring down interest rates; claiming that in fact banks would accommodate a lower demand for credit and rather maintain the real interest rate.[5] In the second place, we recall that Kalecki was also the first to reject Pigou's claim that a wage reduction and the ensuing price drop would stimulate higher spending from creditors who, with lower prices, would feel richer. He objected that debtors would instead feel poorer; adding that generalized and persistent wage and price decreases would likely bring about a "crisis of confidence" which would slow down private spending.[6] His third objection came from his argument that a wage reduction would likely imply a smaller proportional fall in prices than in wages, and that the consequent drop in the wage share would depress workers' consumption, thus amplifying the original situation of unemployment.

Kalecki's view of higher wage share as playing a positive impact on demand and employment, together with his general socialist inclination, explain why redistribution of income was one of his preferred measures in a progressive economic strategy. Greater government expenditures, deficit financed or financed with higher taxes on profits was the other one of the measures he supported; while he was skeptical regarding monetary policy. He dismissed the notions that a higher deficit necessarily entails higher interest rates, or that it would inevitably raise the burden of the national debt. But even if the latter were to be the case, he showed that a rising share of interest payments on the national debt could be financed with higher taxes which, if properly devised, need not slow down the pace of private investment. Anyway, he advocated financing higher government expenditure with higher taxes on profits, rather than by deficits, because he argued that the former would contribute also to redistribute income in favor of wage-earners and the poor.

In developed capitalist economies stimulating effective demand, for example with government expenditure, would encroach upon unemployment; however, this "financial trick" would not be available in backward capitalist economies. Kalecki's analysis of *the economics of underdeveloped countries* was another one of his lasting contributions. He showed that in the latter, capital equipment is insufficient to make employment possible for the potentially active population. Moreover, there are sectors, like agriculture, where because of institutional obstacles supply does not respond to stimuli of growing demand or favourable shifts in relative prices and profitability. In this last type of economies, then, rapid capital accumulation, along with structural transformations and institutional reforms, are previously required.

More generally, Kalecki considered that in developed economies, with an adequate planning of government expenditure, business cycles could be mitigated, and even avoided. However, he doubted that this would be feasible under capitalism, mostly due to political reasons. He foresaw that a state of permanently high employment would alter power equilibrium within society; and, in particular, would improve the bargaining power of workers. "In this situation a powerful alliance is likely to be formed between big business and rentier interests, and they would probably find more than one economist to declare that the situation was manifestly unsound. The pressure of all these forces, and in particular of big business – as a rule influential in government departments – would induce the government to return to the orthodox policy of cutting down the budget deficit" (Kalecki 1943a [1990]: 355). Thus he envisioned a *political business cycle* whereby government expenditure would fluctuate according to the condition of political forces.

The *political* business cycle would act simultaneously with the *pure* business cycle within which Kalecki had embedded his formulation of the principle of effective demand. In fact, Kalecki did not believe that the problem of effective demand could be studied from a static perspective, but rather should be viewed within the context of the dynamics of the system.

The *business-cycle theory* is the last one of Kalecki's enduring contributions we single out in discussing his intellectual legacy; and in fact it was also his life-long passion; which he considered to be the central *pièce de résistance* of economics. Right from his first theoretical paper, Kalecki was convinced that any short period is shaped by what happened in the past and determines, though not mechanically, what will take place in the future. He thus put forward his theory of growth and the business cycle, with the purpose of summarizing the dynamics of the capitalist economy in a mathematical model whose solution ought to simulate what he perceived to be the real evolution of these economies; that is, a solution containing both the *trend* as well as the *business cycle*.

During his lifetime, Kalecki proposed several versions of his growth *cum* cycle model, all of them referring to a private economy.[7] Consequently, the speed and pattern of economic growth are in a way *spontaneous*. To achieve this purpose, he abstracted from the role of the State, and of the political and the international environment. Moreover, in all the versions he assumed that solely the evolution of aggregate demand matters, without supply factors interfering. That is, in contradistinction to the now-popular "real business-cycle theory", he considered that demand expansion is not only a *necessary* condition for growth, but also a *sufficient* condition. Thus, in general Kalecki assumed that the level of effective economic activity is always below potential levels, and at all times there are unused productive capacities, even in the upswing. Kalecki rationalized his methodological option pointing out "a laissez-faire capitalist economy used to achieve a more or less full utilization of resources only at the top of the boom, and frequently not even then. Nor did these full-employment booms fill a major part of the cycle" (Kalecki 1968a [1991]: 438).[8]

Now, the general logic of the operation of Kalecki's models is that, the cycle and the trend are determined by the evolution of investment, which follows with a lag previous investment decisions. Even though the first models he specified referred to a trendless economy, he always strove to overcome the usual limitation of models which start off from a situation of uniform growth; instead, he tried to build a model that simultaneously determines trend and cycle. In this context, he considered that growth is not endogenous to capitalism, but depends on the existence of semi-endogenous elements, within which technical progress (appearance of new products or new productive methods which require investments for their improving; discovery of new markets or new sources of raw materials; etc.) occupies a central role.

To grasp the economic logic of the cycle, it is useful to start from the first version given by Kalecki, which is a "pure" business-cycle model; that is, under the assumption that the system is devoid of a long-run trend. The rate of investment decisions per unit of time is determined by the profit rate; and more concretely by total profits, which have a positive impact, and by the capital stock, which has a negative impact, on investment decisions. Now, investment produces a double effect. While on the one hand it raises output and profits, which would by themselves stimulate new investment decisions, on the other it results (after a lag) in a delivery of new means of production which increase the mass of capital among which profits must be distributed. As profits do not rise again if there are no new investment orders, and thus new production of investment goods, the capital increase will act as an element that will depress investment. The effect of investment on profits is positive in a first moment, when there is demand of production goods; but later, as capital increases and the profit rate tends to fall, it will have a negative effect on investment decisions.

The inflection points occur precisely due to this double effect of investment. When the latter, after having grown, stabilizes at a higher level than depreciation, then profits stabilize too. However, the mass of capital keeps growing. This causes a fall in the profit rate, which tends to generate a fall of investment decisions and later on investment. On the other hand, when investment, which has been falling, stabilizes at a lower level than depreciation, the volume of profits also stabilizes, but the mass of capital is reduced. Hence, the profit rate rises, with which investment is stimulated.

Kalecki later enriched his theory of investment decisions, to account for factors not previously considered. In particular, he included business savings among the factors stimulating investment, adding that under normal conditions and unless other factors intervene, businesses do not tend to completely reinvest their savings. He also incorporated innovations, as another factor stimulating new investments due to its beneficial effect on the profit rate of recent investments. Finally, since he was conscious that the mathematical solution of his model might not be robust, in the sense that small changes in the values of the parameters could damp the cycle, he introduced random shock that would ensure the persistence of the cycle.[9] However, in spite of these changes, the essentials of his cyclical model did not change much.

As mentioned many times in this book, Kalecki was the first to propose a rigorous, and mathematical, business-cycle model based on the principle of effective demand. Accordingly, he received wide recognition and exerted an important influence in this area of economics during that period when attempts to bring dynamics into the principle of effective demand were in vogue; particularly during the 1930s, 1940s and 1950s.[10]

But afterwards mainstream economics abandoned this subject almost entirely. In a posthumous paper, the author contrasts his view with the one hegemonic at the time, and still hegemonic today:

> From the time the discussion of economic dynamics has concentrated on problems of growth the factor of effective demand was generally disregarded. Either it was simply assumed that in the long run the problem of effective demand does not matter because apart from the business cycle it need not be taken into consideration; or more specifically the problem was approached in two alternative fashions: (i) The growth is at an equilibrium (Harrodian) rate, so that the increase in investment is just sufficient to generate effective demand matching the new productive capacities which the level of investment creates. (ii) Whatever the rate of growth the productive resources are fully utilized because of long-run price flexibility: prices are pushed in the long run in relation to wages up to the point where the real income of labor (and thus its consumption) is enough to cause the absorption of the full employment national product. I do not believe, however, in justifying the neglect of the problem of finding markets for the national product at full utilization of resources either in fashion (i) or (ii). (Kalecki 1970 [1993]: 111–112)

Fortunately, there are still authors, especially associated with the Post-Keynesian school, that view the development of the capitalist economy as cyclical in nature. The first name to come to mind is Hyman Minsky, who formulated a very important theory of the business cycle emphasizing the financial inter-relationships of a capitalist economy; and which has gained much audience during the present crisis.

But even among writers closer to the mainstream, and especially among members of the so-called New Keynesian school, the cyclical nature of capitalism has been recognized and explored. In some recent literature of that inspiration, they have sought to revive the Kaleckian approach to dynamics within a market clearing environment, except that they assume imperfections in the financial markets. For borrowing constraints to have any effect upon the economic dynamics, it is necessary to assume that agents are not all identical. At certain times some agents would wish to borrow on terms at which others would be willing to lend. Amongst others, Woodford thus suggested to refer to Kalecki's approach by distinguishing two types of agents: workers who supply labour and capitalists who own the capital stock: "The constraint upon financial intermediation assumed here is given less attention in traditional accounts but is implicit in the treatment of the decisions of the two classes of agents by authors such as Kalecki. If workers lend to capitalists through a complete and fully competitive set of financial markets, they can effectively accumulate capital themselves, so that the distinction between the two roles is negated" (Woodford 1989: 20). Furthermore, such a financial constraint allows describing an economy in which each class's expenditures in a given period are constrained by the income of that class. Again, Kalecki is explicit about it: "some such financial constraints is [...] implicit in all models which assume that workers consume exactly their wages each period, and that capitalist accumulate out of their profits" (quoted by Woodford 1989: 20). The kind of financial market imperfections of primary interest are restrictions upon the ability of economic units (households or firms) to finance expenditures other than out of their own current or past income. That is, there is no assumption of the existence of a single, economy-wide competitive market for claims to future income (including claims to income contingent upon various possible events, as in the Arrow–Debreu framework) to which all agents have equal access. In the extreme case of an absolute inability of any economic unit to obtain external finance at all, no financial assets are exchanged at all, so that each unit must spend an amount equal to its income in every period.

We conclude here our book of what we consider to be the most important chapters of Michal Kalecki's intellectual legacy. Of course, no individual can alone cover the whole field of economics. But the heritage that Michal Kalecki bestowed to us economists is really enormous. We are sure that his theories will be studied, and will remain alive, for many years to come; and that they will be further developed by his disciples, and by all serious students of the reality of capitalism.

Notes

Preface

1. All references to Kalecki give, first, the date of the original publication, and afterwards, between square brackets, the date of publication in the *Collected Works of Michal Kalecki* (seven volumes), edited by Jerzy Osiatynski, Clarendon Press, Oxford.

1 Michal Kalecki's Life and Work

1. According to Prof. Kazimierz Laski (personal communication to the authors), one of Kalecki's closest collaborators in Poland, Kalecki's Polish was perfect. Thus he did not belong to that large section of the Polish – Jewish minority, so vividly described by I.B. Singer, who were culturally isolated from Poles and whose mother tongue was Yiddish.
2. We do not know much about his reading in his early period. However, we do know that his preferred authors were Rosa Luxemburg and Tugan-Baranovsky.
3. Ignacy Sachs, who would become one of Kalecki's closest collaborators in Poland in the late 1950s and the 1960s, tells the story of how Kalecki got his post at the Institute: "At the beginning of the 1930s, [Kalecki] sends a letter to the director of the Institute saying more or less 'Please find enclosed a memo where I propose some scenarios for Poland's recovery from the crisis. Signed: Kalecki, third-year student of engineering'. Edward Lipinsky, the director of the Institute... recalls his impression upon opening the envelope: 'I read the memo and I do not understand anything except that the author is a genius!' And immediately he hired Kalecki" (Sachs 2007: 182).
4. His papers on mathematics are reprinted in his *Collected Works*, Vol. VII, part 4.
5. In those years Kalecki used the term "monetary inflation" to refer to credit or monetary expansion.
6. *Pace* Joan Robinson (1965: 95), who wrote "[Kalecki] had never learned orthodox economics". By the way, Robinson's opinion may reflect "the attractive Anglo-Saxon kind of un-necessary originality" (Ohlin *dixit*). At the beginning of the 20th Century, Polish economic thinking was equally or more influenced by German and Scandinavian than by British economic ideas. Anyway, Kalecki's (1934a [1990]) paper remained unpublished in English until 1990.
7. Ragnar Frisch and Jan Tinbergen, born in Norway and in the Netherlands, respectively, were awarded Nobel Prizes in Economics in 1969 "for having developed and applied dynamic models for the analysis of economic processes".
8. According to Prof. Rolf Henriksson (personal communication to the authors) Kalecki did not mingle much with his Swedish colleagues and was not only intellectually but also socially very isolated.

9. He had resigned from the Institute, due to his disagreement with repressive measures that had been taken there.
10. Surely he got this post because he had already worked on prices and profit margins, while elaborating his theory of the determinants of the distribution of national income (Kalecki 1938a [1990]). As we discuss in Chapter 4, in this theory the relationship of prices to costs plays a central role; and the post he obtained at Cambridge University allowed him to improve his theoretical views.
11. Many years later he would write "The assumption of an almost horizontal short-run prime cost curve was made in my *Essays on the Theory of Economic Fluctuations,* back in 1939. Since that time it has been proven by many empirical enquiries, and has played, explicitly and implicitly, an important role in economic research" (Kalecki 1954a [1991]: 210).
12. In this he differed from Keynes who believed that the marginal cost should include the "user cost". For due to its inclusion "[...] a point must surely come, long before plant and labour are fully employed, when less efficient plant and labour have to be brought into commission of the efficient organisation employed beyond the optimum degree of intensiveness" (Keynes 1939: 405).
13. "The Supply Curve of an Industry under Imperfect Competition" (Kalecki 1940a [1991]) is a summary of his work on the Cambridge Research Scheme of the National Institute of Economic and Social Research into Prime Costs, Proceeds and Output. In that article, Kalecki gave mark-up pricing better theoretical foundations and greater empirical content.
14. The story runs that Kalecki used to say that Dobb and Sraffa were the only two native gentlemen he had known in England; the first was a communist and the other an Italian.
15. Robinson probably refers to Kalecki (1935b [1990]).
16. In 1944 members of the Institute of Statistics published the book "Economics of Full Employment", where Kalecki had the paper "Three ways to full employment" (Kalecki 1944a [1990]). Upon receiving that book from Kalecki, Keynes wrote to him: "When one gets a book like this, one feels that economics is really making progress... Your own contribution seems to me the most striking and original... and also most beautifully compressed. It is a great comfort to read something so short and so much to the point" (Kalecki 1990: 579).
17. The paper (Kalecki 1941 [1991]) was finally published in the *Review of Economic Studies.*
18. One of us (JL) asked Kalecki once why he had not included his article on the Blum experience (Kalecki 1938b [1990]) in a collection of papers on capitalist economies he had published in Poland. His answer was: "Look, in that paper I said that my analysis was based on Keynes's theory, while in fact I was applying my own theory". This tells a lot about his difficult relationship with Keynes, and with Keynes's theory.
19. Feiwell (1975) summarizes nicely Kalecki's papers on the subject.
20. The only US economists contributing to Kalecki's *Festschrift* in 1964 were Lawrence Klein, and Paul Sweezy and Paul Baran (Baran had recently died and their joint paper was given by Sweezy).
21. Gomułka had been a Deputy Prime Minister from 1945 to 1947. However, between 1951 and 1954, he was denounced as right-wing and reactionary,

and expelled from the Polish Communist Party (Polish United Workers' Party).

22. His closest collaborators were Adam Szeworski and Zofia Dobraska.
23. Here is a beautiful story of his engagement at the SGPiS: "I tried to convince [Kalecki] that he should move to teaching and share his knowledge with students. It was not at all easy to persuade him, considering that he had never had a teaching position in academia, but at last I got him to agree to give a one term course (of two hours a week) in the Central School of Planning and Statistics (SGPiS) on his theory of dynamics of a capitalist economy, and another course on his in statu nascendi theory of growth of a socialist economy. I felt very happy until only a few days later Kalecki told me he could not accept my proposal because he had not enough material to lecture for two hours a week. It must be noted in this context that Kalecki almost never referred to other authors and their theories; he presented only results of his own research. I proposed he lectured only one hour and the second one would be devoted to questions and answers and this he accepted" (Laski 3).
24. Some notes (in Polish) from his lectures circulated amongst attendants to Kalecki's 1967–1968 course. We have been unable to recover these notes; but in the Appendices to some of the following chapters we have reproduced some fragments from the notes taken by one of us (JL).
25. Here is a brief account of the circumstances: "Gomulka was giving a discourse at a congress of trade unions when he received a note informing him that in the offices of a Warsaw newspaper, Jew reporters had organized a party to celebrate Israel's victory over the Arabs... Gomulka, who was impulsive, pronounced the expression 'fifth column Zionist'. He was immediately countered by the President, who was also a communist; however, the evil had already been done" (Sachs 2007: 191–192).

2 Kalecki's Theory of Profits and Output

1. In the main text we conduct our reasoning in purely verbal terms. In the Appendix we formalize the ideas.
2. Realization is a word coming from Marx's terminology, who distinguished between the production and the realization of profits; the second referring to a situation when commodities are sold at their value or production price. Kalecki sometimes used the expression.
3. It would do no harm if we suppose that more optimistic entrepreneurial expectations are the consequence of a flexible labour market, which eases the firing of workers at the will of entrepreneurs.
4. We show below that reducing prices with given money wages, entails a change in the distribution of income against profits.
5. Profits certainly have an influence on capitalist investment and consumption, but in future periods, not in the same period in which they are realized. This happens because both capitalist investment and consumption react with a certain time-lag to the changes in current profits.
6. To the best of our knowledge, only Keynes clearly perceived the importance of this assumption of Kalecki for his whole theory of profits. See the Kalecki – Keynes exchange in Kalecki (1990: 557–563). Steindl (1990: 276–302) also

remarked on the difference between Kalecki and Keynes regarding the importance attributed to time-lags and temporary sequences.

7. Kalecki did not consider in his theoretical framework crisis of confidence.
8. Regarding the irrevocability of investment decisions the author said: "It should be noticed that investment decisions are not strictly irrevocable. The cancellation of investment orders, although involving considerable loss, can and does take place" (Kalecki 1954a [1991]: 281).
9. In this paragraph, we are implicitly assuming that changes in income distribution do not induce changes in *P*. We discuss this assumption later on.
10. In a later chapter we will study how Kalecki analysed the case of semi-industrialized countries, where excess productive capacities do not always suffice, or where these do not exist in important sectors of the economy.
11. See Sawyer (2001), and Toporowski (2005), for two excellent and very comprehensive expositions of Kalecki's view of finance and money.
12. In reality this is a virtual equilibrium, which will not necessarily be reached. In fact, the discrepancy between production and sales could create a change in capitalist expenditure.
13. In a private and closed economy, the proportion of profits in income has an inversed relation to that of wages in income. In effect, it would be

    $$w = W/Y$$

    given that

    $$(W+P)/Y = w + e = 1$$

    then

    $$e = 1 - w$$

    We will study the mechanism that establishes income distribution in a later chapter. For the moment we consider that the income distribution is given (or exogenous).

3 Genesis and Originality of Kalecki's Theory

1. See the Appendix to this chapter for a formalized presentation of Kalecki's 1934 paper. Unlike the other Appendices in this volume, this one *is not* based on Kalecki's lectures at SGPiS.
2. "I must point out, though, that by free competition I understand a system in which changes in the supply of one entrepreneur does not influence the market [...]. Thus in my model prices equal marginal costs [...]" (Kalecki 1934b [1990]: 493).
3. With iso-elastic curves and increasing cost curves, changes in aggregate demand increase the share of profit. As with perfectly competitive firms, this is because profit margins rise because of the progressive divergence of marginal from averages cost.
4. $\mu/(1-\mu)$, in the original notation.
5. Later, Kalecki alters slightly this conception by distinguishing between the short and long-term rate of interest and referring to the principle of increasing risk.

6. Both production sectors operate with a constant and historically given capital stock. He assumes profit maximization under perfect competition so that prices equal marginal costs. More up-to-date equipment has higher productivity of labour and lower labour costs. Utilization of different vintages of capital equipment depends on their profitability. Thus, overall, marginal productivity of labour is negatively associated with the level of output (i.e., decreasing returns to labour obtain). Other assumptions include a closed economy and no government sector.
7. Kalecki characterizes Say's law as follows: "In System I, the principle of preservation of purchasing power is pushed to the extreme: all income must be spent immediately on consumer or investment goods. This model is in fact accepted by all classical economists" (Kalecki 1934a [1990]: 201).
8. The notation used by Kalecki has been replaced by the more usual one.
9. After having presented in detail his second system, Kalecki dealt with the implications of increasing the money supply on interest rates (Kalecki 1934a [1990]: 213–214).
10. The interested reader is referred to Kalecki (1934) for the analysis of a decrease in capitalists' consumption, or a rise in the inducement to invest.
11. "A macroeconomic model is said to dichotomize if a subset of equations can determine the values of all real variables with the level of the money supply playing no role in determining the equilibrium value of any real variable" (Sargent 1987: 46).
12. Kalecki also showed that a decrease in capitalists' consumption can reduce investment and drive the economy into a position where unemployment is higher.
13. In the model set up by Kalecki, the relationship between the real and monetary sector is analysed in a rigid credit system, where additional investments are financed only through the acceleration of the velocity of money. Kalecki was, however, well aware that an elastic credit system allows the creation of additional financial means, which moderates changes in the interest rate.
14. Aggregation matters if the marginal propensities to spend from wealth are lower for creditors than for debtors. Commentators on the Kalecki – Pigou debate have given strong arguments in favour of this hypothesis, and for Kalecki's outlook in general (see, e.g., Tobin 1980).
15. Kalecki had considered the possibility of "crises of confidence" in the early stages of developments of his theory. For example: "in the analysis of the money market we must still consider a 'crisis of confidence' which can break out during the depression in the context of a sudden fall in prices, making it difficult or impossible to service debts and pay interest" (Kalecki 1933a [1990]: 98).
16. Note there is a typo in this paragraph in the otherwise careful edition of Kalecki's *Collected Works*, Vol. I.
17. We acknowledge here our debt to Assous (2006, 2007) and Chapple (1995).
18. Kalecki conducted his analysis of the business cycle assuming a given money wage rate. Would not a wage fall, induced by higher unemployment in the course of the cyclical downswing, induce a recovery of investment and bring about the cyclical upswing? Kalecki answered in the negative to this question. Thus, downwards wage flexibility would not necessarily eliminate the cycle. We will see below that, after he developed his theory of income

distribution, he gave a further reason why downward wage flexibility may not ensure full employment.

19. See in particular Robinson (1947), Robinson (1964); see also Klein (1952).
20. We define here as general equilibrium *models*, those that take into account different markets and their interactions. This we distinguish from general equilibrium *theories*, which we define as those where, besides this interaction, everything happens simultaneously. Of course Kalecki's theory, which pays due attention to time-lags and time-sequences, is definitely not a general equilibrium theory.
21. In this model, surprisingly, an increase in the quantity of money, by raising nominal income, will cause an increase in employment. Accordingly, this first model, is neither dichotomic nor neutral. This characteristic comes from the fact that it is nominal investment and nominal savings and not real investment and real savings that depend on the interest rate. Thus the investment function is not homogeneous of degree one vis-à-vis nominal variables. This, as D'Autume (2000: 421) has remarked « translates a generalised money illusion », a characteristic that can be found in each of these models.
22. Which came later to be labelled the LM curve.
23. As real savings do not depend on interest, the distribution of employment between sectors will not be affected.
24. However, Keynes (1964: 207) though that the situations where the liquidity trap rules are seldom found in real life: "There is the possibility, for the reasons discussed above, that, after the rate of interest has fallen to a certain level, liquidity-preference may become virtually absolute in the sense that almost everyone prefers cash to holding a debt which yields so low a rate of interest. In this event the monetary authority would have lost effective control over the rate of interest. But whilst this limiting case might become practically important in the future, I know of no example of it hitherto".
25. Current real profits by unit produced in each production sector depend respectively on p_c/W and p_I/W; they in turn determine expected profitability and hence investment.
26. In Kalecki's analysis, investment can be increased in response to a Schumpeterian "new production combination". (Kalecki 1934b [1990]: 492).

4 The Theory of Prices and Income Distribution

1. Abba Lerner (1934) proposed the concept "degree of monopoly", which can be expressed as the difference between price and marginal cost, divided by price. When the theory of monopolistic competition applies, given the equality between marginal cost and marginal revenue, which is the necessary condition for profit maximization, the degree of monopoly is equal to the reciprocal of the price elasticity of demand. We come back to this issue later on.
2. Let us recall here a remark which is important for understanding the formula $\bar{p} = k\bar{u}$. "The degree of monopoly *may* but need not necessarily, increase as a result in overheads in relation to prime costs. This and the emphasis on the influence of prices of other firms constitute the difference between the

theory presented here and the so-called full-cost theory" (Kalecki 1954a [1991]: 216; emphasis in the original).

3. Hence his assumption that in setting their price, firms include their own output and price in the weighted average price $\bar{p}$.
4. Game theory is also an alternative approach to the one based on the optimizing behaviour of firms. However, to reach any meaningful result it, too, has to assume firms have an enormous amount of information.
5. To simplify, in this paragraph we assume that *j*, the ratio of aggregate cost of materials to the wage bill, does not change.
6. We can develop an analogous type of reasoning using conventional Keynesian analysis. Simplifying, the well-know multiplier equation states (*s* is the saving propensity; which we assume depends on the share of wages in value added):

$$Y = \frac{I}{s(\omega)}, s' < 0$$

A fall in the share of wages (a rise in the share of profits) in income, reduces demand and output for a given level of investment, because the saving propensity rises.

7. Kalecki writes: "i) with given average price *P* the elasticity of demand for the product of a firm e_i is uniquely correlated with its price p_i and ii) when the average price *P* and the firm's price p_i change in the same proportion, this elasticity remains unchanged" (Kalecki 1940a [1991]: 52). As Carson notices: "The assumption that the demand elasticity is homogenous of degree zero in p_i and *P* is restrictive, but analogous homogeneity assumptions are by no means unknown in orthodox writings – the assumptions of a constant elasticity of demand being an extreme case of this" (Carson 1995: 669).
8. We leave aside the technical details.
9. A slightly modified version of it was integrated by Kalecki in his 1939 *Essays on Economic Fluctuations*.
10. We refer the interested reader to D'ASPREMONT, Claude & DOS SANTOS FERREIRA, Rodolphe & GERARD-VARET, (2007) excellent presentation of the theoretical arguments developed by several authors.
11. Recall again Lerner's (1934) proposition.
12. "Since the fear of loss is more powerful than the hope of gain, the tendency towards restrictive combinations is stronger in a slump than in a boom" (Robinson 1936: 59–60).

5 Kalecki's Long-Run Theory of Effective Demand: The Trend and Business Cycles

1. The paper was originally published in 1937 and was reproduced with amendments in Kalecki 1939a [1990]. This latter one is the version we will be referring to in this chapter.
2. Most "Keynesian" business-cycle model follow one of Kalecki's models. Kalecki himself very rarely cited or discussed other business-cycle models.
3. Besides the literature cited in the text, we acknowledge our debt to more general evaluations of Kalecki's business-cycle theory, and especially to Assous (2003a and 2003b), Sawyer 1985, Tew 1999, Sordi 1989.

4. In the preface of his *Essay on the Business Cycle Theory*, Kalecki wrote: "the aim of this study is to provide an explanation, indeed one of several possible explanations, of the automatic mechanism of business fluctuations in a closed economy [...]. Moreover, the automatic mechanism of business fluctuations is defined here much more strictly than usual. We do not, for instance, seek to examine an automatic restoration of equilibrium which has been distorted by disproportions of development. Instead, we want to set out a mechanism which would explain the relative *regularity* of business fluctuations" (Kalecki 1933 [1990]: 66; author's emphasis).
5. Kalecki dealt with unemployment equilibrium when he discussed the validity of Say's Law in Kalecki 1934a [1990].
6. In addition, the analysis is based on the proposition that income distribution is determined by the degree of monopoly, which permits expressing national income as a linear function of investment.
7. See also Fazzari and Mott (1986–87) and Fazzari and Peterson (1993), for attempts to validate empirically Kalecki's hypothesis on the influence of past profits on investment.
8. This is precisely what Kaldor showed in the appendix of his 1940 article, on which the following discussion is based.
9. Kalecki's paragraph comes immediately after a statistical section where he tests his theory with data from the US; and presents the scatter diagram alluded to in that paragraph.
10. "It seems reasonable to assume that larger shocks have a smaller frequency than small shocks. Thus, the assumption of normal frequency distribution appears to be more reasonable than that of even [i.e., uniform, JL and MA] frequency distribution" (Kalecki 1954a [1991]: 319).
11. In Kalecki (1968 [1991]), in his last contribution to this subject, he does not make reference to the importance of erratic shocks to keep the cycle alive. However, he considered the issue in his lectures on "Growth and Cycles in the Capitalist Economy", reproduced in the Appendix to this chapter.
12. "We have identified innovations here with developments in technology. However, the definition of innovations can be easily broadened to include kindred phenomena, such as the introduction of new products which require for their manufacture new equipment, the opening up of new sources of raw materials which make necessary new investment in production and transportation facilities, etc". (Kalecki 1954a [1991]: 354). However "Innovations in the sense of gradual adjustment of equipment to the current state of technology are assumed to be part and parcel of 'ordinary' investment as determined by the 'normal' factors" (Ibid).
13. In his earlier models it was the *average* rate of profit which affects investment.
14. We follow Kalecki's terminology here, and we use the letter *e* to denote the proportion of total savings accruing to entrepreneurs.
15. Many years later he referred to these developments as follows: "I modified in my later work [of my theory of the business cycle] only the factors determining investment decisions...Incidentally, this development of my theory...which was quite laborious hardly earned any applause. It was frequently maintained that the first version was more lucid and elegant. I myself consider that the modifications introduced meant some progress

since the later version of the theory seems to me better founded and more realistic." (Kalecki 1966; foreword).

16. Kalecki (1968b [1991]: 464) argued "Marx did not develop such a theory [i.e. a theory of the determinants of investment], but neither has this been accomplished in modern economics". As we mentioned, he was also critical of Keynes theory of investment, pointing out (Kalecki 1936 [1990]: 231): "it is difficult to consider Keynes' solution of the investment problem to be satisfactory. The reason for this fallacy lies in an approach which is basically static to a matter which is by its nature dynamic".
17. Thus for example Blinder (2006: 27/28) puts it as follows: "I will adhere to the consensus view by assuming that the macroeconomy has a natural-rate property, by which I mean... that output returns to potential".
18. This is equivalent to assuming that workers do not save.
19. In a private and closed economy national income equals the sum of wages plus profits, $Y = W + P = wY + \varepsilon Y$ thus $1 = w + \varepsilon$ and $\varepsilon = 1 - w$. It must be noticed that if *e* grows then *w* must diminish, and viceversa. That is why we call *e* the exploitation rate.
20. This assumption will be discussed later.

6 Kalecki's Macroeconomics of Public Finance and of Monetary Policy

1. As Lerner (1978: 67) recounts: "[A]t a lecture to the Federal Reserve in Washington in 1944, [Keynes] showed concern that there might be 'too much saving' after the war. When I pointed out that the government [by increasing its spending or reducing taxes] could always induce enough spending by incurring deficits to increase incomes, he at first objected that this would only cause 'even more saving' and then denounced as 'humbug' my suggestion that the deficits required to induce enough total spending could always be financed by increasing the national debt. (I must add here that Evsey Domar, at my side, whispered: 'He ought to read the *General Theory*' and that a month later Keynes withdrew his denunciation.)"
2. Lerner devised three laws of functional finance. First, government spending and taxes should be adjusted so that aggregate demand is just sufficient to purchase the full employment level output at current prices. Second, incurring or repaying the national debt should only occur if it is desirable to change the interest rate. Third, the amount of money in circulation should be adjusted to accommodate policies enacted in adherence to the first two laws (Scitovsky 1984).
3. The following coincidence of opinions is so striking that it deserves to be brought to light. At about the same time as Kalecki, Keynes (1933 [1971–1982]: 172) wrote: "The effects of an increase or decrease of £100,000,000 in our loan-expenditure are, broadly speaking, equal to the effects of an increase or decrease of £100,000,000 in our foreign balance." One cannot but subscribe here to Joan Robinson's (1977: 7) remark: "In the history of economic thought, there is one notable example of this phenomenon [i.e., the same

discovery to come almost simultaneously from two independent sources] the discovery of the theory of employment by Maynard Keynes and Michal Kalecki".

4. It seems to us useful to remind readers how Keynes (1964: 200) discussed the issue: "The relation of changes in M to Y and *r* depends, in the first instance, on the way in which changes in M come about. Suppose that M consists of gold coins and that changes in M can only result from increased returns to the activities of gold-miners who belong to the economic system under examination. In this case changes in M are, in the first instance, directly associated with changes in Y, since the new gold accrues as someone's income. Exactly the same conditions hold if changes in M are due to the Government printing money wherewith to meet its current expenditure; – in this case also the new money accrues as someone's income. The new level of income, however, will not continue sufficiently high for the requirements of M, to absorb the whole of the increase in M; and some portion of the money will seek an outlet in buying securities or other assets until *r* has fallen so as to bring about an increase in the magnitude of M, and at the same time to stimulate a rise in Y to such an extent that the new money is absorbed either in M_2 or in the M_1 which corresponds to the rise in Y caused by the fall in *r*".
5. As mentioned earlier in this chapter, here Kalecki anticipated a reasoning later developed and formalized by Domar (1944).
6. In that same paper, Kalecki (1944a [1990]: 364) considered also the possibility of a modified income tax as an alternative. Keynes thought highly of Kalecki's proposal, and wrote: "I am very much taken by your modified income tax... Why don't you apply it, however, to working capital also?" (In Kalecki 1990: 579).
7. In the midst of the deepest world recession since the 1930s, Robert Barro, a leading member of the New Classical School recently wrote: "The theory [underpinning the plea for a fiscal push] implicitly assumes that the government is better than the private market at marshaling idle resources to produce useful stuff. Unemployed labor and capital can be utilized at essentially zero social cost, but the private market is somehow unable to figure any of this out. In other words, there is something wrong with the price system... A much more plausible starting point is a multiplier of zero. In this case, the GDP is given, and a rise in government purchases requires an equal fall in the total of other parts of GDP – consumption, investment and net exports. In other words, the social cost of one unit of additional government purchases is one" (*The Wall Street Journal*, January 22, 2009).
8. This notion has been denoted the "Ricardian equivalence".
9. Concerning the empirical part of the issue, the notion that agents will somehow react in anticipation to government policies, is closely related to the so-called Lucas-critique (Lucas 1976) to "naïve" econometric models. This hypothesis states that when the public expect or observe a rise in government expenditure, they anticipate that this will be followed in the future by higher taxes to finance that expenditure, and they reduce their expenditure today. However, Ericsson and Irons (1995) have analysed a great number of papers dealing with the "Lucas critique" and found no confirmation for this hypothesis.

10. See also Mott and Slattery (1994), as well as Laramie and Mair (1996) on this point.
11. "By indirect taxes we mean the actual revenue from this source minus subsidies for private businesses plus profits from government enterprises" (Kalecki 1956 [1997]: 282).
12. An analogous case will take place when state firms raise prices. If they produce final goods, the price increase will directly reduce the real purchasing power of the population. If they produce intermediate goods, private firms' costs will rise and they will increase prices to maintain their "degree of monopoly". Thus the real purchasing power of the population will also diminish.
13. This is only approximately correct. As we discuss in the next chapter, if the additional government expenditure financed via taxes on profits leads to an expansion of effective demand, imports tend to rise and net exports are reduced, which diminishes profits.
14. Kalecki refers to a paper by Szeworski (1962) in support for his "assumption that an increase on corporate profits is not passed on to the consumer through price increases" (Kalecki 1962a [1991]). Szeworski's paper is the only one we have been able to find in which the association between profit taxes and prices is investigated. Surely, we would need additional empirical research, using the more refined statistical techniques now available, to adequately asses the validity of Kalecki's assumption. Anyway, such empirical studies as we have been able to consult, where prices appear to closely track unit prime costs, with profit margins over unit direct costs more or less constant, seem to us to indirectly validate Kalecki's guess.
15. Note, that under these conditions, the degree of monopoly, or price prime cost ratio, and the unit gross profit before taxes (determined by the relation between the new prices, which rise, and unit prime costs, which remain constant), both increase. See Mott and Slattery (1994) for an extension of Kalecki's theory of taxation to the cases where workers save and where taxes may lead to higher mark-ups.
16. But, the question may arise, will not the tax negatively affect future investment, and hence output and employment in the medium- and long-run? Here the following argument can be maintained. *Since the after-tax profits of the current period have remained unchanged,* the spending decisions of the capitalists for later periods have no reason to be modified due to the implementation of the profit tax. That is, if the capitalists do not immediately diminish their expenditure when the tax is implemented, there is no reason that they diminish it in future periods.
17. It may still be argued that the budget multiplier may work even if workers' disposable income is affected, because workers do save.
18. Kalecki was assuming, of course, a closed economy. In an open economy profits would fall owing to the increase in the trade deficit (We show in the next chapter that in Kalecki's theory, where workers do not save, in an open economy profits are equal to investment plus capitalist consumption plus the budget deficit plus the foreign trade surplus).

19. See also Asimakopulos (1990), and López and Mott (1999) for further details about this exchange.
20. Of course, Kalecki was not the only economist to advocate rationing.
21. "Inflationary" finance was the term that he used to refer to deficit spending or credit expansion.
22. Kalecki (1962b [1991]) applied the same methodology for a short piece on the Western German economy. Also, during the 1950s he directed a small team of economists at the Polish Academy of Sciences, devoted to the study of the economic situation in capitalist countries, which published a series of papers and books on the subject (See, e. g., Kalecki and Szeworski 1957; Dobrska and Szeworski 1958 and 1959; Dobrska et al. 1960. See also Szeworski 1965).

7 Kalecki's Open Economy Macroeconomics

1. The case of an import surplus is symmetrical. Drawing inspiration from Kalecki, Bhaduri and Skarstein (1996) beautifully discuss the case of a country recipient of foreign aid which uses that aid to simply substitute domestic production, without raising effective demand, such that an import surplus appears that reduces output, employment and profits.
2. See the Appendix to this chapter for details.
3. Kalecki (1939b [1990] and 1967 [1991]) reminds us that this outlook played a great role in the theory of the prominent Marxist revolutionary Rosa Luxembourg (2003).
4. In several other places Kalecki discussed the political economy of the export surplus in advanced capitalist countries. The interested reader may refer to, for example, Kalecki's (1962c [1991]) thoughtful remarks of the economic and political aspects of the West Germany export surplus after World War II.
5. Also, in either case the rise in profits stimulates an additional expansion of private expenditure, which reinforces the business upswing.
6. Kalecki is here using the term "domestic exports" to denote the budget deficit.
7. The case of a wage fall is symmetrical.
8. See the Appendix for a formal discussion of the issues considered later.
9. See the Appendix to this chapter for details.
10. The same reasoning can be used to discuss the impact of a currency depreciation on output and employment (see López and Perrotini 2006).
11. See, for example, Bhaduri and Marglin (1990); Bowles and Boyer (1995); Blecker (1999); and the literature cited therein.
12. One year later, Keynes published in *The Times* a series of four papers, which would later appear as "The Means to Prosperity" (Keynes 1933 [1971–1982]). In those papers Keynes argued along similar lines to Kalecki, but with greater optimism. To overcome the world crisis, countries should embark on large-scale loan-financed expenditure, and this would necessitate international coordination among leading capitalist countries. Keynes

put forward these ideas to influence the public opinion, but especially the participants of the World Monetary Conference, organized by the League of Nations in 1933.

13. Keynes made several versions of his proposal, and we select here paragraphs from that version where it seems to us the ideas are more clearly articulated.
14. The quotas he proposed were quite generous.
15. The paper was published in a special issue of the *Bulletin of the Oxford University Institute of Statistics*, devoted to the discussion of these plans. Kalecki and Schumacher, as well as T. Balogh, the other contributor to the volume, worked at the Institute.
16. Note there is a typo in this sentence in the reproduction of this paper in Kalecki's *Collected Works*.
17. Thomas Balogh, the third member of the trio to write in the special issue of the *Bulletin of the Oxford University Institute of Statistics* previously cited, kept alive for several years the debate on the New International Economic System. See his papers collected in Balogh (1963).
18. A and λ are the autonomous part of capitalist consumption and the parameter relating capitalist consumption to profits, respectively, and e is the share of profits in income. G_k is total capitalist expenditure.
19. If we used instead a conventional Keynesian specification, we would have (abstracting from the autonomous part of consumption and from government expenditure):

$$Y = \frac{I + (X - M)}{s}$$

where s is the saving propensity.

20. In Kalecki's extended profit equation, saving out of wages reduce profits, and the budget deficit increases profits.
21. If we used instead the conventional Keynesian specification:

$$Y = \frac{I + (X - M)}{s}$$

we would conclude that if the wage fall entailed a change in the distribution of income against wages, s would rise, offsetting the rise in the trade balance.

8 Michal Kalecki: A Pioneer of Development Economics

Julio López would like to express his deep gratitude to Ignacy Sachs, whom he considers probably the person who more consistently has applied Kalecki's analysis for the understanding of developing economies.

1. Before leaving Poland in 1936, Kalecki conducted important empirical research on Poland, which was clearly underdeveloped at the time. See Kalecki (1931 [1996]), Kalecki (1934c [1996]), Kalecki (1934d [1996]), Kalecki (1935d [1996]) and Kalecki (1935e [1996]).

2. In Kalecki's works during the early 1940s we have not found any other piece concerning underdeveloped economies. However, we surmise that he exchanged ideas on the subject with Josef Steindl, his closest collaborator at the Oxford Institute of Economics and Statistics, while Steindl was writing his report "The impact of the war on India". We reproduce here some relevant parts of Steindl's paper: "In contrast to other countries engaged in the war, India has an abundant supply of labour. This takes the form of 'disguised unemployment', (...), a considerable part of the present population being completely surplus, so that their withdrawal from agriculture would not involve any reduction in the output. (...). A considerable increase in war production (which would, in fact, amount to a part-industrialization), [and] (...) a substantial transfer of labour from 'disguised unemployment' to industrial employment will therefore increase the demand for consumption goods, amongst other things, also the demand for food. (...) [However] It seems to be a feature of agricultural production in India that it is rather inelastic (...) Owing to the inelasticity of agricultural production, an expansion of purchasing power in India must very largely have the effect of increasing prices" (Steindl 1942 [1946]: 129–131).
3. Dell (1977) singles out some of the official materials where the opinions can be attributed to Kalecki. Thus we can find a very typical Kaleckian statement: "Any estimate of the course of events in India and Latin America in the near future must take into account the large-scale development schemes upon which these countries are likely to embark (...) If direct taxation is not increased, inflation will follow just as it did during the war. However, even if development expenditures are offset by direct taxation, the problem of inflation in food prices will not be solved, because taxation of higher incomes will hardly reduce the demand for food. In the long run, an increase in food production will doubtless constitute a very important part in the development programme of under-developed countries. This will require fundamental social and technical changes in the agricultural economies" (Dell 1977: 40).
4. We will take the opportunity here for a personal reminiscence. One of the authors (JL) approached Kalecki with a question concerning an issue that was very much in vogue in Latin America in the late 1960s. "Do you think that in underdeveloped countries agrarian conditions are really semi-feudal, or are they not simply capitalistic?" His answer, in his usual laconic style, was "Do you think this is really important?"
5. We refer the interested reader to Fitzgerald's (1990: 183–203) excellent formalization and extension of Kalecki's main ideas.
6. Recalling the period when Keynesian economics was dominant, neoclassical economists not only agreed with this conclusion, they took it further, in what became a very enriching cross-fertilization of ideas. Indeed, it was accepted that, in the presence of domestic distortions, a decentralized market economy will not achieve its Pareto optimum and so resources may be left idle; which would entail a waste from the perspective of the economy as a whole. With the decline of prominence of Keynesian economics, these ideas disappeared from neoclassical economics.
7. Prebisch (1951) also emphasized this feature of developing economies.
8. Kalecki's conclusion must be amended when we consider an open economy. For in such a situation the fall in unit labor costs improves

competitiveness, and exports and the trade balance are likely to improve, bringing about a rise in profits and in aggregate demand. Thus employment may also rise. But this point was not considered either by other development economists at the time, possibly because industrial exports from developing economies were not considered feasible in any case.

9. The authors would like to thank Martin Puchet, for his collaboration in the elaboration of this section.
10. J. Osiatynski, the editor of Kalecki's *Collected Works*, suggests that, in the elaboration of his theory of "intermediate regimes", Kalecki received inspiration from I. Sachs, his close collaborator at the Centre of Research on Underdeveloped Economies, of Warsaw. See Kalecki 1993; esp. 199–204.
11. The idea that lack of sufficient import capacity prevents fuller use the productive establishments is based on the notion that "foreign currency... is the scarcest factor in the Israeli economy" (Kalecki 1951 [1993]: 103). By the way, this same idea was independently formulated somewhat later by two Latin American economists, Schydlowsky (1967) and Diamand (1973). They took it as a point of departure for their proposal of an economic recovery and employment policy for semi-industrialized Latin American countries. Foreign exchange as the scarcest resource in poor countries is also central to Prebisch and the Latin America structuralist school thinking (López 2008), as well as to the dual-gap analysis pioneered by Chenery (Chenery and Bruno 1962).
12. We want to mention here Kalecki's position on "popular front" policy for countries like France and Italy, discussed in a Polish – Italian workshop held in Ancona in 1965. Kalecki's paper was never published, but according to I. Sachs (personal communication with the authors), who attended this workshop, he was of the opinion that excessive wage rises may jeopardize workers' real income due to price rises.
13. On this point, Kalecki was critical of Dobb (1960) and Sen (1960); who rather advocated capital-intensive techniques in underdeveloped countries, to stimulate the rate of accumulation.
14. "The modernization of old factories acquires a special significance. Such modernization enables their productive equipment and workforce to be better employed, at the cost of relatively small investment outlays" (Kalecki 1960 [1993]: 213). And also, referring to the Israel economy: "Investment in branches of industry where unused capacity still exists, even though this process would involve considerable modernization, is a luxury that the Israeli economy cannot afford for the time being. This is especially the case because (...) there is no scarcity of labour at present" (Kalecki 1951 [1993]: 103).
15. As already shown, in his study for Israel, Kalecki recommended diverse medium- and long-run measures to balance external accounts under rapid growth conditions. For instance, "It is (...) clear that a considerable saving in imports may be achieved by investment in basic industries. In many instances, the cost of investment is small in relation to the saving in imports, the value added per annum being up to three to four times as much as the value of the machinery required" (Kalecki 1951 [1993]: 102).

9 Kalecki: The Socialist Economist

1. In fact, he was never a member of any political party.
2. "Expanded reproduction" denotes a situation in which capital accumulation is taking place; or, to state it differently, net investment is positive.
3. The equivalence between accumulation and net investment may seem strange, since Marxian economic theory also includes in accumulation the increment of variable capital from one period to the following. We, however, exclude this last element from our definition of accumulation, because we assume that the workers advance their labour to the capitalists, and that they are paid for their work at the end of the productive period. As a consequence, for each period, the surplus value not consumed by the capitalist, and which is used for the expansion of the production in the following period – that is, that which accumulates – exclusively encompasses the increment of constant capital. This increment is nothing other than net investment (see Steindl 1952: 243–244 footnote 3).
4. Marx's clear perception of the "realization problem" made it natural for his followers to understand that a capitalist economy cannot ensure full utilization of its productive resources, manpower in the first place. Coming from that culture, Kalecki, when he formulated his version of the principle of effective demand, probably did not feel it too important to demonstrate why capitalism did not normally ensure full utilization of the available labour force; rather, for him this was taken for granted. This is unlike Keynes's approach, who having been brought up in the classical and the neoclassical tradition, considered that first of all he should delve into the reasons why full employment is normally not achieved in a capitalist economy.
5. In fact, Marx never explicitly defined the "Law of value". But from his work we take it that our inference regarding what he meant is correct.
6. In modern parlance, the organic composition of capital could be made equivalent to the ratio between cost of materials plus depreciation allowances, over total wages.
7. Marx never pretended to "explain" capitalist exploitation on the basis of the discrepancy between labour time and the value of labour power. His explanation depends more on economic, political and social factors which give rise to this discrepancy.
8. In his lectures on the economics of capitalism at the Central School of Planning and Statistics, he used the term "rate of exploitation" in reference to the relative share of profits in income.
9. Marx was referring here mostly to the monopoly caused by the land rent. But nothing prevents us from extending the notion to include monopoly power arising from market conditions.
10. It is instructive to compare Kalecki's ideas from this paper, with those put forward by Keynes in the last chapter of his *General Theory*, "Concluding notes on the social philosophy towards which the General Theory might lead". Here one can see at glance how distant in their overall view of capitalism the two founding fathers of the principle of effective demand were.
11. It is worth pointing out, that at the time (1943) he put forward theses ideas the concept of the capitalist state implicit in Kalecki's ideas was totally foreign to the official Marxist view (whereby the State is the simple instrument

of the dominant classes), and correspond better with the notion of the "relative autonomy of State", that was developed later by Marxian authors.

12. Kalecki's theory of the political business cycle has inspired a lot of work. Probably the most original one can be credited to M. Salvati (1984).
13. Let us indulge here on a personal recollection. One of us (JL) can recall a Kalecki's seminar at the Advanced School of National Economic Planning, probably in 1966. Luigi Spaventa the invited speaker, presented a paper, where he argued in favour of a more disaggregated model to plan the Italian economy. Kalecki's intervention at the end of the presentation was simply: "Why such a great effort when you are not going to plan the economy anyway!". Let us recall that during the 1960s Italy was living in a period characterized by heavy State intervention and fast growth.
14. The paper was originally published in a journal of the Italian Communist Party, and was preceded by a critical note from A. Pesenti, a leading economist of that party. We can see that even the most "liberal" amongst the Western communist parties of the time was not open enough to accept Kalecki's ideas.
15. Prof. Laski (personal communication to the present authors) is of the opinion that Kalecki was in fact "allergic" to any discussion about the Law of Value!
16. Immediately after the publication of the *Essay on Business Cycle Theory* (Kalecki 1933 [1990]), Aleksander Rajman, professor of mathematics and a member of the Polish communist party, issued a very critical reply to that work, condemning in particular Kalecki's notion that wages could rise without profits falling. See Kalecki 1990: 478.
17. As far as we have been able to ascertain, this "law" is mentioned only once in Kalecki's works. In his words: "The government spending policy...permits the overcoming of one contradiction in the capitalist system: that of insufficient effective demand. But if technical progress causes productive capacity to rise more slowly than the accumulation of capital, i.e. if the capital intensity of production increases, there comes into picture another contradiction of the capitalist system formulated by Marx in his law of falling rate of profit" (Kalecki 1945 [1990]: 385).
18. Note the similarity with Keynes's concept of saturation of capital.
19. If resources are fully employed, resources used to produce capital goods must be diverted from the production of current consumption goods.
20. This is similar to Harrod's (1939) model of equalizing the warranted and natural growth rates.

10 Michal Kalecki's Intellectual Legacy

1. We note here that some New Keynesian authors (see for example Greenwald and Stiglitz 1988 and 1993, and Blinder 1987) have taken up Kalecki's principle of increasing risk. They have also extended it to the demand for working capital, originating the notion of effective supply failures. It is unfortunate, but also very illuminating of prejudices in our discipline vis-à-vis non-mainstream, and especially radical authors, that Kalecki's name is rarely cited in this literature.

2. Minsky (1975: 57) remarked: "Keynes put forth an investment theory of fluctuations in real demand and a financial theory of fluctuations in real investment".
3. This conclusion is not compatible with the diminishing returns story within which Keynes set forth his *General Theory.*
4. We referred in Chapter 1 to Kalecki's use of the term "Keynesian".
5. This idea, which Kalecki put forward for the first time in 1943, to a certain extent anticipates the New Keynesian notion that credit rationing prevents adjustment in the interest rate to equilibrate the demand for and the supply of credit (e.g., Stiglitz and Weiss 1981).
6. Some years before, Fisher (1933) had put forward his "Debt-deflation theory of great depressions", which also emphasizes crises of confidence. However, Fisher's view is richer, in that he also called attention to distress selling of assets which lowers their prices and deepens the depression.
7. In the Introduction to his collection of essays, *Selected essays on the Dynamics of the Capitalist Economy, 1933–1970,* Kalecki wrote "It is interesting to notice that the theory of effective demand, already formulated in the first papers, remains unchanged in all the relevant writings, as do my views on the distribution of national income. However, there is a continuous search for new solutions in the theory of investment decisions, where even the last papers represents – for better or for worse – a novel approach (Kalecki 1991: 590).
8. Kalecki did not neglect the possibility of potentially explosive cases. In such situations, fluctuations in actual output would be constrained between a "ceiling" along which the (growing) resources are fully utilized and a "floor" set by the fact that gross investment cannot become negative.
9. Some of Kalecki's models also make use of non-linearities. In his 1939 and 1943 models, investment is a sigmoid function of output with much lower positive slopes at both extremes than in the broad middle range of the output scale. Investment is deterred by surplus capacity in slump, rising construction and financial costs in booms and most importantly by waves of pessimism and optimism. Saving has a linear shape due to the stability of the degree of monopoly which determines income distribution and the social propensity to consume. Given output, investment depends inversely on the capital stock. There are three possible equilibriums, two of which are stable. The result is a self-sustained cycle in real aggregates, from stable to unstable to another equilibrium. Although the dynamics is more complicated, it allows for stable closed cycles which are generated independently of time-lags, initial conditions or random shocks. These "limit cycles" are characterized by the fact that no matter how the system is initiated, it will tend to a certain type of the cycle. Thus it is no exaggeration to postulate that Kalecki actually anticipated contemporary non-linear business-cycle models.
10. Most of the business-cycle model inspired on Kalecki are based on the capital stock adjustment (or "flexible accelerator") principle: current investment equals some fraction of the gap between the desired and the actual capital. The desired stock varies directly with output (taken as a proxy for the expected demand for output that the capital is to help produce). Net

investment therefore depends positively on output and inversely on the initially available stock of capital. Since profitability depends positively on the output–capital ratio, the role of profits in the investment function is implicit in these models. The dynamics then comes from lags, from non-linearities, or both.

Bibliography

Arestis, P. and Sawyer, M. (2003) "The case for fiscal policy". *The Levy Economics Institute Working Paper* No. 382.

Asimakopolous, A. (1990) "Kalecki and Keynes: their correspondence", *History of Political Economy*, 22: 49–64.

Assous, M. (2003a) "Kalecki's contribution to the emergence of endogenous business cycle theory: an interpretation of his 1939 *Essays*", *History of Economic Ideas*, XI, 1: 109–123.

Assous, M. (2003b) *Sous-emploi, cycles et concurrence imparfaite*, Ph. D. Thesis, Université de Cergy-Pontoise.

Assous, M. (2006) "Kalecki était-il keynésien avant Keynes?", *Revue économique*, 57, 2 : 165–184.

Assous, M. (2007) "Kalecki's 1934 model vs. the IS-LM model of Hicks (1937) and of Modigliani (1944)", *European Journal of the History of Economic Thought*, 14, 1: 97–118.

Balogh, Th. (1963) *Unequal partners*. Basil Blackwell, Oxford.

Barro, R. (1974) "Are government bonds net wealth?", *Journal of Political Economy*, 82, 6: 1095–1117.

Barro, R. (2009) "Government spending is no free lunch", *The Wall Street Journal*, January 22.

Beveridge, W. (1944) "Full employment in a free society". George Allen & Unwin, London.

Bhaduri, A. (1986) "Macroeconomics: the dynamics of commodity production". Macmillan Education LTD, Hampshire.

Bhaduri, A. and Falkinger, J. (1990) "Optimal price adjustment under imperfect information", *European Economic Review*, 34, 5: 941–952, July.

Bhaduri, A. and Marglin, S. (1990) "Unemployment and the real wage: the economic basis for contesting political ideologies", *Cambridge Journal of Economics*, 14: 375–393.

Bhanduri, A. and Skarstein, R. (1996) "Short-period macroeconomic aspects of foreign aid", *Cambridge Journal of Economics*, 20: 195–206.

Blecker R.A. (1999) "Kaleckian macro models for open economies", in *Foundations of International Macroeconomics*, edited by J. Deprez and J.T. Harvey, Routledge, Londres: 116–149.

Blinder, A. (1987) "Credit rationing and effective supply failures", *Economic Journal*, 97, June: 327–352.

Blinder, A. (2006) "The case against the case against discretionary fiscal policy", in *The macroeconomics of fiscal policy*, edited by R.W. Kopcke, G.M. Tootell and R.K. Triest, The MIT Press, Cambridge, MA.

Bowles S., and Boyer, R. (1995) "Wages, aggregate demand, and employment in an open economy: an empirical investigation", in *Macroeconomic policy after the conservative era*, edited by G.A. Epstein and M.G. Gintis,Cambridge, Cambridge University Press: 143–171.

Brus, W. (1999) "Great debt and a few grievances: a note on Michal Kalecki as my adopted mentor", *Review of Political Economy*, 11, 3: 257–260.

Carpenter, R., Fazzari, S. and Petersen, B. (1994) "Inventory investment, internal-finance fluctuations, and the business cycle", *Brookings Papers on Economic Activity*, 2: 75–138.

Carson, J.D. (1995) "Kalecki's pricing theory: Marginalist to the end ?", *History of Political Economy*, 28, 4, Duke University Press: 661–690.

Chamberlin, E.H. (1933) *The theory of monopolistic competition*. Harvard University Press, Cambridge, MA.

Chapple (1995) "The Kaleckian origins of the Keynesian model", *Oxford Economic Papers*, 47, 3: 525–537.

Chenery, H. and Bruno, M. (1962) "Development alternatives in an open economy", *Economic Journal*, 72, 1962: 79–103.

D'ASPREMONT, Claude & DOS SANTOS FERREIRA, Rodolphe & GERARD-VARET, Louis-André, 2007. *"Imperfect competition and the trade cycle: guidelines from the late thirties," CORE Discussion Papers* 2007079, Université Catholique de Louvain, Center for Operations Research and Econometrics (CORE).

D'Autume, A. (2000) "L'essor de la macro-économie", in *Nouvelle histoire de la pensée économique*, edited by A. Béraud et G. Faccarello, Vol. 2, La Découverte. Paris.

De Vroey, M. (2000) "IS-LM a` la Hicks versus IS-LM a` la Modigliani". *History of Political Economy*, 32: 293–316.

Dell, S. (1977) "Kalecki at the United Nations. 1946–1954" *Oxford Bulletin of Economics and Statistics*, 39: 31–45.

Diamand, M. (1973) 'Doctrinas económicas, desarrollo e independencia', Editorial Paidos, Buenos Aires.

Dobb, M. (1960) *An essay on economic growth and planning*, Routledge and Kegan Paul, London.

Dobrska, Z. and Szeworski, A. (1958) *Sudia z zakresu koniunktury wspólecznego kapitalizmu,* vol. 2., Panstwowe Wydawnictwo Naukowe, Warsaw.

Dobrska, Z. and Szeworski, A. (1959) *Sudia z zakresu koniunktury wspólecznego kapitalizmu,* vol. 3, Panstwowe Wydawnictwo Naukowe, Warsaw.

Dobrska, Z., Kalecki, M., Kudlinski, R. and W. Sadzikowski (1960) *"Sudia z zakresu koniunktury wspólecznego kapitalizmu"*, vol. 4. Panstwowe Wydawnictwo Naukowe, Warsaw.

Domar, E. (1944) "The burden of the debt and national income", *American Economic Review*, December: 798–827.

Dunlop, J.T. (1938) "The movement of real and money wage rates", *Economic Journal*, 48: 413–434.

Ericsson, N. and Irons, J. (1995) "Theory without measurement", in *Macroeconometrics: developments, tensions, and prospects*, edited by Kevin D. Hoover, Kluwer, Boston, MA.

Eshag, E., (1977) "Kalecki's political economy: a comparison with Keynes", *Oxford Bulletin of Economics and Statistics*, 39, 1: 79–85.

Evans, M. (1969) *Macroeconomic activity*. Harper and Row, New York.

Fazzari, S. and Mott, T. (1986–87) "The investment theories of Kalecki and Keynes: an empirical study of firm data, 1970–1982", *Journal of Post Keynesian Economics*, 9: 171–187.

Fazzari, S. and Petersen, B. (1993) "Working capital and fixed investment: new evidence on financing constraints", *Rand Journal of Economics*, 24: 328–342.

Feiwell, G. (1975) *The intellectual capital of Michal Kalecki. A study in economic theory and policy.* The University of Tennessee Press, Knoxville.

Fisher, I. (1933) "The debt-deflation theory of great depressions", *Econometrica,* October: 337–357.

Fitzgerald, E.V.K. (1990) "Kalecki on financing development: an approach to the macroeconomics of the semi-industrialized economy", *Cambridge Journal of Economics,* 14: 183–203.

Frisch, R. (1935 [1990]) "The characteristic solutions of a mixed difference and differential equation ocurring in economic dynamics", reprinted in *Collected works of Michal Kalecki,* Vol. II, edited by J. Osiatynsky, Oxford University Press, Oxford.

Galbraith, J.K. (1975) "How Keynes came to America", in *Essays on John Maynard Keynes,* edited by Milo Keynes, Cambridge University Press, Cambridge.

Goodwin, R. (1989) "Kalecki's economic dynamics: a personal view", reprinted in Sebastiani (1989), *M. Kalecki's relevance today.* Macmillan, London.

Greenwald, B. and Stiglitz, J. (1988) "Imperfect information, finance constraints, and business fluctuations", in *Finance constraints, expectations and macroeconomics,* edited by Kohn, Meier and S.C. Tsiang, Oxford University Press, Oxford: 103–140.

Greenwald, B. and Stiglitz, J. (1993) "Financial market imperfections and business cycles", in *Quarterly Journal Economics,* February: 77–114.

Haavelmo, T. (1945) "Multiplier effects of a balanced budget", *Econometrica,* XIII: 311–318.

Hall, R.L. and Hitch, C.J. (1939) "Price theory and business behaviour", *Oxford Economic Papers,* 2: 12–45, reprinted in *Oxford Studies in the Price Mechanism* (1951), edited by T. Wilson and P.W.S. Andrews, Clarendon, Oxford.

Harrod, R. (1936) *The trade cycle.* Oxford University Press, Oxford.

Harrod, R. (1939) "An essay in dynamic theory", *Economic Journal,* 49, June: 14–33.

Hicks, J. (1937) "Mr. Keynes and the 'Classics': a suggested interpretation", *Econometrica,* 5: 147–159.

Kaldor, N. (1940) "A model of trade cycle", *Economic Journal,* March: 78–92, reprinted in *Essays on economic stability and growth* (1960), edited by N. Kaldor, Gerald Duckworth & Co. Ltd., London.

Kaldor, N. (1955–56) "Alternative theories of distribution", *Review of Economic Studies,* 23, 2, reprinted in *Essays on value and distribution,* edited by N.Kaldor,Gerald Duckworth & Co. Ltd., London: 209–236.

References to Kalecki

Kalecki, M. (1931 [1996]) "An estimate of investment activity in Poland" (with Ludwik Landau). in *Collected Works of Michal Kalecki,* Vol. VII, edited by J. Osiatynsky, Oxford University Press, Oxford.

Kalecki M. (1932a [1990]) "Reduction of wages during crisis", in *Collected works of Michal Kalecki,* Vol. I, edited by J. Osiatynsky, Oxford University Press, Oxford.

Kalecki M. (1932b [1990]) "On the papen plan", in *Collected works of Michal Kalecki,* Vol. I, edited by J. Osiatynsky, Oxford University Press, Oxford.

Kalecki, M. (1932c [1996]) "Inflation and war", in *Collected works of Michal Kalecki,* Vol. VI, edited by J. Osiatynsky, Oxford University Press, Oxford.

Kalecki, M. (1932d [1990]) "Is a capitalist overcoming of the crisis possible?", in *Collected works of Michal Kalecki,* Vol. I, edited by J. Osiatynsky, Oxford University Press, Oxford: 53.

Kalecki, M. (1933a [1990]) "Essays on the business cycle theory", in *Collected works of Michael Kalecki,* Vol. I, edited by J. Osiatynsky, Oxford University Press.

Kalecki, M. (1933b [1990]) "On foreign trade and domestic exports", in *Collected Works of Michael Kalecki,* Vol. I, edited by J. Osiatynsky, Oxford University Press.

Kalecki, M. (1934a [1990]) "Three systems", in *Collected works of Michal Kalecki,* Vol. I, edited by J. Osiatynsky, Oxford University Press, Oxford.

Kalecki, M. (1934b [1990]) "Rejoinder", in *Collected works of Michal Kalecki,* Vol. I, edited by J. Osiatynsky, Oxford University Press, Oxford.

Kalecki, M. (1934c [1996]) "Fluctuations in industrial output and consumption" (with Ludwik Landau), in *Collected works of Michal Kalecki,* Vol. VII, edited by J. Osiatynsky, Oxford University Press, Oxford.

Kalecki, M. (1934d [1996]) "An estimate of social income in 1929" (with Ludwik Landau), in *Collected works of Michal Kalecki,* Vol. VII, edited by J. Osiatynsky, Oxford University Press, Oxford.

Kalecki M. (1935a [1996]) "Stimulating the business upswing in Nazi Germany", in *Collected works of Michal Kalecki,* Vol. VI, edited by J. Osiatynsky, Oxford University Press.

Kalecki M. (1935b [1990]) "A Macro-dynamic theory of business cycle", in *Collected works of Michal Kalecki,* Vol. I, edited by J. Osiatynsky, Oxford University Press.

Kalecki, M. (1935c [1990]) "The essence of the business upswing", in *Collected Works of Michal Kalecki,* Vol. I, edited by J. Osiatynsky, Oxford University Press.

Kalecki M. (1935d [1996]) "Social income in 1933 and the foundations of periodic studies on changes of income" (with L. Landau). Included in *Collected works of Michal Kalecki,* Vol. VI, edited by J. Osiatynsky, Oxford University Press.

Kalecki M. (1935e [1996]) "Fluctuations of prices and costs and fluctuations of industrial production in Poland" (with L. Landau). Included in *Collected works of Michal Kalecki,* Vol. VI, edited by J. Osiatynsky, Oxford University Press.

Kalecki, M. (1936 [1990]) "Some remarks on Keynes's Theory", in *Collected works of Michal Kalecki,* Vol. I, edited by J. Osiatynsky, Oxford University Press, Oxford.

Kalecki, M. (1936–37 [1990]) "A theory of the business cycle", in *Collected Works of Michal Kalecki,* Vol. I, edited by J. Osiatynsky, Oxford University Press.

Kalecki M. (1937 [1990]) "A theory of commodity, income, and capital taxation", in *Collected works of Michal Kalecki,* Vol. I, edited by J. Osiatynsky, Oxford University Press.

Kalecki M. (1938a [1990]) "The determinants of distribution of the national income", in *Collected works of Michal Kalecki,* Vol. I, edited by J. Osiatynsky, Oxford University Press, 1990.

Kalecki M. (1938b [1990]) "The lessons of the Blum experiment", in *Collected works of Michal Kalecki*, Vol. I, edited by J. Osiatynsky, Oxford University Press, 1990.

Kalecki, M. (1938c [1993]) "Foreign trade and the national forces of production", in *Collected works of Michal Kalecki*, Vol. V, edited by J. Osiatynsky, Oxford University Press.

Kalecki M. (1939a [1990]) "Essays in the theory of economic fluctuations", in *Collected works of Michal Kalecki*, Vol. I, edited by J. Osiatynsky, Oxford University Press.

Kalecki, M. (1939b [1990]) "The Principle of increasing risk", in *Collected works of Michal Kalecki*, Vol. I, edited by J. Osiatynsky, Oxford University Press.

Kalecki, M. (1939c [1991]) "Money and real wages", in *Collected works of Michal Kalecki*, Vol. II, edited by J. Osiatynsky, Oxford University Press.

Kalecki, M. (1940a [1991]) "The supply curve of an industry under imperfect competition", In *Collected works of Michal Kalecki*, Vol. II, edited by J. Osiatynsky, Oxford University Press.

Kalecki, M. (1940b [1997]) "A scheme of curtailment of consumption", in *Collected Works of Michal Kalecki*, Vol. VII, edited by J. Osiatynsky, Clarendon Press, Oxford.

Kalecki, M. (1941 [1991]) "A theorem on technical progress", in *Collected Works of Michal Kalecki*, Vol. II, edited by J. Osiatynsky, Oxford University Press.

Kalecki M. (1943a [1990]) "Political aspects of full employment", in *Collected works of Michal Kalecki*, Vol. I, edited by J. Osiatynsky, Oxford University Press.

Kalecki, M. (1943b [1997]) "International clearing and long-term lending", in *Collected works of Michal Kalecki*, Vol. VII, edited by J. Osiatynsky, Oxford University Press.

Kalecki, M. (1943c [1991]) "Studies in economic dynamics", in *Collected works of Michal Kalecki*, Vol. II, edited by J. Osiatynsky, Oxford University Press.

Kalecki, M. (1944a [1990]) "Three ways to full employment", in *Collected works of Michal Kalecki*, Vol. I, edited by J. Osiatynsky, Oxford University Press.

Kalecki, M. (1944b [1990]) "Professor Pigou on 'The classical stationary state' ", in *Collected works of Michal Kalecki*, Vol. I edited by J. Osiatynsky, Oxford University Press, Oxford.

Kalecki, M. (1944c [1997]) "The White paper on employment policy", in *Collected Works of Michal Kalecki*, Vol. VII, edited by J. Osiatynsky, Clarendon Press, Oxford.

Kalecki, M. (1944d [1997]) "Economic implications of the Beveridge Plan", in *Collected Works of Michal Kalecki*, Vol. VII, edited by J. Osiatynsky, Clarendon Press, Oxford.

Kalecki, M. (1945 [1990]) "Full employment by stimulating private investment?" in *Collected works of Michal Kalecki*, Vol. I, edited by J. Osiatynsky, Oxford University Press.

Kalecki, M. (1946 [1990]) "Multilateralism and full employment", in *Collected works of Michal Kalecki*, Vol. I, edited by J. Osiatynsky, Oxford University Press.

Kalecki, M. (1951 [1993]) "Report on the main current economic problems of Israel", in *Collected works of Michal Kalecki*, Vol. V, edited by J. Osiatynsky, Oxford University Press.

Kalecki, M. (1954a [1991]) "Theory of economic dynamics", in *Collected works of Michael Kalecki*, Vol. II, edited by J. Osiatynsky, Oxford University Press.

Kalecki, M. (1954b [1993]) "The problem of financing economic development", in *Collected works of Michal Kalecki*, Vol. V, edited by J. Osiatynsky, Oxford University Press.

Kalecki, M. (1956 [1997]) "The economic situation in the USA as compared with the pre-war period", in *Collected works of Michael Kalecki*, Vol. VII, edited by J. Osiatynsky, Oxford University Press.

Kalecki, M. (1960 [1993]) "Observations on labour productivity", in *Collected works of Michal Kalecki*, Vol. IV, edited by J. Osiatynsky, Oxford University Press.

Kalecki, M. (1962a [1991]) "The economic situation in the USA, 1956–1961", in *Collected works of Michael Kalecki*, Vol. II, edited by J. Osiatynsky, Oxford University Press.

Kalecki, M. (1962b [1991]) "Economic aspects of West Germany rearmament", in *Collected works of Michael Kalecki*, Vol. II, edited by J. Osiatynsky, Oxford University Press.

Kalecki, M. (1962c [1991]) "Economic aspects of West Germany rearmament", in *Collected works of Michael Kalecki*, Vol. II, edited by J. Osiatynsky, Oxford University Press.

Kalecki, M. (1962d [1992]) "Outline of a method of constructing a perspective plan (Based on Polish experience)", in *Collected works of Michal Kalecki*, Vol. III, edited by J. Osiatynsky, Oxford University Press.

Kalecki, M. (1963 [1993]) "Introduction to the theory of growth in a socialist economy", in *Collected works of Michal Kalecki*, Vol. IV, edited by J. Osiatynsky, Oxford University Press.

Kalecki, M. (1964a [1992]) "Observations on the 1966–1970 economic plan", in *Collected works of Michal Kalecki*, Vol. III, edited by J. Osiatynsky, Oxford University Press.

Kalecki, M. (1964b [1993]) "Observations on social and economic problems of 'intermediate regimes'", in *Collected Works of Michal Kalecki*, Vol. VII, edited by J. Osiatynsky, Clarendon Press, Oxford.

Kalecki, M. (1966a) *Studies in the theory of business cycles. 1933–1939.* Basil Blackell, Oxford.

Kalecki, M. (1966b [1993]) "The difference between crucial economic problems of developed and underdeveloped non-socialist economies", in *Collected works of Michal Kalecki*, Vol. V, Edited by J. Osiatynsky, Oxford University Press.

Kalecki, M. (1967 [1991]) "The problem of effective demand with Tugan-Baranovsky and Rosa Luxemburgo", in *Collected works of Michael Kalecki*, Vol. II, edited by J. Osiatynsky, Oxford University Press.

Kalecki, M. (1968a [1991]) "Trend and the business cycle", in *Collected works of Michal Kalecki*, Vol. II, edited by J. Osiatynsky, Oxford University Press.

Kalecki, M. (1968b [1991]) "The Marxian equations of reproduction and modern economics", in *Collected works of Michal Kalecki*, Vol. II, edited by J. Osiatynsky, Oxford University Press.

Kalecki, M. (1968c) *"The last phase in the transformation of capitalism"*. Monthly Review Press, New York.

Kalecki, M. (1970 [1993]) "Theory of growth in different social systems", in *Collected works of Michael Kalecki*, Vol. IV, edited by J. Osiatynsky, Oxford University Press.

Kalecki, M. (1971 [1991]) "Class struggle and the distribution of national income", in *Collected works of Michal Kalecki*, Vol. II, edited by J. Osiatynsky, Oxford University Press.

Kalecki, M. (1990) *Collected works of Michal Kalecki*, Vol. I, edited by J. Osiatynsky, Oxford University Press, Oxford.

Kalecki, M. (1991) *Collected works of Michal Kalecki*, Vol. II, edited by J. Osiatynsky, Oxford University Press.

Kalecki, M. (1993a) "Contribution to the debate on 'The main problems of political economy and teaching it' ", in *Collected works of Michal Kalecki*, Vol. IV, edited by J. Osiatynsky, Oxford University Press.

Kalecki, M. (1993b) *Collected works of Michal Kalecki*, Vol. V, edited by J. Osiatynsky, Oxford University Press.

Kalecki, M. (1997) *Collected works of Michal Kalecki*, Vol. VII, edited by J. Osiatynsky, Oxford University Press.

Kalecki, M. and Kowalik (1971 [1991]) "Observation on the 'Crucial Reform' " in *Collected works of Michal Kalecki*. Vol. II, edited by J., Oxford University Press.

Kalecki, M. and Kula, M. (1970 [1993]) "Bolivia – an 'Intermediate regime' in Latin America", in *Collected works of Michal Kalecki*, Vol. V, edited by J. Osiatynsky, Oxford University Press.

Kalecki, M. and Sachs, I. (1966 [1993]) "Forms of foreign aid: an economic analysis", in *Collected works of Michal Kalecki*, Vol. V, edited by J. Osiatinsky, Oxford University Press.

Kalecki, M. and Schumacher, E.F. (1943 [1997]) "International clearing and long-term lending", in *Collected works of Michal Kalecki*, Vol. VII, edited by J. Osiatinsky, Oxford University Press.

Kalecki, M. and Szeworski, A. (1957) *Sudia z zakresu koniunktury wspólecznego kapitalizmu*, Vol. 1. Panstwowe Wydawnictwo Naukowe, Warsaw.

Keynes, J.M. (1939) "Relative movements of real wages and output", *Economic Journal*, 49, 193: 34–51.

Keynes, J.M. (1940) "How to pay for the war", reproduced in Keynes (1972–1982), Vol. 22.

Keynes, J.M. (1964) *The general theory of employment, interest and money*. Harcourt Brace & Company, New York.

Keynes, J.M. (1933 [1971–1982]) "*The collected writings of John Maynard Keynes*", edited by Moggridge and Johnson. Macmillan, London.

Keynes, J.M. (1933) *The means to prosperity: Mr. Keynes's reply to criticism*. London: Macmillan, first edition; reproduced in Keynes, J.M. (1971–1982), Vol. 9.

Klein, L. (1952) *The Keynesian revolution*. Macmillan, London.

Kriesler, P. (1987) *Kalecki's microanalysis*. Cambridge, Cambridge University Press.

Laramie, A. and Mair, D. (1996) "Taxation and Kalecki's theory of the business cycle", *Cambridge Journal of Economics*, 20, 4: 451–464.

Laski, K. (1987) "Kalecki, Michal", *The new Palgrave: a dictionary of economics*, edited by J. Eatwell, M. Milgate and P. Newman, Macmillan, London: 8–14.

Laski, K. (2006) "Kalecki's place in my career as economist", *EAEPE Newsletter*, 36: 2–5.

Lerner, A.P. (1934) "The concept of monopoly and the measurement of monopoly power", *Review of Economic Studies*, June: 157–175.

Lerner, A.P. (1943) "Functional finance and the federal debt", *Social Research*, 10: 38–51.

Lerner, A.P. (1978) "Keynesianism: alive, if not so well", in *Fiscal responsibilities in a constitutional democracy*, edited by James Buchanan and Richard Wagner, Martinus Nijhoff, Boston: 63–69.

Lewis, W.A. (1954) "Economic development with unlimited supplies of labour", The Manchester School, 22, 2: 139–191.

López, J. (2008) "Keynes in Latin America and Latin American structuralism", in *Keynes for the twenty-first century. The continuing relevance of* The General Theory, edited by M. Forstater and L. Randall Wray, Palgrave, New York.

López, J. and Mott, T. (1999) "Kalecki versus Keynes on the determinants of investment", *Review of Political Economy*, 11, 3: 291–302.

López, J. and Perrotini, I. (2006) "On floating exchange rates, currency depreciation and effective demand", *Banca Nazionale del Lavoro Quarterly Review*, LIX, 238, September: 221–242.

Lucas, R. (1976) "Econometric policy evaluation: a critique", *Carnegie-Rochester Conference Series on Public Policy*, 1: 19–46.

Luxemburg, R. (2003) *The accumulation of capital*, Routledge Classics edition, London.

Manoilescu, M. (1931) *The theory of protection and international trade"*, P.S. King & Son, London.

Marris, R. (1991) *Reconstructing Keynesian economics with imperfect competition: a desk-top simulation*, Aldershot, Hants, England; Brookfield, Vt., USA: E. Elgar.

Marx, K. (1993) *Capital: A critique of political economy, Vol. 3*. Penguin, London.

Minsky, H. (1975) *John Maynard Keynes*. Columbia University Press, New York.

Mott, T. (2004) "Kalecki's principle of increasing risk, the distribution of income, and consequences for macroeconomics", in *Kalecki's Economics Today*, edited by Z. Sadowski and A. Szeworski, Routledge, London.

Mott, T. and Slattery, E. (1994) "Tax incidence and macroeconomic effects in a Kaleckian model when profits finance affects investment and prices may respond to taxes", *Journal of Post Keynesian Economics*, 16: 391–409.

Noyola, J. (1956) "El Desarrollo Económico y la Inflación en México y otros Países Latinoamericanos." *Investigación Económica*. XVI:4; 603–648. A new version appears in Desequilibrio externo e inflación. *Investigación Económica*, ed. UNAM, 1987.

Nurkse, R. (1953) *Problems of capital formation in underdeveloped countries"*. Oxford University Press, New York.

Osiatynski, J. (1989) "A note on Kalecki's and Keynes's unemployement equilibrium", in *Kalecki's relevance today*, edited by Sebastiani, Macmillan, London.

Osiatynski, J. (1991) *Collected works of Michal Kalecki*, Vol. II, edited by J. Osiatynsky, Oxford University Press.

Osiatynski, J. (1992) *Collected works of Michal Kalecki*. Vol. III, edited by J. Osiatynsky, Oxford University Press.

Patinkin, D. (1982). *Anticipations of the General Theory? and Other Essays on Keynes*. University of Chicago Press, Chicago.

Prebisch, R. (1951 [1982]) "Problemas Teóricos y Prácticos del Crecimiento Económico", in *La Obra de Prebisch en la CEPAL,* edited by Gurrieri, Adolfo, Fondo de Cultura Económica, México.

Robinson, A. (1947) "John Maynard Keynes 1883–1946", *The Economic Journal,* 52, 225, March: 1–68.

Robinson, J (1936) "Review of R. Harrod 'The trade cycle' ", The *Economic Journal,* 46: 690–693.

Robinson, J. (1933) *The economics of imperfect competition.* Macmillan, London.

Robinson, J. (1964) "Kalecki and Keynes", in *Problems of economic dynamics and planning: Essays in honour of Michal Kalecki,* Warsaw, PWN-Polish Scientific Publishers, reprinted in *Contributions to Modern Economics,* Blackwell, Oxford.

Robinson, J. (1966) "The economics of full employment. By members of the Oxford Institute of Statistics", in *Collected Economic Papers,* Vol. 1. Basil Blackwell, Oxford.

Robinson, J. (1977) "Michal Kalecki on the economics of capitalism", *Oxford Bulletin of Economics and Statistics,* 39, 1: 7–17.

Robinson Joan (1965) "Kalecki and Keynes", in Joan Robinson, *Collected Economic Papers,* Vol. Three, Basil Blackwell, Oxford.

Rosenstein-Rodan, P. (1943), "Problems of industrialization of eastern and south-eastern Europe", *The Economic Journal,* 53, 210: 202–211.

Sachs, I. (1977) "Kalecki and development planning", *Oxford Bulletin of Economics and Statistics,* 39: 47–56.

Sachs, I. (2007) *La troisieme rive.* Bourin Editeurs, Paris.

Salvati, M (1984) "Political business cycles", in *Long Waves in The World Economy,* edited by C. Freeman, London, Frances Pinter.

Sargent, T. (1987) *Macroeconomic theory.* Second Edition. Academic Press, Sand Diego.

Sawyer, M. (1985) *The economics of Michal Kalecki.* Macmillan, London.

Sawyer, M. (2001) "Kalecki on money and finance", *European Journal of History of Economic Thought,* 8, 4: 487–508.

Schydlowsky, D. (1967) "From import substitution to export promotion for semi-grown up industries: a policy proposal", *Journal of Development Studies,* III, 4, July.

Scitovsky, T. (1946) "Review of Kalecki's studies in economic dynamics", *Economic Journal,* 56: 451–452.

Scitovsky. T. (1984) "Lerner's contributions to economics", *Journal of Economic Literature,* 22, December: 1559–1560.

Sebastiani, M. (1989) *Kalecki's relevance today.* Macmillan, London.

Sen, A.K. (1960) *Choice of techniques.* Basil Blackwell, Oxford.

Solow, R. (1975) "Review of 'The intellectual capital of Michal Kalecki: a study in economic theory and policy' ", by George R. Feiwel", *Journal of Economic Literature,* 13, 4, December: 1331–1335.

Sordi, S. (1989) "Some notes on the second version of Kalecki's busines-cycle theory", in *M. Kalecki's relevance today,* edited by Sebastiani, Macmillan, Londres.

Steindl, J. (1942 [1946]) "The impact of the war on India", in *Studies in war economics,* edited by A.J. Brown, Oxford University Press, Oxford.

Steindl, J. (1981 [1991]) "Some comments on the three versions of Kalecki's theory of the trade cycle", reprinted in *Collected works of Michal Kalecki,* Vol. II, edited by J. Osiatynsky, Oxford University Press.

Steindl J. (1990a) *Economic papers, 1941–88.* Macmillan, London.

Steindl, J. (1990b) "Reflections on the present state of economics", in *Economic papers 194–88,* edited by J. Steindl, St. Martin's Press, New York.

Stiglitz, J. and A. Weiss (1981) "Credit rationing in markets with imperfect information", *American Economic Review,* 71: 393–410.

Sunkel, O. (1960) "Inflation in Chile; an unorthodox approach", in *International Economic Papers,* 10: 107–131.

Sweezy, P.M. (1939) "Demand under conditions of oligopoly", *The Journal of Political Economy,* 4: 568–573.

Sweezy, P.M. (1942) *The theory of capitalist development. Principles of marxian political economy.* Oxford University Press, Oxford.

Szeworski, A. (1962) "On the consequences of taxing monopoly profits", *Ekonomista,* 3: 27–55 (in Polish).

Szeworski, A. (1965) *Cykl koniunkturalny a intervencia Panstwa,* Panstwowe Wydawnictwo Ekonomiczne, Warsaw.

Tarshis, L. (1939) "Changes in real and money wages", *Economic Journal,* 48: 150–154.

Tew, B. (1999) "Kalecki's essays in the theory of economic fluctuations", *Review of Political Economy,* 11, 3: 273–282.

The Oxford University of Economics and Statistics (1944) *The economics of full employment.* Basil Blackwell, Oxford.

Tinbergen, J. (1935) "Annual survey: suggestions on 'Quantitative business cycle theory' ", *Econometrica,* 3, 3: 241–308.

Tobin, J. (1980) *Asset accumulation and economic activity.* University of Chicago, Chicago.

Toporowski, J. (2005) *"Theories of financial disturbance".* Edward Elgar, Cheltenham, UK.

Vatter, H. and Walker, J. (1997) *The rise of big government in the United States.* M.E. Sharpe, Armonk, New York.

Wolfson, M. (1994) *Financial Crises.* M.E. Sharpe, Armonk, New York.

Worswick, G.D.N. (1977) "Kalecki at Oxford, 1940–44", *Oxford Bulletin of Economics and Statistics,* 39, 1: 19–29.

Woodford, M. (1989) "Finance, instability and cycles", in *Financial Dynamics and Business Cycles,* edited by W. Semmier, M.E. Sharpe, New York: 18–37.

Wray, L.R. (1998) *"Understanding modern money: the key to full employment and price stability".* Edward Elgar, Cheltenham, UK.

Wray, L.R. (2008) "Demand constraints and big government", *Journal of Economic Issues,* 42, 1: 153–173.

Author Index

Subject Index